A GRAND TOUR

In 1794, after the recent inheritance of his father's fortune, the twenty-two-year-old John Bacon Sawrey Morritt departed his native Yorkshire on a Grand Tour during which he travelled through Greece, Austria, Hungary, Asia Minor and Italy. He returned in 1796, whereupon he settled down to lead the life of the influential country squire of Rokeby Hall—situated between Richmond and Barnard Castle, and described by his friend Sir Walter Scott as 'one of the most enviable places I have ever seen'. Perhaps its attractions explain the fact that Morritt never again repeated the grand scale of the venture recorded and celebrated in this book, though he lived until 1843.

A Grand Tour was not published until 1914: it forms an edited collection of Morritt's letters, written while en route, to his mother, sister and aunt. At once instructive, anecdotal and entertaining—whether dwelling on the balls and cafés of Vienna, or the pilfering of classical remains in Athens ('some we steal, some we buy')—this correspondence allows us to journey in the company of 'a man made on purpose to travel with', in the words of a contemporary who had done just that.

This edition of *A Grand Tour* includes an introduction by Peter J. Hogarth, who is a lecturer at York University. In addition to his many articles and publications, Dr. Hogarth is also the author of a book on dragons. He is himself well travelled in the footsteps of J. B. S. Morritt.

Also available in the Century Lives and Letters series:

A GRAND TOUR

Letters and Journeys 1794–96

JOHN B. S. MORRITT
OF ROKEBY

EDITED BY
G. E. Marindin
INTRODUCTION BY
Peter J. Hogarth

CENTURY PUBLISHING
LONDON
LESTER & ORPEN DENNYS DENEAU
MARKETING SERVICES LTD
TORONTO

Introduction copyright © Peter J. Hogarth 1985

First published in Great Britain in 1914
by John Murray (Publishers) Ltd

This edition published in 1985 by
Century Publishing Co. Ltd,
Portland House, 12–13 Greek Street,
London W1V 5LE

Published in Canada by
Lester & Orpen Dennys Deneau Marketing Services Ltd
78 Sullivan Street, Ontario, Canada

ISBN 0 7126 0993 8

The painting on the cover is 'Mount Tomohrit' by Edward Lear

Reprinted in Great Britain by
Richard Clay (The Chaucer Press) Ltd,
Bungay, Suffolk

INTRODUCTION

JOHN BACON SAWREY MORRITT inherited Rokeby Park, on Teesside, in 1791; and with it the considerable fortune that enabled him, at the age of twenty-two, to undertake the journey through the Levant that he describes so graphically in these letters to his mother, his sister Anne, and his aunt Frances Morritt.

His father, John Sawrey Morritt, had added Rokeby to other family properties in 1769, a few years before his son was born, and seems to have lived there the uneventful life of a country landowner. There is no great evidence of leanings towards literary or scholarly pursuits; if we except his sole published work *On Carrots and their use in fattening Hogs*. One of John Sawrey Morritt's sisters, Ann Eliza Morritt, was a needlewoman whose speciality—copies in woolwork of paintings by famous artists such as Poussin and Salvator Rosa—earned her a fashionable reputation as 'a lady of a most surprising genius', and attracted many visitors to Rokeby. Another sister, Frances, is described by her nephew as 'an advocate of petticoat independence' with 'strange notions . . . about the advantages of travel for ladies': it is with Frances that J. B. S. Morritt discusses the detail of the topography of Troy, and a book that she had lent him was 'as great an incentive to my touring as any I had read'. Frances must have been a lady of some character, and not a little learning. In other respects, however, the Morritt family seem to have been fairly unexceptional members of the Yorkshire gentry of the period.

J. B. S. Morritt himself was educated in Manchester and admitted to St. John's College, Cambridge, in June

1789. While still an undergraduate, he found time to serve as lieutenant in a militia regiment in Lancashire, where the family had property, and cheerfully drilled in anticipation of having to repel a French invasion. His Colonel, Thomas Stanley, had a younger sister named Catherine who was later to become Morritt's wife.

Shortly after leaving Cambridge, Morritt set off on his journey. Previously, it had been to Italy that the English 'milord' looked to indulge a taste for cultured travelling. With the onset of the continental wars, however, 'The exclusion of Englishmen from those parts of the continent which were formerly the chief objects of inquiry to the curious, has of late years induced many of our travellers to direct their attention to a country highly interesting from the wrecks of ancient grandeur, and from the contrast between its former state of glory and its present degradation. No man is now accounted a traveller who has not . . . tasted the olives of Attica; while . . . it is an introduction to the best company, and a passport to literary distinction, to be a member of the "Athenian Club", and to have scratched one's name upon a fragment of the Parthenon.'

Having, indeed, a taste for the 'wrecks . . . of ancient grandeur', Morritt accordingly joined the 'Levant lunatics' and directed his steps towards classical Greece. Accompanying him as companion and tutor was Robert Stockdale, his senior by ten years, the son of a York clergyman and a Fellow of Pembroke College. The two friends left London in February 1794, crossed Europe by way of Brussels, Dresden, Vienna (where they added a draughtsman to the party, much as one might today buy a camera), and Bucharest, to arrive at Constantinople at the beginning of August. After several busy weeks in and around the City, they set off to inspect Troy and other ancient sites, before sailing by way of Lemnos to the monastic community of Mount Athos, then travelling by land through Thessaly, eventually to Athens. Here the party spent some time, visiting the classical ruins and collecting classical remains—'some we steal, some we buy'. Some (such as portions of the Parthenon friezes later acquired by Lord Elgin) they attempted to obtain by 'negotiation' with a corrupt Turkish official, until thwarted by a Frenchman ('such a blackguard') who, on behalf of the Republic, had his own designs on the remains.

From Athens, Morritt turned southwards to the Peloponnese, through ancient Sparta and the isolated peninsula of the Mani, then to Tiryns, Epidaurus, Rhodes and Crete, before again sailing northwards to the Ionian islands. From there he left Greece for Italy; where, in the course of a prolonged stay in Naples he showed himself as appreciative of the charms of Emma, Lady Hamilton, as of those of the Parthenon or the Troad. Sidestepping Napoleon's armies, he passed rapidly through northern Europe and eventually sailed safely into Yarmouth harbour, a little over two years after leaving England.

For the remainder of his long life (he lived until 1843) Morritt showed little inclination to travel. His only subsequent excursion out of England was a very different affair from the adventurous tour of the Levant; shortly after the Bourbon restoration of 1814 we find him in Paris to attend the first levée held in the Tuileries by Monsieur, brother of Louis XVIII (and later himself crowned as Charles X).

Apart from this glittering interlude, Morritt discharged the traditional duties of a landed gentleman; as High Sheriff, Colonel-Commandant of the local Volunteers, and as a Tory Member of Parliament. Morritt gained his first seat, Beverley, at a bye-election in 1799, and lost it three years later, 'beaten by a combination of bribery & mobbing', as he complains in a letter to a friend. After some attempts to find an influential patron with a vacant constituency in his gift, and who 'w$^{d.}$ possibly not be much disinclined to bring forward a Yorkshire Gentleman' to represent it, Morritt was eventually 'brought forward' unopposed as Member for Northallerton. His patron there was the Earl of Harewood; but when in due course the Earl's son came of age, Morritt had to vacate

Northallerton in his favour, and finally became M.P. for Shaftesbury. In the course of this nomadic parliamentary career, he seems to have made little impact on the House of Commons.

Partly because of his parliamentary activities, Morritt acquired a town house in London, at 24 Portland Place; this was also convenient for his involvement in the Society of Dilettanti. At the foundation of the Society in 1734, its members were 'gentlemen who had travelled in Italy, desirous of encouraging a taste for those objects which had contributed so much for their entertainment abroad'. Subsequently a visit to Greece was allowed as an additional qualification for membership. In its early days, the principal activities of the Society consisted of meeting every month in the *Star and Garter* to drink toasts to 'Grecian Taste and Roman Spirit'; Horace Walpole aptly described it as a club 'for which the nominal qualification is having been in Italy, and the real one, being drunk'.

By the time of Morritt's election in 1799, the Society's raffish days were over; its meetings were more sedate, its membership more respectable, and its interests scholarly as well as social. In 1831 Morritt became 'Arch-master of the Ceremonies to this Society' and his only known portrait shows him 'in the long crimson taffety-tasselled robe of that great and respectable officer'—a far cry from the romantic and high-spirited youth of thirty-five years previously.

Most of the more prominent scholars and eastern travellers were members of the Society of Dilettanti at this time; one who was most pointedly *not* elected (until 1831, when he equally pointedly declined) was the Earl of Elgin, erstwhile Ambassador to the Sublime Porte. The 'Elgin Marbles' then, as now, provoked controversy. Because of his reputation as a classical scholar, not to mention as one who had visited the Parthenon and failed where Elgin was later to succeed, Morritt was summoned in 1818 to give evidence before the Select Committee of Parliament on the Elgin Marbles, 'appointed to inquire whether it be expedient that the Collection . . . should be purchased on behalf of The Public, and if so, what Price it may be reasonable to allow for the same'. Morritt ventured no opinion on the latter point, but strongly supported the former; in contrast to the majority of influential members of the Society, which had determined the sculptures to be of no great merit.

The Society of Dilettanti apart, Morritt was much involved in the intellectual and social life of the capital. In journals and letters of the period, we frequently glimpse him dining with Theodore Hook, Robert Southey, or Sir Humphry Davy, disputing the authenticity of Homer with Samuel Taylor Coleridge, or accompanying Sir Walter Scott on a visit to Hampton Court.

Many of these friends also visited Morritt at his beloved Rokeby, to inspect the latest improvements in the pathways that he constructed along the picturesque banks of the Tees, or his collection of curiosities: 'rude remains of Roman Britain . . . completely thrown into the back-ground by the collection of Greek and Roman inscriptions, urns, &c in marble, brought . . . from Greece or Italy'; or his paintings, which included the famous *Rokeby Venus* by Velasquez, now in the National Gallery.

A vignette of life at Rokeby, combining intellectual discussion with the more conventional pursuits of the landed gentry, comes from the journal of Colonel Roderick Murchison, veteran of the Peninsular war, and later an eminent geologist. Rokeby seems to have been a turning point in Murchison's career:

'In the Summer following the hunting season 1822/3, when revisiting my old friend Morrit (*sic*) of Rokeby, I fell in with Sir Humphrey (*sic*) Davy, and experienced much gratification in his lively illustrations of great physical truths. As we shot partridges in the morning, I perceived that a man might pursue philosophy without abandoning field sports and Davy . . . encouraged me to come to London and set to at science.'

One of Morritt's closest friends was Sir Walter Scott.

In his Journal, Scott records in 1808 the visit of 'a very pleasant English family, the Morritts of Rokeby Park'; as they walked round the Scottish countryside, Scott was much impressed by his guest's learned discussion of the location of ancient Troy, and more than a little relieved—being himself 'but a slender classical scholar'—to find Morritt's erudition 'not of an overbearing kind'. This auspicious first meeting led to many later visits by Scott to Rokeby Park and Portland Place, and by Morritt to Scott's houses of Ashestiel and, later, Abbotsford. Scott was so struck by Morritt's home that he wrote *Rokeby*, an epic poem of considerable length, about Morritt's medieval predecessors; Morritt in turn contributed *The Curse of Moy* to Scott's *Minstrelsy of the Scottish Border*. The two men, through visits and a copious correspondence, developed a warm friendship which lasted until Scott's death in 1831.

Towards the end of his life, Scott declared Morritt to be 'one of my oldest, and, I believe, one of my most sincere, friends, a man unequalled in the mixture of sound good sense, high literary cultivation, and the kindest and sweetest temper that ever graced a human bosom'. The qualities that so endeared Morritt to Scott shine through his letters from the Levant, which enable us also to share the learning, the affectionate wit, the vitality and the unbounded zest of (in the words of one of his travelling companions) 'a man made on purpose to travel with'.

PETER J. HOGARTH
1985

CONTENTS

LETTERS OF MR. MORRITT
OF ROKEBY

CHAPTER I

JOURNEY FROM OSTEND TO DRESDEN

A FEW notes on the position of affairs in Europe when
Morritt started on his travels, at the end of February
1794, may help to an understanding of some allusions
in his letters.

In France the destruction of the Girondists four
months before had left the various Jacobin parties
in power, and Robespierre was engaged in removing
his rivals—the extreme party of the Hebertists on the
one side, and the less immoderate section headed by
Danton on the other. The month of March, just as
Morritt reached Dresden, saw the overthrow and
execution of both Hebertists and Dantonists, leaving
the supreme power for the time in the hands of Robespierre and his coadjutors, St. Just and Couthon,
acting through the Committee of Public Safety. The
Terror was at its height.

The frontier warfare had surged backwards and
forwards. More than a year earlier, in November 1792,
Dumouriez's victory at Jemappes had opened all
Belgium (still the Austrian Netherlands) to the
French, who occupied Brussels and other Belgian
towns through the winter; but with the spring campaign came reverses. The Prince of Coburg in March
1793 moved forward; the siege of Maestricht was
raised; the French army was driven beyond the
Meuse, routed near Liége, fell back on Tirlemont and
then on Louvain. On March 18 Dumouriez suffered

1793

a severe defeat at Neerwinden; and, by a convention of March 21, the French evacuated Brussels and fell back towards their own frontier. Dumouriez was intriguing with the Austrians, partly from a genuine disapproval of the Jacobin excesses, and partly because he foresaw that want of success in any campaign would lead to the guillotine, as was found by Custine and Houchard not long afterwards. He failed to carry over his troops, and was forced to take refuge with the Austrians. The French armies, still further discouraged and disorganised by his desertion, retired to Valenciennes, Lisle and Condé, within the French frontier. They also formed an entrenched camp at Famars, about three miles to the south of Valenciennes commanded by General Dampierre, who attempted an advance, but was driven back to his camp. The camp of Famars itself was stormed three weeks later by a combined British and German army; Valenciennes was taken ; and it appears that only the jealousies and separate interests of the Allies prevented a march upon Paris.

The tide then turned again. Carnot, " the Organiser of Victory," became military member of the Committee in August 1793. In the same month the British, under the incapable Duke of York, sat down before Dunkirk,

1794

and narrowly escaped destruction when Houchard defeated the Hanoverian troops under Freitag at Hoondschoote on September 8. But Houchard failed in the decision which would have completed his success, and paid for the failure with his head. Jourdan, his successor, defeated the Austrians at Wattignies in October, and so compelled Coburg to raise the siege of Maubeuge. This marked the end of the Austrian advance. They retired into winter quarters across the Sambre, while the French armies were encamped for the winter on the Belgian frontier.

Such was the position of the armies in the North when Morritt travelled from Ostend to Dresden—in sixteen stages, as his diary shows. The chief places on his route were Ghent, Brussels, Tirlemont, Liége, Aix-la-Chapelle, Düsseldorf, Cassel, Erfurt, Leipzig. It will thus be seen that much of the country over which he travelled had been fought over in the previous year, as he describes in some of his letters. Later in the same year it was again overspread by French armies within ten or twelve weeks of Morritt's passage.

At Dresden Frederick Augustus, Elector of Saxony, had his Court. He was grandson of Augustus III., King of Poland, and great-grandson of Augustus II., Elector of Saxony, and afterwards King of Poland, surnamed "The Strong," who formed the famous collection of art treasures which Morritt found at Dresden. Frederick Augustus abstained as much as possible from war against France, and only took up arms when he was called upon to furnish a contingent for the defence of the German Empire. After Jena he made peace with Napoleon, and received the title of King of Saxony in 1806, as a member of the Confederation of the Rhine.

SITTINGBOURNE,
February 27, 1794.

DEAR MOTHER,

Though I did not trouble you with any descriptions of London and its environs (for, to say the truth, the subject has been so fully treated of by *Master Jacky Curious* in his letters *to his mamma* that I thought it needless), yet now I have begun my tour you may depend upon hearing regularly from me. However, to give some account of London, which the afore-mentioned writer has, I believe, omitted, you may tell Anne that Bond Street is as gay as usual, the dear Mount undeserted by any of its adherents, and Warren's Hotel frequented by all the beau-monde of the present day, amongst whom I first enumerate Mr. Bert Champneys, who, in his *pretty* way, desired his very best compliments.

Stockdale and I set off to-day at three o'clock on our journey after having amused our friends in Pall Mall with our mode of packing, and setting off for such a tour, not a little. Augusta and Elizabeth came in with Mrs. J. Stanley just before we set out, and send their love. We are now, after supper, or in reality dinner, at the inn at Sittingbourne, and I take the opportunity of his being in a comfortable nap to write to you and tell you of our motions. We shall arrive at Dover to-morrow, and sail at twelve o'clock at night for Ostend, from which place you shall certainly have a note from me to say I am safe, though not a very long letter, unless I write it at Dover, as I did the last time I toured. We have got all sorts of letters, and have been presented to the Mussulman, so we are more determined on our Grecian tour than ever, especially as we have met with men who themselves have made it and who represent the dangers of it as entirely imaginary.

I was much obliged to you for the letters you got me, though, as we do not mean to stop before we arrive at Dresden, they will many of them be useless. I left all my papers and worldly concerns with Walton, so you will hear all that sort of thing from him. Perhaps you would hear he has for some days been extremely ill, though he was much better when I left town.

I must tell you the character we go in to the Sublime Porte, as it will give you some idea of the understandings of the Faithful. The Ambassador asked Mr. Frederick North if we as Englishmen were not very well acquainted with the art of fortification, as he would give us letters to his own brother, the Grand Master of the Ordnance in Turkey, whom he hoped we should enrich with some very valuable secrets about European tactics. Mr. North represented us as great engineers, and says that they know so little of the matter that we may keep up our character with ease out of an old German almanac on fortified towns, so do not be surprised if you hear of General Stockdale and me fortifying the Dardanelles. We shall very soon, I hope, be equal to the Duke of Richmond in making batteries against buckram men, and ramparts with nothing to defend.[1] I believe the Duke of York sails at the same time we do to-morrow,

---

[1] The third Duke of Richmond was Master-General of the Ordnance, 1782-95.

and I only hope the kind wishes that attend his return may not endanger us in a storm, for never man was half so hated by his brother officers ; tell Frances this is not democrat intelligence, but the general cry of them all.   I left Henry in London very well this morning, and Edwardiki also.   As this is the most interesting intelligence I have, I shall conclude with Stockdale's respects and my love to you all.   I will write constantly.   Adieu.

Your affectionate son,
J. B. S. MORRITT.

Tell Burgh not to forget me or be idle, but do his lessons like a good boy.   I meet Bootle and Wilbraham [1] at Vienna.   Old Bootle is better, for he makes jokes as usual.   Emma and Eliza *à l'ordinaire*.   Direct Dresden, poste restante.

DEAR MOTHER,
    I just stop one moment longer here to tell you that we arrived safe last night at eleven o'clock, without danger, fatigue, or sea-sickness, after a voyage of about twelve hours.   We are setting off for Brussels instead of going by Antwerp, as there is, I hear, almost as much to see, and Antwerp is less likely to be in the hands of the French at our return.
We are in high health and spirits, and you shall some of you hear again very soon.   Adieu.

Your affectionate son,
J. B. S. MORRITT.

OSTEND,
    March 2,
        Sunday morning.

---

[1] These two friends of Morritt, who appear often in the letters, and who gained some repute as travellers, were brothers, sons of Richard Wilbraham Bootle, of Lathom House, Lancashire, who had assumed the name of Bootle with the Lathom property.   His second son Randle retained the name Wilbraham.   The elder at this time was Edward Bootle, but he afterwards resumed the name of Wilbraham, and was created Lord Skelmersdale.

BRUSSELS,
May 4, 1794.

DEAR ANNE,

Though I told you all from Ostend we were safely arrived in the Continent, yet, as I promised to write you an account of everything queer we meet with, I can't do less than give you some account of our proceedings at Brussels. We travelled post from Ostend here in two days, being sixty-eight miles, a distance which in Germany is about equal to two hundred between London and York, for the more you scold in French the more the postillions smoke, a Flemish answer to all sorts of language.

We got here on Tuesday evening, and have employed two days in gapeweed, of which here is plenty. The ridiculous *mélange* of English, French, and Austrian manners here is completely laughable. "Venez ici si vous voulez voir nos manières et nos modes étrangement travestiées par des maladroits singes et des gauches poupées," for we went last night, being the last of the carnival, to what they call a Ridotto and Grand Bal at the theatre, dressed *à la mode de Londres*, and were not a little amused to find half the room in boots, slouch capes, and hunting coats by way of being *à l'Anglaise* in an evening, all walking in the true slang step and taking us for *émigrés*, I dare say, because we had cocked hats on. On the contrary, another half of the room abounded with Croix of St. Louis, dirty laced ruffles and bags, muffs, and cockades—I never wished so much for Bunbury in my life. We stayed till one o'clock, but though there needed no introduction to ask a lady to dance on this side of the water, yet none of the Flemish ladies were charming enough to overcome our national modesty, so we walked out again after quizzing the ball a little, without sporting a toe among such clodhoppers.

We were surprised to find everything as we came along so flourishing and so little damaged by the French as it has been. Tell Mrs. Frances nothing in the whole way here announces the late seat of war. At Brussels all the French had taken from the churches was restored before they evacuated the place (by Dumouriez), and all the furniture and ornaments of which they had stripped the palace were sold to individuals of whom the Court have again bought them, so that the whole is just as it was before. Indeed Dumouriez, by their accounts, seems to have had nothing to do but to counteract the folly and violence of his army, and to restore what they plundered. We are now within forty miles of the French army, and within about thirty of that of the Allies, yet all here is just as gay and as quiet as they are in London. I can't help thinking how your Aunt Mary would feel if General Van Damme was at Catterick. We have been all yesterday and to-day employed in seeing some very fine pictures in different churches and cabinets here, particularly some by Rubens, Vandyck, and Rembrandt. Pictures can't be described, but the Rubens here give you a much better idea of his skill in drawing than any I have seen, and are equal to almost any pictures I know.

One picture, however, I will describe to you as it was described to me this morning. The subject was Abraham, Sarah, and the three angels—" Voilà, Monsieur, un tableau qui représente *Jacob* et les trois anges. On lui dit que *Sarah sa femme* deviendra grosse (elle en rit, voyez-vous), et on lui commande de faire baptiser son enfant par *Saint Jean le Baptiste*." This will give you some idea of their accuracy in Bible chronology. The rest of the things we have seen are a beautiful château of the Archduke's a league from the town, the rooms charmingly fitted up, and I think as good as the best English houses; and what is not very 'common here, the walks are crinkum-crankum, as Lord Ogleby says, with many fountains or lead statues. There is a large coffee-house here filled with French aristocrats, who choose to stay here at other people's expense while the Austrians and

English fight their battles, within thirty miles of them. But they are the same here as in England, and wage no war but in the coffee-room. Our *laquais de place* recommended us to go there " parce qu'il y avait des Archévêques, des Évêques, et *tous les diables*." We presented Mrs. Gore's letter to the Princesse de Horne, but she was ill, so we did not see her; the Countess Ferrari is at Vienna, which will be better for us. As our stay here is so short, we had no need of letters, and did not even call at the Ambassador's. To-morrow we hope by early rising to reach Aix-la-Chapelle, sixty-nine miles, but I have great doubts; then through Düsseldorf to Dresden. I do not pass near Weimar, where Miss Gore is, so shall send her letter by the post, from the nearest place to Frankfort.

The weather is as fine for us as possible, everything in our favour, and I saw two magpies immediately on setting off; so if we do not get to Greece the devil's in it. I shall receive no letters from you till we get to Dresden, where I am heartily anxious to be now. We shall stop, however, one day at Düsseldorf to see our old acquaintance in the gallery there. I have seen nothing very pretty to be bought either living or dead, so have not begun either of our collections yet. Give my best love to my mother and aunts; we are both ¡very well, and you may depend upon hearing constantly from your affectionate brother,

J. B. S. Morritt.

Naumberg,
March 19, 1794.

Dear Frances,

Though we have been rolling on so long, yet we are not yet arrived at our journey's end, for of such travelling you cannot have any idea. An English heavy-loaded wagon is sometimes flying, if compared with the pace we come in parts of our journey, and in the very best we hardly go four miles an hour. But though I am tired of our trailing, I will endeavour to get you on through part of our journey more pleasantly. So, to begin, after we left Brussels, we came forward through Liége and Aix-la-Chapelle by St. Tron, Tongres, and Tirlemont, all names which you recollect pretty much talked of in English newspapers in the summer; but we were a good deal surprised at the perfect composure of the people, and the cultivation of the country, though the French were within twenty miles, and it had been the scene of so many engagements already.

The camp of Famars is not far off Tirlemont, I believe,[1] so there had been pretty hot work; we were shown a hill where the French encamped, when Prince Coburg drove them from Louvain, but, excepting some broken and overturned crosses, the country looked as little damaged as any part of England by either army, and I believe forage, etc., sells so high they rather gain by being the seat of war, by selling at so good a market as the camps are. I wonder the French ever were suffered by the Brabanters, for they committed continual outrages upon their churches, though little upon private property; and I think it completely shows the influence and share their monks had in stirring them up against the Emperor, for they let a good deal of their property alone—so that the Brabanters opposed the Emperor when he tried to destroy the convents, without ever minding the French, who were pulling down their very altars.

DRESDEN.

I was obliged to leave off here by the arrival of supper, and have never had half an hour's time to take up my pen again till now. We arrived here yesterday; that varlet Abney, not receiving any of my letters (by what accident I cannot imagine), only stayed here two days, went to Berlin, from which he sets off in about a week for Hanover, and afterwards

[1] Here he is misinformed: it was more than seventy miles from Tirlemont. See p. 2.

for England. You may be sure we were a good deal disappointed. Lord Porchester, however, is here, and stays some months; we have been introduced to Elliot,[1] the Envoy, by him, and mean to stay here and look about for a week or two. Not any of our letters from England have arrived here yet; but as the post is very slow, I hope they will still arrive soon, as I long to hear of you all. We have not yet begun to hunt lions in Dresden, for we arrived only yesterday, and have been busy in settling and presenting our letters to the Envoy, etc. This I hear is a very fine show-place, particularly for pictures, of which we have not yet seen enough to be tired.

We did not explore anywhere as we came from Cassel here except for a few hours at Leipzig, which is like all trading towns almost, very rich with nothing to see; when I say *nothing* I mean it literally, for I cannot tell you one single thing worth notice. The roads from Düsseldorf to Cassel, and indeed to Leipzig, beggar all description; they often go through a pretty country, but more frequently over wide downs, or through thick forests. The quantity of wood is inconceivable; you travel between hills covered with it for days sometimes, and in summer it must in places be beautiful. Tell Mrs. Mary that we were often in roads which she would not like; indeed, we broke our springs, and bruised our carriage strangely; however, we have not been overturned, though more than once on the balance with the wheels in the air.

Dresden is indeed beautifully situated in a large plain on the Elbe, bounded with pretty cultivated hills and vineyards. The drollery and absurdity of the figures and equipages here exceed anything I ever saw, and, like true Englishmen, we have been

[1] Hugh Elliot was Minister at the Court of Saxony from 1792 to 1802. Greater interest attached to his diplomatic work previously in Sweden in the reign of Gustavus III., and subsequently at Naples 1803–6. His last public office was the governorship of Madras.

employed all the morning in quizzing the natives. However, it is hardly worth while, for it quite fails of its effect with a German, as if you were to spit in a man's face here he would only wipe it off. I always thought what I had heard of the phlegm and sleepy temper of these people exaggerated; but it is enough, I assure you, to look at them, and see the scenes we sometimes do: you would swear the whole nation was asleep. The composure with which they let you scold them is inconceivable; and when we have done we might have better held our tongues, as a German is never in a hurry, and I believe cannot conceive anybody else is. Voltaire somewhere calls them the old men of Europe; and it is drawing their picture at once. Some of my friends I know will not agree with me, but I like the French better by half, having a natural propensity and partiality for folly in preference to stupidity. We shall be presented to Mr. and Mrs. Saxony as soon as possible; and when we see what the higher society is you shall hear more what we think about it, though by the accounts we hear from Lord Porchester it is exactly the same.

I have hardly left myself room to tell you that when you answer this you must direct *à la poste restante, Vienne*, for our letters are so long in going that it is most probable we shall have left Dresden. Indeed, we must not attempt to have a question-and-answer correspondence, but write as often as we feel inclined. I will in a day or two write again to my mother or sister. Make Burgh remember his promises, and give my best love to the whole circle, Rover not excepted. We are both as well and in as good spirits as possible; and every inquiry confirms our Grecian schemes. Believe me, my dear aunt,

Most affectionately yours,
J. B. S. MORRITT.

DRESDEN,
March 22.

DRESDEN,
Saturday, March 29.

DEAR MOTHER,

By the letter I wrote my Aunt Frances some days since, you would see I was arrived safe and sound at Dresden; as we are now established there, I will give you some farther account of our motions. Abney, from never receiving my letters, which arrived here but two days since, though I sent them in January, had only stayed here two days, and proceeded to Berlin in his road home, where he means to arrive in the course of next month; and if he travels through Westphalia, as we did, he had better set off directly to accomplish that.

Read the account of Baron Thundertentronck's château in "Candide," you have no bad idea of the

BARN AND KITCHEN ALSO DOOR	COW HOUSE
PIG STY	ENTRANCE	HOUSE

country there. In the villages the houses are built upon the adjoined plan; there is not a chimney in all Westphalia, and the smoke goes out at the windows. If you only observe the vicinity of the house and cow stable, I think you will give Anne a comfortable idea of a Westphalian bedchamber; the cows have their heads very often through the partition, and indeed Lord Porchester found a white cow one night in his bedroom; do not you think Anne would have passed a comfortable night if she had made the same discovery?

Saxony, however, at least that part of it which lies near Dresden, is a very fine and beautiful country. The Elbe, which is here a large and rapid river, runs through the town; the plain is very extensive, and bounded by pretty hills, and towards Bohemia by very bold and craggy mountains. The society here is small in the higher orders, and consists entirely of the Court and Corps Diplomatique. Mr. S. Milnes wrote for letters for us to the old Countess Bentinck, who, however, has not yet sent them, and the post is so slow and uncertain we possibly shall not receive them until we are tired of Dresden. Elliot, however, who is our Envoy here, has been very civil to us.

I was presented at Court last Sunday to about thirty or forty people; so have had engagements ever since in plenty. The chief meetings here are card assemblies and suppers, and one o'clock dinners, which do not at all suit my taste. Yesterday I dined at Court, which is a pretty awful ceremony. I sat next the Electress, and I must say found her more chatty and pleasant than I thought sovereigns were in general. Conceive me going about here dining at one o'clock, in a bag and sword, for you go almost everywhere in full dress; and I cannot say but I feel a very great quiz in my striped velvet.

A German dinner lasts about three hours and a half, for when you are all seated round the table it is conceived you are all much too great people to make use of your hands, or to carve; so every dish is cut up by the servants at a sideboard, and handed round on plates one after the other, an excellent contrivance for getting the meat perfectly cold and prolonging a great beastly party, when you have nothing to say. I speak very feelingly, as I have just returned with Lord Porchester from dining with one of their Ministers, and have just been stripping off my fine things in no very good humour with them. I am going to Court again to-morrow, and dine with the Spanish Ambassador, but I hope we shall not be quite so stupid there as with the natives. I go to-night to the Bavarian Minister's, who has, I hear, the best society in the place, so I hope the supper will make some amends for the dullness of the dinner.

The principal lion here is the Picture Gallery, which is the best in Europe out of Italy, and, I hear, many say fully equal to any there. I will never tease you however, by attempting to describe pictures: I feel too strongly how very little language can do justice to some I have seen here. There are five Correggios which are esteemed his best works, and the finest Raphael I have yet seen; judge, then, if I can give you any idea of what we felt on seeing them. At Court here there is not much form (for a Court, that is), and the Elector and Princes seem pretty affable, to strangers particularly; he talked to me a great deal yesterday about England and the alarms there, for he seems to know everything that is going on.

As for business, will you tell Walton I will thank him to lodge six hundred pounds in Hammersley's hands, and tell him to transmit me the sum in circular notes to Vienna through his agent there. It is not that I suppose I shall want so great a sum, but I would wish to make sure of not being stopped in the Greek Isles, where I can get no remittances. Tell Ward, too, that on second thoughts I would have him sell the horse I bought at Doncaster, if he can get sixty guineas for him, but to ask eighty. I do not think he will quite suit me. He must pay no Cambridge bills; all of them are about 40 per cent. too dear and ought to wait. Best love to all at York. I will write again in a day or two.

Believe me, affectionately yours,

J. B. S. Morritt.

Dear Anne,

I was just taking my pen to give you a little intelligence of our motions, when a letter arrived from you in answer to my Brussels gazette. This, you may be sure, did not stop me, especially as Dresden is altogether as ridiculous as Brussels; and while there are quizzes in the world there will always be subjects for a letter to you.

I told you in my mother's letter part of the agreements of this place, such as Court-going and dining at one o'clock. I visit about a good deal, as you would see, and of course meet with some figures which, walking up St. James's Street, would be most numerously escorted. To be sure, Court figures (like Court cards) are ridiculous enough in England as elsewhere, but we have not yet discovered the luxury of walking in a morning with our hair full dressed and our hats under our arm, neither are we fully sensible of the happiness of a coat without a cape or a bag and sword. I often wished that I had you with me to take a walk on the great bridge, which is here the principal walk, but oftener that I could by magic convey them all into Bond Street for half an hour. As that may hardly be, I will just give you some idea of a few characters in our society. *Imprimis*, an Italian count, much the figure of my friend Townley, with a voice like Lord Arundel's. You would take him for a buffoon: *point du tout*, he would tell you himself he has too much feeling to be ever happy, and is deeply in love with a woman that laughs at him to his face. She, clever, elegant, and lively, you would think meant to do anything rather than marry him; *au contraire*, he has eight thousand a year, and she is determined to have him. This, however, is common enough, you will say, in England. Secondly, a lady that asked me after English fashions, and thought herself *à l'Anglaise*. She is a good deal like Miss Kitty Catterick in person and face, and she wears a riding-habit jacket with a coloured calico, muslin, or cotton petticoat; item a hat and feather morning and evening, and I believe she sleeps in it. I hear she has fifteen suits. Thirdly, her friend and companion, who is sentimental, and never sees anything that is not *singulier*, *superbe*, *charmant*, *magnifique*, or *délicieux*. Fourthly, a figure exactly like our friend Mr. Constable, who walked in at my aunt's one night, only he always has on a sword and striped velvet coat, and though hardly broader than a penknife, is indebted for that little substance to a tin belly and a pair of false calves. He is the gallant man of the party

Were I to describ all, there would be no end of them; the women here are all free-and-easy, and among the rest of their agreements all take snuff and spit about the room they sit in. I must say that, take the party all together, they are excellent; but though nasty enough often for French women, they have neither their liveliness nor their manners. Many of them are content with holding their tongues and walking about staring at you, and I begin to be of the mind of a lively little woman (the only one of the party) who asked me last night if I did not think "qu'on montoit bien les automates dans ce pays-ci." You will see by this that, however charmed I am with pictures and statues, I do not admire the living figures much here, and as my opinion is backed by that of all the foreigners that I meet here, I suppose it is right; for Elliot, who has been here these three years, says that they are just as stiff and stupid to him.

We do not make any great advances in talking German, for all the higher ranks here speak French, and of course we do not hear much of the other. Indeed, I can't say I regret it much, for the language is very difficult, and as their books are in general books of information, not of amusement, you lose little pleasure by reading them in a translation. Amongst other pictures I have seen in the road here there was one of our Saviour at Brussels which is undoubtedly very curious. It was painted by Rubens, from an *original painting by St. Luke*, burnt at Antwerp in 1768. This was the account we heard of it there. Don't you think their believing such a story delightful? His highness of Banbury at Hornby Castle quite yields to the picture history of foreign parts, you see. However, I wish I could only give you an idea of the pictures we have admired, as well as of those we laugh at; but when I think of describing a picture of Raphael's we have seen here, and find no words to express myself with but beautiful, graceful, fine, etc., etc., I give up the cause in utter despair.

I am nevertheless studying attitudes, and as I always admired Mrs. Hart, and Mrs. Parsons her *élève*, I do not give up all hopes of being able to represent by my figure and drapery ye Madonna; and I hope Abney and Stockdale will remember enough of the group to play Pope Sixtus and St. Barbara, who are adoring her. As I can't draw, this will be the only way I can tell you of the sights we have seen when I come back; so I desire you will prepare all sorts of shawls and flowing robes, as there is a great deal of very fine drapery to be represented, and many of the figures are really in old-fashioned drapes, for I take it that your remark on the fashionable dress for figures holds here as well as in the Orléans Gallery.

My best love to all the York party, and I hope this will find Henry with you at York. You seem very much alarmed about his going abroad; it is a circumstance both he and we should make up our minds to, as it is both very probable, and inseparable from his profession. I think it, and I hope he does, much more respectable than being a holiday soldier, and I own I also think it less dangerous for him, a great deal, than London. We are very well and very happy, but wish to hear often from you. Adieu.

Your very affectionate brother,

J. B. S. MORRITT.

DRESDEN,
April 4, 1794.

DRESDEN,
April 12, 1794.

DEAR MOTHER,

Be assured that we run no dangers, notwithstanding the alarms English people have about outlandish tours. Mr. Elliot, the Envoy here, and his Secretary, Mr. Grey, have both been at Constantinople and encourage us in our schemes very much. We have received infinite civilities from the first during the whole of our stay, and a very agreeable man he is.

Our mornings have been spent generally in seeing pictures and statues or the country, which is charming. We have an English mess with Lord Porchester, a Mr. Ferguson (Scotch) and a Baron de Roldkirk (a young Prussian who has lived in England and speaks very good English), at three every day, unless we are engaged out to dinner: after dinner we play billiards, go to the coffee-house, walk, and at eight or nine I go to the Bavarian Minister's, who opens his house every night, and assembles the little society there is here to cards and supper. They have no idea in the circles here of meeting in an evening to cards or tea with supper, as they had in France, by which means, as they are often poor, very few people open their house to society at all. Elliot talks soon of setting the fashion of conversaziones, but it is a bold attempt, for German intellects are great enemies to innovation. The manners here are but dull to a stranger, and I think in about a week we shall set off again for Vienna; in a day or two we are to make a party to Königstein, a small fortress about fifteen miles from this place: it is on the summit of a high rock, and so inaccessible from situation that the King of Prussia, in the Seven Years' War, left it behind him blocked up, as he despaired of taking it, though only defended by about 300 Saxons. Perhaps it and Gibraltar are the only really impregnable fortresses, as sieges are now conducted. It is a state prison, and an Irish Captain Brown, in the Saxon service (who was confined there a small time), goes with us to do the honours of the party, but *vivent les Paddy* for forgetting those little anecdotes.

The weather here has been as fine as possible, and is quite spring. Very few days we have had any rain, and, even at this time of the year, three or four days without literally seeing a speck in the air like a cloud. We often walk on the promenade after supper at twelve or one o'clock, ladies and all, so you may think it is very fine. Tell Mrs. Frances that the story Strickland told us of Major Semple is literally true. He now calls himself M. de Lille, and by some means has got brevets and commissions in the Dutch service. He served in Flanders, was detected by some English-men, afterwards was a spy for Prince Coburg, came over to Leipzig, attempted to swindle Lord Porchester and Lord Riversdale, who is also there, but fortunately failed; he has since been here, cheated through almost all Germany, and is at last in limbo again in Bavaria, where he has been introduced at Court, and showed off so well that he was hand-and-glove with the Elector. Elliot, who saw him here, knows him very well, and always lends him some money by way of getting rid of him.

After being discharged of our hulks (for he was not sent to Botany Bay) he went to Russia, rose by his wits at Court, and showed forged recommendations to everybody, for he knows all the world. Being in great favour with Potemkin, and through him with the Empress, he persuaded them that the English companies of light infantry never wore their hair behind, and looked much more martial for being close trimmed. By these representations he got orders to go round and cut off all the tails of the light infantry in the service. If the colonels were addicted to the old fashion enough to ransom their soldiers' queues with a handsome present, he let their heads alone; if not, he docked them all, and, having an amazing quantity of good hair, he shipped it off from Petersburg to Paris, where the barbers at that time gave a great price for it; and received at the same time a present from the Empress for the improvement he had suggested in her military establishment. He really is so ingenious one begins to respect him, and I think it is a great pity swindling is contrary to law, as it would sharpen our wits so very much.

The Russian story is Elliot's, so I give you my authority; however, I was highly amused with it. There is, I see by the papers, great bustle about expected invasion in England; tell me in your next what is really true about it, and if you are very much afraid I will not be saucy now. The reviews at Berlin are on the 15th of next month, but it will throw us so late at Vienna that I do not think we shall go to them. They are, to be sure, prodigious by all accounts, but as I am no judge of military manœuvres (notwithstanding my service in the Royal Lancashires) I do not think they are so well worth going to see. Perhaps we should be something like an English gentleman, who was there last year, and being told with a sneer, by a great Prussian officer, "qu'il n'y avoit rien comme cela en Angleterre," answered very composedly, "C'est vrai, mais j'aime mieux la chasse du Renard." Adieu, once more; tell Anne I wrote to her the other day, and depend upon it you shall hear from me constantly.

Believe me most affectionately yours,

J. B. S. MORRITT.

CHAPTER II

Vienna—The Polish Insurrection

Morritt reached Vienna early in May 1794, to find the Polish insurrection at its height. The iniquitous Partitions of 1772 and 1793 left the Poles no hope of preserving any remains of independence, except by an armed rising. The titular king, Stanislaus Poniatowski, was Catherine's nominee, and had acted as a mere puppet in her hands. All the hopes of the patriotic party were fixed on Thaddeus Kosciusko, the one man who could rouse his countrymen and keep them together. He had some military experience; for he had been trained in France, and then had served under Washington and Gates in the American war; and he had shown his powers at Dabienka in 1792, when with 4,000 Poles he held his post against 18,000 Russians. The order for disbanding Polish regiments, in March 1794, was the signal for revolt. Madalinski marched off his brigade from Pultusk, and formed a nucleus for the insurgents. Kosciusko returned from Dresden to Cracow, was proclaimed General-in-Chief on March 24, and defeated a Russian force at Raclawisze on April 4. On April 18, Warsaw was in the possession of the insurgents, and a few days later the citizens of Wilna rose, and killed or made prisoners all the Russian garrison. At Grodno the same thing happened, and all the Polish regiments deserted the Russian service and joined Kosciusko. In May, therefore, all seemed to be going well; but before Morritt left Vienna there was a change for the worse. The King of Prussia had withdrawn most of his troops from the French war to co-operate with Russia. On June 15 the Prussians occupied Cracow, and Austria also began to send troops against the Polish insurgents. After a few trifling successes Kosciusko was defeated in the fatal battle of Maccejowica on October 10, and himself wounded and taken prisoner. This was the real "Finis Poloniae," though the struggle was kept up for a few weeks, until, with the storming of Praga and the capitulation of Warsaw on November 8, and the defeat at Radoczya ten days later, the insurrection came to an end.

In the months of May and June 1794 the French armies of the Sambre and Meuse and of the Rhine had made considerable progress, thanks in great measure to the vigour with which Carnot reinforced them and pushed them forward. After severe fighting on the river Sambre, the successes of the French in the engagement at Turcoing on May 17, and still more the victory of Fleurus on June 26, resulted in the fall of Charleroi and the retreat of the Austrians from Flanders and beyond the Meuse, while the English under the Duke of York retired to Antwerp. But in the early part of the campaign the Allies had had a temporary success on April 26, when a force composed of the British under the Duke of York and some Austrian troops repulsed the French near Cambrai. The news of this reached Vienna on May 3, and Morritt refers to it when he writes of the French being "drubbed" and of English bravery being praised at Vienna. Another apparent success noticed in the letters was the capture of Landrecy on April 30, the French having left that siege unrelieved, for the sake of a more important plan of campaign. There is no reference in the letters of this year to Lord Howe's naval victory of June 1.

May 4 *I believe,*
1794.

DEAR ANNETTE,
Stockdale and I are at last got to Vienna. Just when we were going to leave Dresden arrived Wilbraham and Inge in their road to Petersburg from Vienna, which you may be sure induced us to defer our departure for a day or two. Old English friends are not the less agreeable for exportation, and very happy we were. When I got here I met Bootle, to whom of course I introduced myself. From letters

having miscarried, etc., he had just missed his brother, who expected his coming to Dresden, from thinking Poland impassable. Bootle, however, has taken the Polish route, and come near Warsaw here, where he equally expected to find Wilbraham. As Polish news of any authority is not to be had even here, I must tell you the particulars he himself saw, and heard. When he was near Warsaw, within six miles, the town was in a state of the utmost insurrection. Nobody could come out or in by the gates. He was at the head-quarters of the Prussian troops near the place, and saw some Russians, who escaped from the town. The citizens and people had risen and massacred the Russian garrison, of which very few had escaped. The place in consequence is once more in the hands of the Poles. Their army, under Kosciusko, has twice beat the Russian troops, and was advancing to Warsaw, which will now perhaps fall into their hands.

We heard at Dresden before he had with him about 10,000 men, and another army of about 8,000 in another part of the country has declared for him. Many of these are the regular Polish army, which the Russians had in part disarmed and disbanded. The peasants from all sides were flocking to the insurgents, and their only want was arms for them, which if they get to Warsaw they will have. Kosciusko, who commands them, bears the highest character both as a man and a general. He left Dresden just before we got there to go and make this stand once more, and what everybody at first thought a mere riot amongst the peasantry has proved a serious insurrection by his abilities. The Poles are as unanimous as possible now, for they who last year opposed them are now chiefly with Kosciusko, thanks to Russian oppression. He was the man who, before the King gave up the cause, performed such wonders, and not Poniatowski; Bootle says the Prussian officers speak of him in the highest terms, though an enemy, and the Poles to a man adore him. In the last short war with 4,000 men he drove before him from the Vistula a corps of 20,000 Russians, and has always beat them hitherto.

You know it was the fashion in England to talk of the hard fate of the poor King of Poland. Having heard from revolutionary Poles, and others here and at Dresden, the whole of the affair, I must undeceive you. The King was never sincere from the first, and has all along played a collusive game with the Empress. The Poles at the end of the last war had more advantages over their enemies than ever, and were in a strong state of defence along their frontier. They called on him to head them and join the camp. He made all the parade that a hypocrite sovereign could on taking the field, and formed a camp near Warsaw by withdrawing the troops from the frontiers, which he left exposed to the Russians. The consequence was they advanced into the country, and he then had an opportunity of saying with truth that all hopes were over, and making the disgraceful truce [July 23, 1792] which has ended in the slavery of himself and his country. It was an entire mistake to suppose the Poles unable to hold out any longer at that time, and it was owing to his want of honesty that they were deserted. At present they will, I fear, only irritate the rascals that plunder them, but their commanders are sincere, and they are in the right, so *nous verrons*.

You see, I am, *à l'ordinaire*, wild, but don't wonder at it, I dare say ; if they succeed it will perhaps make the Empress Catharine and the King of Prussia feel that oppression is not the safest way of governing a newly conquered country ; if not—

> By fairy hands their knell is rung,
> By forms unseen their dirge is sung.

I saw a letter from a noble Pole to a friend in Dresden, in which the expressions were very sanguine ; he says : "Vous voyez nos greniers sont les magasins de Kosciusko, et tous nos biens sont ses trésors." With this spirit they all talk, and act; so drink their healths, as we do. If you think all this a bore I beg your pardon; but as the facts even here are not generally known, and I dare say misrepresented both here and in England, I cannot help sending you the story as it is, not so much for you as your mother and Frances, who are, I believe, glad to hear good news of these poor people. I am sure, if bad usage gives men a claim to pity, none have it more, for, backed by the Empress, the insolence of the Russian troops had gone to seizing on private property just as they liked. It is a real fact that their officers, if they saw a fine horse or anything of the sort, made no scruple of taking it as plunder in a country where they entered under the pretence of alliance. Can these men succumb, or will they fight like men? If they do not I am sure men's hearts are changed lately, or a just cause does not make men fight as it used to do. We just heard, too, yesterday of the French being drubbed,[1] and have the pleasure of hearing English bravery recorded at Vienna in the highest terms. I am as glad of this as of the other, for I hate oppression either from kings or sans-culottes. In my next you shall hear something more about Vienna, and ourselves; in the meantime tell my mother that we are as well as possible if she will take our words for it, though she may not see anybody that has seen us. I shall make a trip to the mines in Hungary at Schemnitz and Cremnitz; they are both gold and silver mines. We return here, and soon after proceed to Constantinople. Direct here, and I shall leave directions to forward my letters wherever I may be. My mother shall hear from me very soon; in the meantime be easy about us, for the humbugs one hears about dangers by an English fireside are too ridiculous. The passage from hence to Constantinople is as regular as from Edinburgh to London, and as safe, and almost as commonly

[1] See page 22.

travelled; rather *worse roads*, but I believe nowhere so dangerous as over Finchley common.

Your very affectionate brother,

J. B. S. M.

SCHEMNITZ, HUNGARY,

May 22, 1794.

DEAR MOTHER,

Though I date my letter from the mines of Hungary, we shall probably return to Vienna before I can put it into the post, so do not wonder if it is rather long upon the road.

To take up our story where I left off, I wrote to Anne an account of our arrival at Vienna, but we had seen too little to give you any account of the place. We had been there about a fortnight when we set out on our present expedition, and flatter ourselves we can give a most excellent and accurate description of it. Perhaps of all the great towns I ever was in Vienna is the very pleasantest, particularly at this time of the year. The number of people of fashion who reside here, the ease with which we were introduced, and the many places of public lounging, are beyond those of any town we have seen on the Continent. Bootle introduced us to some friends he had been acquainted with at Petersburg who happened to be here, and we presented our letters to Stratton, the chargé d'affaires. Such an introduction for an Englishman is quite sufficient, as the only question ever asked about you is, "Est-il aimable?" which I presume is the reason why Lord Porchester preferred Dresden, as there can otherwise be no comparison. A few evenings after our arrival we were carried to a great ball at a Madame de Saldaignac's; as she had assembled everything that was gay amongst the *haute noblesse* here, we began in a fair way. The dances in vogue here are the walses, and English country dances, so Heaven be praised we need not, as in France, torture our legs into cotillons, or have a dancing-master to teach us to hold up our heads. The walse, however, we have not yet dared to attempt. I showed Anne one day how it was danced, and if she has forgot Martignier can tell her; but in doing it the other day as part of a country dance I gave my partner such a kick that we were very near both falling together. They dance them so well here that I assure you it was a great subject of lamentation to us that we could not join in them. The night after we were at another ball, which was given in a *superbe bosquet* in the middle of Prince Lichtenstein's garden, but which, choosing unfortunately to be *vastly rural*, was extremely cold. What with a German play and Battel given in an alley of the garden, all lighted with lamps, it was very magnificent, but we were obliged to teach the natives to dance Country Bumpkin by way of keeping ourselves warm. Besides the plays in German, and an Italian opera, there are more public places of resort, and more frequented, than in any town I have seen. There are lounges for every hour of the day, almost equal, I think, to Bond Street. In the different public walks and drives of the Prater and Schönbrunn there are great public saloons and coffee-rooms, where people of all ranks breakfast, dine, or sup, and where there are *traiteurs*, and refreshments of ice, etc., at all hours. You here meet everybody, for the weather has been uncommonly fine, and people here dare amuse themselves, because it is not thought vulgar. In London it would be certainly thought rather odd, but in a broad, open street like St. James's Street I have seen women of fashion, and even princesses with a hundred thousand quarterings, sitting eating ice at a coffee-house door after ten o'clock at night.

The history of our day was in general this: After breakfast we went seeing sights, or playing tennis, or walking in the gardens, which occupations lasted till dinner. If not engaged out we always dined with Bootle and his friend at three. At five go in our carriage to the Prater, the Hyde Park here, but much prettier, and walk about seeing our friends, or playing the fool in swings and merry-go-rounds, with which the place abounds. We afterwards go to the opera sometimes, or on the ramparts, where there are music, ices, and another assemblage of everything that is gay till ten o'clock, when, if we do not contrive in the course of the day to be asked to a ball or a supper, we march home, and shut up shop. The Emperor not being here there is no Court, so our bags and swords are unemployed, as we did not choose to be presented at Prince Kaunitz's dinners, which are very stupid, and not necessary unless you mean to stay. There is less form of that sort here than in any metropolis except London, and in most places, as in England, you cannot be too undressed to be genteel.

Indeed, if an Englishman wore his shoes on his head I believe he would have imitators here, as we are in high vogue and received with great cordiality. We presented Mrs. Philips's letters to Madame Ferrari and the Bishop of Nancy, and met with much civility, and offers of more if we stayed. I was so extremely tired of being quizzy in a dress coat that I followed the example at last of every single Englishman I have met, and made up once more my uniform. As it is a custom in most corps here for a man to be allowed to wear any uniform he has once had, though he is no longer in the corps, there is nothing improper in it. However, don't tell Stanley, as he makes a fuss about these things. Elliot and everybody advised me to do it, and I found that all foreigners, English and others, make a practice of it with less right than I have. Stockdale has sported a grave black dress coat, and looks *Doctor Stockdale* at least. I only wish you could see either of us full dressed, as our figures are excellent.

We have now been from Vienna about a week, and are returning to-morrow from a tour to the mines of Hungary. So take up your map and follow us. I left off here to go and see the mines, and have not had time to take up my pen till now I am again at Vienna, May 27. The mines we have been to see are in the north part of Hungary, at Schemnitz and Cremnitz, and no trace of history, I believe, ascertains how long they have been worked. We passed through Presburg, the capital of this province, where there is a large palace, in which the Emperor's son or brother, as Palatine of Hungary, sometimes keeps his Court. It is built on the Danube, which is here very broad and handsome, and which we crossed on one of the *ponts volants* or boat bridges you have heard me mention as on the Rhine. Presburg is not large, and stands along the river under a steep, prominent hill, on which is the castle. The country from here to near Schemnitz is not interesting, but made us reflect a little on the situation of all kingdoms that are not themselves the seats of government; for the great rambling châteaux of the *noblesse* are everywhere almost deserted, and often put me in mind of our drive to Scarborough from Doncaster. Some old frontier castles and woody hills adorned the Danube near Presburg, but the country in general is a large, flat plain, sometimes marsh, or down, but more generally covered with corn. All over it are great well-conditioned convents, and their inhabitants are the only people in the country that seem to live comfortably.

The national dress of the Hungarian nobles is a handsome one, and they seem very much attached to it, as few of them lay it aside, even in the circles of Vienna. Hussar breeches, boots and spurs; an Hussar cap with a long tassel at the point hanging down their back, a waistcoat and jacket edged with sables and adorned with small round buttons and Brandenburgs. The Emperor has a guard of them, all nobles, and each attended by his servant, which seems as fine a body of men, I think, as the Royal Lancaster. In revenge, however, for all this dressing, the common people are almost naked, and all beggars. Near

Schemnitz the country is beautiful, and all the tour by Cremnitz to Roden the same. These mountains are very high, and covered with a profusion of different wood ; bold rocks, like those on the edge of Ulleswater, often rise out of it, and here and there we remarked a ruined castle. These hills are the famous mines, chiefly lead, silver, and gold. The two last are generally mixed together, and are in greater or less quantities ; they also find a quantity of coal in the lead. The immensity of the works struck us very much. You will have some conception of them when I tell you that at Cremnitz they go to the depth of 300 fathoms in one part, and that parts of them are joined by subterraneous passages of twelve and fifteen English miles.

We went into one of the mines to the depth of 172 fathoms. The descent is (unless you choose to be let down in a bucket) down long ladders tied end to end, and often perpendicular or bent inwards. They afford, however, such good hold for your hands that we preferred them to the bucket. Little boys go just before each person with candles, and the darkness of the rest prevented the height from having any effect on our heads. You sometimes go down six or eight ladders together before you arrive at a landing-place. The old works are easily distinguished, having been cut with iron instruments ; but since the invention of powder, blasting has been found a speedier method. At Cremnitz is the Imperial mint, where we saw the whole process of coining the gold and silver. As I believe it, however, nothing more than our own, and inferior indeed in machinery, as they everywhere are, I will not describe what you may get better elsewhere. They separate the gold from the silver after smelting off all the drops and scoria from the ore, by applying aquafortis, which absorbs the silver, and precipitates the gold. They afterwards detach the acid from the silver by applying an alkali, but both these are common chemical processes.

The names and richness of the different streams of ore, of which there are five at Schemnitz constantly worked, I wrote down in my journal, but they will not be very interesting here. We were told these mines employed 13,000 people; they are divided into different departments, and very well regulated. Every one who is a candidate for an employment here is obliged to enter at an academy which the Emperor maintains at both Schemnitz and Cremnitz. He is instructed by the professors for three years in the practical part of mineralogy, and then if he can get an appointment as superintendent of any part of the departments, he is salaried accordingly; this is a great resource for some of the inferior *noblesse* here. The appearance of the ore in the mine is little more than that of a different coloured stone, except the lead, which is so broad and so full of ore as to have a very pretty effect by our lamps. For the machinery and dresses, I have drawn them in my journal, but could not make you otherwise understand them by description. The mechanism is, however, I think, much inferior to some in England. The language here being the Wallach, and totally different from German, one often had a difficulty in being the least understood. We found, however, that almost every peasant understood Latin, which is in many parts here almost the common language of the country, so we contrived to make them comprehend what we wanted, though our pronunciation made it a different language. Is it not singular that a place the Romans knew but little of, and which was so early ravished from them by the northern hive, should retain at this day their language as a vulgar tongue, when it is lost in Gaul, Spain, and Italy? The Hungarians and Austrians seem almost to have as great an antipathy as the Scotch and the Irish. I must add a sheet, or you will never read this.

Is it not a curious subject of reflection that nations under the same government, instead of being more united, almost everywhere hate one another? However, perhaps here the jealousy may have some cause, as the Austrians, who are really a flourishing and well-conditioned people, occupying the seat of government, do seem to draw a good part of their riches from their neighbours. As the aristocracy, both of the sword and the gown, seems to be a good deal more aggressive in Hungary, and the people more bigoted, ignorant, and poor, the difference of opinion may have its effect. Can anything be more striking than the perpetual conjunction of superstition and poverty that prevails in many parts of the Continent? The poor wretch with nothing to comfort him on earth has recourse to his beads and ave-Marys, which, in their turn occupying all his thoughts and industry like a dream, continue that misery whose pains they alleviate. In the Prussian and Saxon dominions, on the contrary, at least in parts of them, industry and activity are seen in their villages, which are clean and comfortable even under an arbitrary government, so that despotism borrows part of its effect from religious opinions.

The Emperor Joseph, who is here almost adored by those whom he governed, did suppress many of the convents in Bohemia as well as Brabant and Flanders, and seems to have meant to bring forward his subjects there to a level with the industry, etc., of the Protestant states. His enemies charge him with sansculottism, but is that possible in his situation? You will see my English ideas don't change much, and I can still say with J. J. Rousseau, " Heureux si, en voyant d'autres constitutions, je trouve des nouvelles raisons pour aimer celle de ma patrie." We are now returned to Vienna, which we find as pleasant as ever, and last night were at a great ball to which all the strangers subscribed, and which was *magnifique*. To give you some idea of etiquette, we admitted none but the first *noblesse*—for here they are divided into first and second. The first must have at least thirty-two undisputed quarterings. Does not this put you in mind of Baron

Thundertentronck? We have been dancing and
laughing till eight this morning, though at first the ball
was rather threatened with destruction from the
entrance of two actresses, pretty notorious, to whom
their *chers amis* had given tickets. As none were
admitted without thirty-two quarterings they got
handed out, and the whole went on very well.

I have just received a great parcel of letters, in
which are two from you and one from Anne, which,
being very differently dated, shows how regular the
post is. She talks of her partiality to her own dear
countrywomen; tell her if she will come here, I can
show her as pleasant, as pretty, and as good and well-
behaved girls as ever she saw in her life, and that I
wish some of my English acquaintances were here, as
they might hear "T'other young women speak civilly
to us," as that wag Ben says. Our great adorations at
present are two Princesses de Ligne, sisters to the
poor Prince Charles, who was killed last year in
Flanders, and with whom we have all of us been
making the agreeable at the ball, and I have learnt
several pretty pastimes, such as *pied de bœuf*, etc.,
though not absolutely in the way I taught her it;
however, it improves a ball-room infinitely. On our
return here we found Wilbraham, who had come to
join his brother, so we are extremely pleasant indeed,
and, what I am sure you will all congratulate me upon,
he accompanies us to Constantinople. I have just
seen a most alarming letter from Mrs. Bootle, who,
under the idea that the whole Continent is in com-
motion, wants them at home. Now, lest you should
take the same imaginations, I can only assure you
we have never been so quiet in England for a year or
two as matters are here at present, and seem likely
to be.

You bid me tell you our plans from hence; they
are as followeth. In about ten days I think we shall,
if possible, leave this charming place for Constantinople. We send off our carriage and all our heavy

baggage to Trieste, there to stay till further orders for Italy. From hence across Hungary and Servia there is an established post, so we buy a German carriage, which we shall sell there. The country about Belgrade being at present dangerous on account of banditti, we take the road by Buda, Temesvar, and Bucharest, though I regret very much missing Belgrade. The other road is, besides, near two hundred miles round about. After we are in the Turkish dominions we shall be obliged to ride all the way, though you will believe there is no very mighty matter in the journey when I tell you there is a regular post twice a month from here to Constantinople. You who laugh at my general mode of travelling in England would be highly amused to see us driven here. The man who drives has a long rein fastened to the near horse before, by which of course he has no command over the leaders but to stop them. In consequence of this liberty, they often beg leave to turn, regardless of his voice, to the right instead of the left, etc., but notwithstanding the hourly inconvenience of having to get off merely to turn the horses, they have not the sense to use a double rein. Mr. Burke would delight in a German : he never makes innovations. A pipe of tobacco, a long queue and whiskers, and a pace of three miles and a half per hour make him happy. As, in many parts of our last trip into Hungary, there was not a regular post, we frequently had to sit in our carriage above an hour while the postmaster was mustering all the horses in the village—and all sometimes were not five, which was our number. In this part of our tour, even though we rose at six, twenty-five or thirty miles was our utmost stretch of travelling.

I will reserve my future remarks on the dress and style of driving till we get through Hungary, only it always strikes me as one of those things my Aunt Mary would not like. We shall take the first opportunity of adding to our suite a man who understands

Turkish and modern Greek, though Italian on the coasts of all the Archipelago is so universal that we shall meet with little difficulty, as we can already make ourselves completely understood in it, and shall very soon speak it with ease. I must add one remark here which has been often made at Vienna, that there is no town where languages are so much understood. Most people of fashion here understand four or five, and many more. Everybody speaks French and Italian amongst the tradesmen, even, and the higher ranks almost all speak English and perhaps Hungarian, Polish, or Greek; for the Poles, Russians, Bohemians, and Carinthians, I believe, all speak different dialects of Sclavonian, a perfectly distinct, and more ancient language than the German, I believe, and which, though I have heard that it is very difficult, certainly sounds far more soft and agreeable to the ear than that detestable grunting; for I cannot bring myself to bear German, and only wonder the language is not changed by agreement. Wilbraham has just been making me laugh with an account of his accommodations on his road to Dresden. He passed by Hungary and crossed the Crapack (Carpathian) mountains. In the room where he slept one night the company consisted of himself, Inge, their two servants, the innkeeper, his wife, two postillions, three children, an ass, a sow and pigs, two turkeys, and a hen and chickens. As far as these agreements go, however, I can't say we any of us affect being very fine, though we have once or twice remarked with Touchstone, " Now are we in Germany, more fools we; when we were at home we were in a better place."

I have hitherto chattered away so much on what I have seen and heard that I have hardly taken any notice of your letters.

So Henry is at last in Flanders. When I look at the very small list of officers that have suffered, I hope we have but little to fear, and I am sure that real service of this kind will conduce more than anything in the world to make him a steadier and more manly character. We must make up our minds to that danger which immediately results from the very nature of his profession, and in our present victorious state [1] I hope we shall soon have less to apprehend.

I am glad to hear your apprehensions of an invasion are rather got over. I used to be rather saucy about them, but as, in London, the colonel of the Royal Lancaster was so much greater an alarmist than yourself, I began to entertain a more respectful opinion of your courage than I had done before the comparison. If he and Mrs. Bootle were besieged in Lathom Hall, I very much doubt if old Lady Derby's memory would be very much disgraced by her descendant and successor.

Peisse was so sure we could not get to Constantinople, he bet Stockdale five guineas against it, which in about a month's time we hope to write and claim. You can really not have a notion how ridiculous these bugbear journeys are as you approach nearer to them. You see a great many more Greeks and Turks here than you do Irishmen in London, so the communication, you may be sure, is nothing either very difficult or dangerous. We have been inquiring after a draughtsman, and I hope we have heard of one who will suit us. As we have not yet settled anything, however, about him, you shall have particulars in my next letter, as I will write to Frances in a few days. Our best way of receiving letters from you will still be by the post. Direct your letters to me, "Aux soins de Monsieur le Comte Fries, Vienne." He is our banker, and will forward them to Constantinople, from whence I shall easily order them to Athens or wherever we are by Mr. Liston's [2] assistance. I am heartily glad the country in England has given such general proofs of its loyalty and sense; I must own I

---

[1] See p. 22.

[2] Afterwards Sir R. Liston. He was Ambassador at Constantinople, 1793-6.

never had any fear of the contrary myself, for I do not and cannot believe that any great part of our people can ever be in a French interest.   There have been reports of their emissaries making great attempts on the minds of the lower classes here, and an honest Irishman, Captain O'Connel, told us the other day that to his *sartin* knowledge the national assembly had for a year past employed above thirty emissaries here in making *prostitutes*, meaning probably *proselytes*; but it was a very good Irish reading.

I will give a more detailed account of the lions here in my letter to Frances, but the chief object is what I have so much enlarged upon—the society.   I cannot say that I would encourage you or her to come here for adoration, for since Lady Mary Wortley's time so many English costumes have got here that I do not think *embonpoint* so much admired as it used to be; but if you will proceed to Turkey you may still have a chance of passing for beauties, as they tell me the Ambassador in London was struck with nobody so much as Mrs. Hobart.

Believe me, **my dearest mother,**

Your ever affectionate son,

J. B. S. MORRITT.

CHAPTER III

Journey from Vienna to Constantinople, with some Digressions about Vienna and Styria

KECSKEMET,[1]
June 24, 1794.

Dear Frances,

You will wonder from my date where the deuce I have got to, and, indeed, so do I myself; however, it is a small town, alias village, where we are changing horses between Buda and Temesvar. We left Vienna some days ago, and have come through Buda. However, as I have given you a very imperfect account of our stay and trips at Vienna, I have much previous debt to discharge before I describe our present situation, and this letter will, I suppose, set out from Temesvar. My mother would show you an account I sent her of our tour to the Hungarian mines, and some sketch of Vienna. Of this latter I will now attempt a more minute description. Vienna, though it stands on a very considerable space, contains but about 32,000 inhabitants; this is owing to the suburbs, which are larger even than the town itself, being separated by the ramparts from it, which take up near a quarter of a mile in breadth. Parts of it are well built and neat, though I cannot say there are any squares or streets like those of London and Paris; but then, in return, there are no streets like our *City lanes*, or those of the *faubourgs* St. Marcel. The Court and the principal places of amusement are within the ramparts, on which account everybody endeavours to have a

---

[1] In Hungary, south-east of Buda-Pest, on the present Orient line.

38

house or lodgings in the town, while the *faubourgs* are occupied by tradesmen and mechanics of all sorts, as for these reasons they are considerably cheaper lodgings. We all (viz. Bootle, Wilbraham, and our two selves) lived at Wolf's, a great house where all the English lodge almost, as you are well treated and pay a good deal. The Court at Vienna, though perhaps one of the most active, is one of the least noisy in Europe. The present Emperor, who is now returned from Flanders, keeps up scarce any sort of state, no levees or drawing-rooms but three or four great days in the year, and he frequently walks out in the town or on the ramparts without attendants. The Empress seems as much averse to state as he is, and, if one may now place any confidence in the attachment of subjects, he has but little occasion for guards, as he seems to be extremely beloved by all ranks of people, at least all we have been able to converse with.

Notwithstanding this, however, it is certain there have been conspiracies detected here too, and several persons arrested, though with such privacy nobody knows any particulars about them, and whatever the danger may have been there is neither alarm nor bustle in the town, as except once or twice we never heard it mentioned. As to the town of Vienna itself, it does not abound in fine buildings or lions of that species, but the public walks about it and the general situation is delightful. These were most of them parks of the Emperors, and were thrown open by the Emperor Joseph, with an inscription on one of them which does him infinite honour: " A place of amusement thrown open for all men by *their friend.*" The Augarten, which is one of the principal ones, is a large garden laid out in shady walks, with a fine saloon, where anybody may dine or sup, and where there is music, and the people go there to take refreshments from six in the morning. Schönbrunn, at about a league from the town, is a large palace of the Emperor's, where he resides during the summer months; nevertheless the walks here, which are very extensive, and really pretty though formal, are open to everybody, and there is a coffee-house on the same plan as that of the Augarten.   There are the lounges in the morning and at dinner for those who have nothing else to do. In the evening about five everybody assembles in the Prater, a large park, very shady, with long avenues, where the fine folks display their equipages and the Jemmy folks their riding, in favour of which I cannot say much.   Here everybody walks about, takes coffee, ices, etc., and there is so great a mixture of people that if the fine people (as fine people sometimes will) should happen to be stupid there are always others who love fun.   In consequence of this the place is filled with ups-and-downs, merry-go-rounds, swings, etc., etc., and very pretty little masters we were more than once, all of us having (thank Heaven) no bad knack at playing the fool.   Here are what I never saw elsewhere, a quantity of stags and wild boars, which however from good living and being taken care of are as tame as any other pigs.

Whilst we were at Vienna there were fireworks given in the Prater twice, one of which represented the siege of Landrecy [1] and was pretty enough.   From the Prater, which is about a mile from the town, the people go off to the theatres; there are Italian operas here for five times a week, and one of the theatres is pretty, the singing very good.   There is a German theatre, which of course we did not frequent much, not understanding the language.   Indeed, though German is the universal language, yet French is so much the language of the higher classes that you often hear of a person talking *good or bad German* as you would of an acquired tongue.   Italian is also generally spoken, and with the intercourse they have with Hungary, Bohemia, Russia, and England, Vienna is a perfect Babel, and you meet with many men and women who can speak five or six languages, and almost all three—

[1] See p. 22.

French, German, and Italian.   In the evening after the
theatres all the town assemble on the ramparts, where
there is music, ice, etc.   They stay till ten, and very
often afterwards walk or sit in the Graben, a broad,
open street, eating ices at the coffee-house doors ; and
this is not scrupled by people of the first fashion.
There are in the evening many private assemblies
and balls.   So, with all these places of public resort,
Vienna is one of the gayest scenes in the world.
Another pleasant circumstance, at least in the public
places, is the great strictness of their police, which
keeps the people perfectly quiet : and you here see
nothing of that riot and confusion which infests the
doors of all our public places.   There are also very
severe penalties for all sorts of riot ; every one who
strikes a blow would have to pay forty florins (about
four guineas), and for discharging a pistol within a
certain distance about two hundred florins.   You will
easily perceive these laws would be very inefficacious
with our ideas about quarrels, but the Germans, who
are used to subordination and even corporal punishments, are by no means so nice about the point of
honour between men as we or the French were ;
so that I believe a man might pay his fine for a beating
without being called to account in any other way.
However, though in some respects perhaps agreeable,
I can't help thinking this extreme police very bad in
its effects.

It encourages, like that of Venice, a system of spies
and informers, of which there are, I am told, several in
every place of public resort ; it has likewise a further
and still worse effect on the manners of the people,
for, supported by the soldiery, and armed with entire
power over them by the Government, it keeps them
unenterprising, mistrustful, and phlegmatic.   It is true
our mobs are unruly, but amongst our common
people we find marked, active characters, and all
that spirit and activity of mind which is destroyed
in a German by this one principle of perpetual

subordination. Their military turn encourages this still more, for the Austrians are all soldiers, and almost every postmaster and innkeeper is an officer in the army. Perhaps I have some grudge against the police for keeping us a whole day at Vienna to get our passports signed, which they must be by all of them, or we should have risked being stopped on our journey. All our representations could not prevail upon them to make the least haste either with ours or our servants'. For our draughtsman, who is a native of Vienna, I was obliged to be surety in two hundred florins that he should return in two years.

In society the Viennois are rather French in their manners, and still more so in their morals, which are pretty licentious. No woman here loses her character in society for what would in England banish her from it even now. The frequency of intrigue proceeds, too, from the same cause, for like the French they are often married without being the least consulted, and nothing is more common than living separate by mutual consent; they are also ridiculously nice in their ideas about nobility and descent, and the men are, amongst most of the first *noblesse*, themselves an excuse, or at least a reason, for the infidelity of their wives. The Court, I am told, is now much better in this respect than it was ten or twelve years ago; but it is not confined to the Court, as these ideas seem to prevail through the whole people, and there are few women who are not provided with a lover or two, and that pretty avowedly. As in France, too, Madame here is everything and Monsieur is a very subordinate character. Indeed, how it should be better I do not know, for the men are certainly as stupid a set as I ever saw; and really the women, where they deviate from the above system, and the young ones who, from not being married, have not begun it, are some of them very amiable.

In the way of sights, the chief ones we saw were the cabinets of modern and ancient coins and medals;

the modern ones were very complete, and arranged
from the earliest times. Of the antique ones I will
not give any description, as Bootle has been so kind
as to take charge of a book for you which will do
it better. I could not get you any sulphurs, as they
do not make them here. There is a cabinet of fossils,
which I do not much understand, and a very fine and
large library, which we walked over, and in which
there is a room open to everybody, where you may
go and call for any book you please at certain hours,
but you cannot take them out of the library. This is
common with the library at Dresden and others.
I wonder the King has never adopted so liberal a
system in our libraries. Amongst other curiosities,
they possess here every book that was printed in
Germany from the beginning of printing in the year
1448 to the year 1500. Most of them, according to
the taste of the times, are doctors and divines, but
there are some curious editions of the Classics. There
is a very curious priory here, with a clock of which
all the motions correspond with those of the planets
they represent, and the clock has all the various
movements for the month, year, etc. This machine,
however complicated, was the work of a common
labourer near Vienna, who afterwards was mechanist
to the Court, and enjoyed a well-deserved pension
from Joseph as a reward for his ingenuity.

At the Belvedere, a palace built by Prince Eugène,
the Emperor has a good collection of pictures, though
not equal to the electoral one at Dresden, by any
means. I cannot describe pictures, so you must
excuse this ; but the curious part is a large collection
of specimens of the very old German masters, such
as Alb. Dürer, Holbein, etc., which are very ugly but
striking, as they show the progress of the art.

There is a finer collection at Prince Lichtenstein's,
who has a great house here, particularly in Guidos
and Vandycks. This family is the most considerable
of any in Vienna, where they possess richer and finer

palaces than the Emperor himself. I am told Prince
Louis Lichtenstein is not worth less than £100,000
per annum. There are three or four brothers and
cousins; of one of them, Charles, we heard a very
honourable story. He had been in great favour with
the late Emperor; after his death being not equally
so. After some time the present Emperor sent to
tell him "he had heard his father had offered him
considerable advantages, and that it was his desire
to fulfil his intentions." The Prince's answer was,
with equal generosity, "that he had never *received* or
solicited a promise during the whole of his favour."

Another great man here is the Prince Esterhazy,
who has about the same income. He commands the
guard of Hungarian nobles which is the Emperor's
own, and consists of about four hundred young men
of the first families in Hungary, all *noblesse*. Their
uniform is a scarlet Hussar uniform, their boots, caps,
and clothes embroidered beautifully in silver, with a
tiger's skin over their left shoulder; their housings
and horse-furniture superb, and each attended by a
servant in the Hungarian dress, also on horseback.
The whole are the finest body of men I ever saw.
Except three or four great houses, the rest in Vienna
are all let in lodgings; they are built in separate
stories, with a common staircase of stone through
the house, and one family hires a story. This is
common in Dresden, and indeed in almost every
town in Germany. Here whole streets belong to
individuals, and within the ramparts are a very
considerable fortune. So much for Vienna. (Patience!)

I have filled, as you see, one sheet with Vienna
alone, and shall never get on through my Styrian
expedition, which took place about a week before
I left it, till I send off this letter, as we are now at
Szegedin, and slept last night at Telegyhaza. I can't
help putting down these names for the good of your
teeth and pronunciation. I will endeavour to give
you an account of ourselves since we set off from

Vienna, and will reserve my other trip for another letter, which shall be put on the stocks for some of you immediately, and launched from Hermanstadt perhaps. On Saturday last, then, being determined at all events to leave Vienna, we set out, after fussing all day at the police about our passports, at ten o'clock at night, for Constantinople. A violent storm of thunder and lightning accompanied our exit, which was of course very majestic. You will now begin to think that I shall never travel like other people ; however, it was no bad plan for getting forward, as we lost nothing by travelling all night, having seen the country as far as Presburg before on our Hungarian tour. Our party consists of Wilbraham, ourselves, a draughtsman, and two servants.

Near Attesburg, in a cornfield about eight miles from Presburg, is an old ruined arch extremely in decay, without inscription, which was built by Germanicus. About six miles from Presburg the high road to Buda turns off to the right, and continues through a rich, cultivated country or extensive flat wolds as far as Buda ; about which place it is hilly, and varied though not mountainous. However, though the parts of the landscape were not bad, they everywhere wanted what Mr. Gilpin would call *composition*. The harvest was everywhere in hand, June 22 and 23, and we also have passed through immense plains of Turkey wheat.

The Danube, when you have a view of it, is a fine feature in the prospect, sometimes spreading its branches amongst islands covered with wood, sometimes stretching out in a fine, bold sheet of water not narrower than the Thames at Westminster. He changes his bed perpetually, and seems quite the master of the plain he runs through. This is the only instance, I suppose, in Europe of a river so large at this immense distance from the sea. Raab and Comorn were the only two towns we passed through, and I do not know whether in England they would be honoured with that name, at least Raab; the other stages are positively villages. About that part the country is nothing but sandy wolds for some way, and very thinly peopled; near Buda it is more populous. The race of people, though the men are fine figures, are in general ugly and poor. The villages are collections of huts in long lines on each side of the road, with the gable ends towards the road, and each a little stoneyard, or garden, between them.

To give you some idea of the great authenticity of news in this part of the country; at Gonyos, about six miles from Raab, where we changed horses, the postmaster informed us that there was a general revolution in England, and Mr. Pitt was guillotined; but that though he was not quite sure of this, we might depend upon it there was an insurrection in Poland. This country is wild, and over the heaths the road is not made; however, it is very smooth and good in summer, the rest a fine turnpike road—and they drive like the wind. Where the country is cultivated it seems very fertile, and there are vines on the hills, though the wine is not of a good quality. (Temesvar, June 27.)

Buda and Pest are large towns, situated along a broad part of the Danube, and joined in summer by a bridge of boats, in winter by a flying bridge. I should think they contained together about 50,000 inhabitants, and, though not strikingly built, no one can help admiring them from the river, which is here broader than the Thames, and very rapid. We employed one morning here in seeing the Turkish baths, which, as the ruined mosques are now pulled down, are the only remains of the Turkish occupation here. There are three sets of them; two about a mile from the town and one in it. The water is naturally warm; we did not try it with a thermometer, but found it so hot that we could hardly bear our hands in it near the spring. Indeed I never felt any so hot, and I believe it is slightly impregnated with sulphur.

The plan of their baths is the same in all three, though the *Kaiserbad*, or bath of the Emperor, is the largest and neatest. There is one large circular room arched over with a dome, and a large bath where any one may bathe, and where we found about twenty men and women of all ages washing and bathing, or lying round in the steam, for rheumatisms, etc. Besides this, there are several smaller baths for *solo's*, likewise arched, and painted in fresco, with grotesque ornaments. In many of these they have brought a pipe with cold water so you may make it hot or cooler to your own taste. The common people are bathing here all day long, and seem very fond of the custom, which I suppose has at first been Turkish. Bootle had found it a very general one in Russia and Siberia, where, after a violent steam bath, they would run out and roll in the snow.

When we had got about six miles (one German mile) from Buda, the face of the country was entirely changed. In the Danube is a large island of sand, spotted here and there with a few evergreens, extending for miles, and resembling an African desert. The country one great plain of thin corn or Turkey wheat, often without a tree, without a hut or a human being for miles, except a few poor devils hoeing the Turkey corn here and there; then you pass some way over wide wolds or low, swampy grounds, and then again come to a plain of corn extending every way as far as the eye can reach. These, however, grow less and less, till about twenty miles from Buda the country becomes a perfect plain, without any covering but a short wold grass, except perhaps immediately about the villages, and extends in this state, literally without any rise or wave in the whole as far as the eye can reach, for three days' journey, to near Temesvar, about 130 or 150 miles.

The whole way from Buda there is no road made, though the way across this country in summer is better than any turnpike, and you are driven as quickly as in England. They are, however, so very long in changing horses, we could only make from fifty to sixty miles in a day. In all this plain there are but a few miserable villages, and I think Szegedin and Felegyhaza are the only two as large as Barningham. The post is established as far as Hermanstadt, and the post-house is often one poor solitary hut with a few horses turned loose on the common.

You cannot have an idea of the singularity of this immense plain, where you often see nothing but it and the sky, without a tree or a bush in the whole prospect. Over the whole of it are a number of hillocks, the remains of the Turkish wars, where the dead of each army have been buried in heaps. Where you do not see these there is not a rise in the whole country.

This part of Hungary and the Bannat are allotted for the residence of the French prisoners. At Szegedin there are about two hundred of their officers shut up in the fortress. They at first had the liberty of going about the town, but, having made a bad use of it, were confined to the castle, where they have a large court, and the ramparts to walk on. We attempted to get into the place, by a present to the sentinels, but we were only permitted to stand in the entrance and see them, but could not speak to them. There were several in the red cap, and some very fine-looking men among them; and, in the true French style, they seemed very merry and happy. At Temesvar there are about six hundred more, most of them common soldiers. The Bannat in winter is very swampy and marshy, and we were told at Vienna that one reason why they were sent here was that in this unwholesome climate they died off very quick. This I was sorry to hear in some measure confirmed by an Irish officer at Buda, who said that out of a body of fifteen hundred he had escorted there, he only found four hundred living a short time after. If this is really true it can only be equalled by the late bloody decree of the Convention against the English and Hanoverians.

In our day's journey from Felegyhaza we observed the villages, and huts which were absolutely nothing more than holes in the ground, with a thatched roof over them, the light admitted at one end through a square hole. The people, poor and dirty, more like savages than anything else, made us fancy ourselves in another part of the world from Europe. The only dress the men wear is a short, coarse shirt reaching to their waist and a pair of very wide open trousers to the knees, with a pair of jack-boots and spurs, which they never quit, and which may be the remains of some Tartar custom, when they wandered over these plains on horseback. What induces me more to think so is that these huts and these figures are exactly the same as those of the Crimea and the South of Russia, as we were told by Wilbraham's servant, who had been with Bootle. All the other Hungarians, almost, wear boots, even the women north of Presburg. The Hungarian nobles have short Hussar boots and always wear them, even at Vienna, except they choose to be à l'Anglaise at the balls. Though there are very few huts for many score miles, yet do not think these deserts thinly inhabited.

Besides weasels, which run about all over them exactly like rabbits in a warren, there are birds of prey, and water-birds innumerable near the swamps and streams, where there by chance are any. We saw several vultures, cranes, herons, hawks, storks, and some birds we did not know upon the water, with long, sharp bills, resembling woodcocks. We had no shot with us, so our gun was not very useful, and we were not good shots with a pistol, though we now and then tried our skill. Their sheep, of which they have a peculiar breed, have straight, sharp, spiral-twisted horns, but seem poor and bad. They have a very fine race of large sheepdogs, high and white, with woolly hair and very fierce. You see few huts without a breed of these dogs in all this country. The cattle are almost all a dusky grey, with long, upright horns; and they have a very good breed of horses throughout, much lighter and nearer the blood horse than those of Germany, and some wild horses.

In these plains, too, are several plants which are not in England, or only grow in gardens; but I am no botanist, so all this amusement is for Stockdale. The race of people here are handsomer, though not so numerous as in the north of Hungary. Near Temesvar you do see something like hills at about thirty miles' distance, and the country has some small woods, and appearance of cultivated fields. The town is small though not ill built, and very strongly fortified. We stay a day here as a resting-place, and I am employing it in this long prose, for which you will, I hope, not grudge the postage, as I foresee I have not near finished. We have here the luxury at last of clean water, which for several days we have not had. Here are no springs, and the wells are as thick as a ditch bottom in the deserts, for they are nothing else. We even met caravans of eight or ten wagons, who for want of accommodations stopped all night on the wold, and the people slept while the horses grazed round them, guarded by great dogs in the true caravan style.

The heats you have no notion of, and would laugh heartily at our figures in consequence of them. The thermometer in our room, with windows and doors open, is about ninety degrees, and I am at this moment without either coat or waistcoat, in a loose pair of linen trousers and slippers, and can scarce bear to write. We all are equipped with linen trousers and jackets, wear socks and no stockings, straw hats against the sun, and gauze veils against the dust and gnats. We have beautiful sheet lightning every evening, and have had for above a week. Last night, on entering the town, we saw several French prisoners, who are permitted to go about guarded, and seemed both in good order and very lively and merry. Indeed, had I not known the French pretty well I should have thought them the guard, and the others the prisoners. There are a great many Greeks too, in the town, and we have seen women in the Grecian dress, which is beautiful. The languages spoken here are Hungarian, Wallach, Sclavonian, and a little German. The Hungarian is really harmonious, and with many vowels. The people, too, are evidently less phlegmatic, and livelier than the Austrians or Saxons. Whiskers are a great fashion here, and Stockdale and Wilbraham, who cherish theirs, begin to look very fierce ; for my part I find my pretty face sufficiently hot without them.

At Buda we were told there were banditti beyond Temesvar who would render an escort necessary ; at Temesvar they are beyond Hermanstadt, and I fancy at Hermanstadt will again fly before us. However, escorts are easily procured, and we risk nothing. The truth is, three years ago there were some thousands, who infested all this country, but they have been all cleared away by the army, many of whom were sent down for that purpose, and are now kept off by the *Pandours*, a sort of independent Militia, who ride separately all over the country. We saw one yesterday, and I wish I could give you an idea of his figure. A tall, immense man, with a dirty cocked hat slouched over his shoulders, an old soldier's coat, and wooden boards with stuffing for a saddle, a small grey, lean pony, jack-boots, whiskers, a brace of pistols, powder-horn, pipe, and tobacco-pouch in his cross-belt, and a brass battle-axe at his saddle-bow. I have now finished my narrative, and will say something about other things on a separate sheet.

Anne told me in her last that Hall Wharton was arrested. Is it for high treason, or only sedition ? for she does not say. If your eyes have got so far as this, I will now be generous and release them ; so make my love to your whole fireside, or rather hearth-

side in this weather, and believe yourself sincerely
beloved

By your affectionate nephew,
J. B. S. MORRITT.

TEMESVAR, BANNAT,
June 27.

IZASVAROS, TRANSYLVANIA,
July 1.

DEAR MOTHER,

I write to you at present from a small inn
between Temesvar and Hermanstadt, where we are
stopping to dine and change horses. We have now
made, in ye vulgar tongue, a considerable hole in our
journey, and I hope soon to write to you from Constantinople. *En attendant,* I will give you some
account of our present and past motions. I wrote
to my aunt from Temesvar, and gave her a very
minute detail of all we had seen and observed at
Vienna, and in our road thence to Temesvar. For
these reasons, as you have, I suppose, seen that
elaborate composition, I will not go over my ground
again, but attempt to give you some account of a tour
we made in Styria about a week before we came away,
and which was productive of so much pleasure in
the execution that I hope you will have some in the
history of it.

We set off in a large party, viz. Wilbraham,
Bootle, Parkinson, a friend and companion of B.'s,
Stockdale, and myself. Styria, as you will see in
your maps, lies to the south of Austria, and is the
eastern extremity of the Alps, which here decrease
into the fertile plains of Southern Austria. The
object chiefly proposed in our pilgrimage was Maria-
Zell, a church on the Loretto plan, in a charming
situation, and a great object of pilgrimage to all this
country, as, like her sooty sister, I suppose she can
upon occasion perform miracles. As we did not, however, expect to see any of these, we went rather to
see the country, I believe, than her.

The first day of our tour we only went to Baden ;
indeed, we did not set out till after dinner, as we
meant only to go there that night. Baden is a small
watering-place about twelve miles from Vienna, where
we were that night to have a very pleasant ball in the
rooms, which was attended by all the gay people of
Vienna, and of course was very *charmant*, *délicieux*,
etc. Balls being, however, balls everywhere, I shall
not say what dances were called or who called them.
The next day we set forward on our tour.

The country beyond Baden grows immediately
picturesque, for you there leave the plain and go
between two very woody hills with a torrent in the
bottom. Beyond this, as in every hilly country, the
scene changes continually, and the eye commands
sometimes a very varied scene of hills, fields, and
woods, and at others you travel along deep dells with
every beauty rock, wood, and water can produce. The
rocks vary more than I ever saw them, I think, sometimes standing out of the wood in bold crags, sometimes
hanging over the torrent, and sometimes in immense
scars forming grotesque battlements round the tops of
very high mountains. One great beauty in all these
scenes, which in other places is often the greatest
blemish, is the style of building the cottages and
villages. You remember, perhaps, two little pictures
by Ruysdael in the Orléans Gallery, of cottages, and
trees with water, and Alpine scenery ; these cottages
might have sat for the picture.

The low-raftered walls, the very overhanging eaves,
the roof covered with shingles, and the modest brown
colour with red tiles or white plaster, make them not
only inoffensive objects, but often extremely picturesque, as whoever has seen the two pictures above-
mentioned will easily conceive. Their villages, which
are all built in the same way, sometimes adorned with
a neat, plain church, and placed along the banks of the
torrent aforesaid, produce an effect you can easier
conceive than I describe, till the variety of language

shall correspond better than it does with that of nature.

There are likewise, here and there, ruined fortresses on the hills, which, though but tolerably picturesque in themselves, yet acquire still further beauties from their situation ; for monasteries, which in England are our most beautiful ruins, are here, like their owners, in very excellent and unpicturesque conditions. As you proceed in the mountains towards Maria-Zell the scenes grow more and more bold ; that is, the dells are deeper, the rocks higher, the wood more mixed with firs and pines, and the stream more rapid. At last you see hills at distance, with patches of snow on them.

At and near Maria-Zell we met quantities of pil-grims, and processions with banners, crosses, saints, and Heaven knows what to amuse them on their journey to and from the chapel. The Virgin here is in very great repute, and receives visits from the very first company, both at Vienna and still greater dis-tances; however, when we saw her, her Court was rather numerous than brilliantly attended. She is a fat, chubby, black figure, in a massy silver shrine. Round this are people, as at Loretto, walking about on their knees. We saw a procession (which consisted of some five hundred of all ages, both men and women) make their entrée ; two leading troops were crowned with little green wax crowns, just on the middle of their head. They chanted in turns something we of course did not understand, made the tour of the church once, then went in, all kissing the top step, which must, of course, be very pleasant to those that came in last— made their obeisance to different saints, and then assembled, singing in the three aisles before the shrine, which they address individually afterwards, some on their knees with tapers, some on their faces, some walking on their knees ; in short, I think almost every way but walking on their heads, which I can't say I saw practised.

On Whit-Sunday there were here about 16,000 people on this errand; they generally stay here four-and-twenty hours, praying to all the saints and figures in the neighbourhood.   Indeed, so holy are the figures here that (whether by mistaking it for a saint or not I do not know) I saw one poor fellow pay most devout addresses to a stone lion, which was an ornament over the churchyard gateway.   Many parade out of church on their knees, and, like the junto in the "Critic," *exeunt praying*.

I bought a coloured print of the town and environs, which will give you a better idea of them than I can, and which you will, I hope, some time see. The country all around is delightfully romantic, and we travelled short journeys, having taken four *voituriers* from Vienna.   We crossed two or three steep mountains, where our horses were taken off and oxen put to the carriages, and where we saw the small Alpine huts for summer habitations, with excellent milk, etc.   This part of the country ends in a perfect Swiss scene of mountains, rocks, snow all round, and in the bottom a little peaceful valley like that of Grasmere, only without the lake.   We then returned by a different part of the mountains, which, though very fine, would only admit of the same kind of description I have already exhausted, and which, though various, in reality is very much the same upon paper.

The country is poor and the huts small; the people seem, however, handsome, and a strong race.   Their dress, like that of the Tyrolese, is a green jacket, large-brimmed, shallow green hat, green pantaloons and waistcoat, with short boots.   The roads are everywhere good, as in Austria and Bohemia.   They are made entirely by the army, and it employs them in time of peace better than ours are near London, in either idling or robbery.   When you leave the mountains you return to the wide, fertile plain of Vienna, which, like those Sterne notices, are more pleasing to the traveller than the travel writer or reader. We met no dancing Nannettes on ours, so cannot show our talents at sentimental descriptions. In about seven days from our setting out we returned to Vienna, and went on for a week longer in our old track of gaiety before we set off for Constantinople.

Now for our journey from Temesvar here, for all which you must make up your mind to a double letter. In the evening, while I wrote my aunt's letter, Stockdale and Wilbraham walked over to see the French prisoners walk about, and found the guard civil enough not to hinder their talking to them. They had been taken under Dumouriez, and were not acquainted with anything that had since happened. They by no means conversed irrationally, and were much less violent than we expected. They passed a tacit censure upon the conduct of their countrymen since, particularly with regard to the late bloody decree about English prisoners; they would not believe it possible.

Dumouriez was not popular amongst them, and they said he sacrificed many lives unnecessarily. They were allowed but about three-halfpence a day, and lodge in casemates under the hospital, both very dirty, low, and unwholesome. They spoke with great gratitude of the people of Temesvar, though they said the Government did not treat them well. They here, every evening, hold a convention in form, and debate on different revolutional topics. The order of the day when we were there was about the conditions of peace, and one of them very much insisted on was the *exchange of prisoners.*

You will not wonder at this, though you will be concerned to hear it for the sake of common humanity when I tell you they assured us that out of 5,000 sent here a year ago only 700 remained. Some of them seemed very decent men, and better informed than in their rank of life men usually are. Beyond Temesvar we saw with joy the country become a little uneven, and here and there varied with underwood, though I think it was many miles before it acquired the unevenness of the Crofts at York, or the picturesque beauties of Poppleton fields; however, with hills in the distance it appeared to us a perfect paradise after the flats we had crossed. Before the evening, however, our fields grew cultivated and varied, and (what we could have dispensed with here) our last stage improved from underwood to an immense forest near Tarzed, where we slept. Where the forest was not timber trees you saw hills, and plains of underwood as far as the eye could reach, and where there was timber we saw the finest oaks possible for miles.

As the night came on we perceived the air and the bushes sparkle all round as with fire, and found it proceeded from fireflies, which flew all round us in quantities; at last we arrived safe at our night's lodging in a violent storm of thunder and lightning, which we have either seen at a distance or felt near for many days past. Beyond Tarzed the forest continues for about eighteen miles, over considerable hills, which, with such wood, are of course fine. Near Dobra (for which consult your maps) we change them for a rich, cultivated vale, with a fine, broad river, along which the road winds under shady or cultivated mountains on the right, with the river on the left, beyond this a fine plain and mountains like the former. At Deva, where we slept, is a fine old castle of the Emperor's of which I have a drawing by our draughtsman, as of several other scenes of our journey. You may imagine how much we enjoyed such a country after our journey on the other side of Temesvar. The vale now grows wider, and more cultivated than woody; beyond Szarvaros it becomes open, and afterwards hilly without trees or high cultivation.

Between Muhlenbach and this place (Hermanstadt) we ascend a fine woody hill with a pretty village in the bottom, and the town here stands on the other side of it in an open, large plain. It is old, and part ill-built, though larger than Temesvar—no great matter, however, and not finer or larger than Newark or Retford.   We arrived here yesterday, to-day being Thursday, July 3, and have just now returned to our inn from the playhouse, where we have been showing ourselves and seeing the beau-monde of Hermanstadt ; the theatre is large and not ill-built, much better than we expected, or than suited the company ; the play German.   We have here been told that the dangers we had heard of on our road beyond this place to Bucharest were just as imaginary as those near Temesvar.   Indeed, nothing is so ridiculous as the exaggeration of all these things, for we have all along at a hundred miles' distance heard of dangers which always vanished as we approached nearer.   The only thing that has ever put us out of our way is the cheating and extreme rascality of the postmasters ; these places are often given to the poorer officers in the Austrian service, or Hungarian *noblesse* ; so, pretending to be something like gentlemen, they take every opportunity to plunder and cheat you.   You have frequently to wait two, three, or four hours while they send for their horses from fields three or four miles off ; often pretend there are hills to make you take more horses, and at the next post insist on your continuing to take the same number.   Your only redress is applying to the postmaster-general at Vienna, which is always more trouble than the object is worth, for the punishment of one is nonsense when they are all alike.

The peasants in Transylvania and the Bannat are poor beyond description, often wearing literally nothing but a shirt and trousers.   Their shoes are nothing but a coarse piece of leather tied with thongs round their feet and ankles.   They are a livelier people than the Germans, but seem almost like savages, with a vacant idiot laugh, and senseless beyond conception.   Their language here changes from Hungarian to Wallach, which is very like Italian in sound-pronunciation, and from which it takes many words. Indeed, with Italian you will often be understood. Farther on they talk Greek and Turkish, so between Vienna and Constantinople the language changes six times, viz.: German, Sclavonian, Hungarian, Wallach, Greek, and Turkish, which I do not suppose happens in so short a space in any other part of the world. Transylvania is certainly a fine, and might be a fertile province, but, being a frontier one exposed to the Turks, is not cultivated as it might be, and the Turks have hardly any commerce with them.

I shall now (having travelled thus far) talk about England to you. And first let me thank you with all my heart for subscribing in my name for the internal defence of the country. As you have, I hope nobody will tell you again I am a democrat, in the *present* sense of the word. Be assured I shall always be glad as an Englishman to act as you have done for me, since I look upon the views of our present democrats to be the destruction of all we ought to hold dear; and I can never think that my opinions, however represented, can be supposed to coincide with them. But you know as well as anybody my ideas on this subject, so I am sure you cannot act wrong, as I know how much our opinions coincide. As for the danger of England, I hope it will be found that the preventive measures which have been taken will increase our security though they heighten our alarm. If anything serious happens I would return, that is in case of *invasion*; but of that I have and can have no idea. In the meantime I should be extremely sorry to give up a tour of such pleasure for anything less, as I have now nothing less in view than a complete seeing of Greece and the islands, and hope to have infinite satisfaction from it. Tell Anne that I have not yet begun my collection of pretty things for her, having seen nothing of the sort yet but living creatures, which I think were expressly barred in the commission. My only purchase, I think, except a book or two, has been a black little Hungarian terrier, the beauty of all ugliness. I am at present anxious beyond measure for English news, as I have not heard a syllable since I left Vienna, and shall not possibly before I arrive at Constantinople, where I hope my letters from Vienna will have arrived before me.

DEAR MOTHER,

I write to you from Bucharest, where we are all arrived perfectly safe and well. You will be surprised at the shortness of this letter, but I am in the very hurry of packing off to go to Constantinople. Since we left Hermanstadt we have been travelling in a Greek country, and the whole scene is so new, so extraordinary that we are afraid we are dreaming out of the "Arabian Nights' Entertainments." On arriving here we were fortunate enough to find the couriers for Constantinople just setting off, and have agreed with them to take us. We ride the whole way, and are accompanied by two janissaries, who have the care of us. We pay them here for everything (a great price, to be sure), but they procure us eating, homes, and everything we want the whole way without our taking any trouble or having an interpreter. We hope to be at Constantinople in about nine days; in a carriage it is about fifteen, and very bad road. There is, we are told, no danger, as merchandise and other things go every day, so I hope very soon to write to you from thence. My only reason for writing now is that you may not think us lost, and if my letters are in future long in arriving, remember the posts only leave Constantinople once a fortnight and are not quite so certain as on the Boroughbridge road. However, be assured that I will write as much as I can. If I have not been able on my road from Hermanstadt, the reason is we have hardly ever entered a house, even to eat; for the villages and huts are so poor we have always slept in our carriages or under a tree rather than take a bench (for beds are unknown) and be covered with vermin. To-night we are to go to bed, but our inn at Bucharest is about on a par with Boggle House. We are in high glee, however, and have seen scenes so new they make amends for everything, and we do nothing but laugh and jaw. Adieu. *Voilà l'essentiel*, and I have not time for more. Stockdale's and Wilbraham's best regards.

Believe me,
Your affectionate son,
J. B. S. MORRITT.

BUCHAREST,
July 9 (I believe), 1794.

ZYORLU, ON THE SEA OF MARMORA,
July 25, 1794.

DEAR ANNE,

I write to you in rather an extraordinary situation, being at this moment on the steps of a Turkish inn in a small town some way beyond Adrianople, surrounded by Turks and infidels, all astonished at my writing apparatus, and fingering every part of it. I have just rescued my pen from their paws, and as everything about me is very ridiculous I can't have a better time for writing to you. Wilbraham and Stockdale are trying to sleep, for we were up about half-past two, and the heat now (about two in the afternoon) is intolerable. I, however, have had my nap, and don't feel inclined to renew it, as in the street (where I now am) the figures promise me some amusement. My letter will probably be sent from Constantinople, and so you no doubt expect a longer than my last.

Since I wrote my mother an account of our proceedings from Hermanstadt, we have been almost constantly moving. You will see by your map that very soon afterwards we left Transylvania, and entered the Turkish dominions. Wallachia, which is the first province belonging to the Porte, is under the immediate government of the Prince of Wallachia, and is entirely Christian,[1] no Turk, by the treaty of alliance, being allowed the exercise of his religion or to bring his wives.   Wallachia extends from where we entered it at the pass of Rotherturm, through Bucharest to Sistova, where we left it, about three hundred miles, of which the pass through the mountains from Transylvania is the only part that can possibly amuse anybody.   It is about twenty-five miles, or thirty, of picturesque rock and wood scenery.   Through this, however, there was no way of getting our carriages but by oxen, and we were about two days in going it.   The rest of Wallachia is a miserable, barren, flat country, which, except its being here and there overrun with brambles and thistles, would be exactly another Bannat.   Our road to Bucharest was through the towns of Arjis and Pitesti, which you will perhaps see marked on your map, though they are neither of them larger than Bowes.   On leaving Transylvania we bid adieu to beds, tables, and chairs, the Wallachians, who are Greek Christians, as well as the Turks, never sitting on a raised seat, and always sleeping on carpets in their clothes.

To give you some idea of the manners of the country, I will give you an account of our reception one night at a village near Arjis where we slept.   There was no inn or alehouse in the village, and we were driven to a noble Wallachian's country seat, much such a house as Hanby's.   The gentleman of the house was at Bucharest, and we were received by his lady.   She was seated on a low board sofa which filled the whole of one side of the room, surrounded by five or six Greek slaves in great state.   As this was the first specimen I saw of the Greek dress of which you have heard so much, I will describe you hers.   Her gown

---

[1] Wallachia (like Moldavia) was at this time a vassal State of Turkey, having a semi-independence under its own Rouman Prince, but tributary to the Turkish Sultan, by whom the ruling prince was nominated.   It was not until 1861 that the Rouman States of Wallachia and Moldavia formed themselves into a single State as the Principality of Roumania; and not until 1878 that Roumania became completely independent of Turkey.

was long-sleeved, coming up before no higher than her cestus, which was tied *à la Campbell*. It was gathered round her ankles and legs like trousers, and was made of a spotted light muslin.   On her head she wore a flat-topped high cap with a gold tassel on the top, and a shawl handkerchief round her forehead, her hair hanging loose about her shoulders.   Over her gown she wore a long light blue silk pelisse edged with fur, with half-sleeves; on her feet she had thin yellow-leather boots, with slippers, which she left at the side of the sofa to put up her feet, for they all sit cross-legged, *à la Turque*.   Over her bosom she wore a thin fold of muslin which fastened under her cestus; and I assure you, though not of the *première jeunesse*, it is difficult to imagine a more elegant figure.

We had not dined, and she sent into the village for everything we wanted which she had not in the house, and after dinner two servants walked round with a basin and a pitcher, to pour water on our hands.   She had a little child about four years old with her, with whom we made a great friendship.   She also showed us a little boy of about a year older, whom she had bought of the Turkish soldiers during the last war with the Austrians, and after supper and a little conversation through means of an interpreter, she left us in peaceable possession of the sofa, on which we slept very luxuriously, as it was about six foot broad and as long as the room.   In the morning she came in with her little boy, bringing each of us a teaspoonful of conserve of roses, the best I ever tasted, which is a constant custom amongst them.   We were not suffered to pay for anything but what we had from the village, and left the house delighted with the novelty of the scene and the hospitality we had experienced.   This, however, was but one day of the many we spent in Wallachia, and of the rest I have nothing amusing to say; even Bucharest is not worth noticing; indeed, Constantinople includes every other town.   At Bucharest we quitted our carriages and proceeded on horse-back under the care of the janissaries who conduct the post.

On entering Bulgaria at Sistova we bid adieu to Christianity, and, having been told there was consider-able danger on the road, were surprised at the hardi-ness of our guides, who travelled with us till one in the morning the first day; but indeed we found every-where that the dangers so much talked of were excessively exaggerated, though there certainly are robbers in these hills, as our servants who went with the post in another party saw several, who, however, did not offer to molest them. As our party seldom consisted of less than eight or nine men well armed, we did not think we had much to fear, and our confidence did not deceive us.

On examining my journal I find so many uninterest-ing days that I will not detail them, but just mention what struck us as most worth notice.

(Pera, July 28.) The Danube at Sistova, where we crossed it from Wallachia, is not less than a mile and a half across, and runs down in one large, majestic sheet of a great depth. I fancy this is far the greatest breadth of any European river at the distance of about two hundred miles from the sea, and that a sea where there are no tides, for the Danube is entirely a sweet-water river. Sistova stands prettily along the banks of it, ornamented with orchards, and an old frontier castle on the side of a slope that overhangs the river, and relieves the eye considerably after the tiresome flats of Wallachia. It may not be amiss to tell you that this was the place the last peace was concluded, in 1791, between Austria and Turkey and Russia.[1]

We arrived at Tirnova very late, as I have already mentioned, after a ride of about six hours. It was a clear, full moon, and our ride (though we were tired) was continued delightfully through a close lane over-

---

[1] The peace between Russia and Turkey was concluded in the following year at Jassy, fixing the Dniester as the boundary of Turkey. See page 73.

hung with the largest and finest oaks. On our right was a bank of fine wood crowned with rocks, and lighted up by the moon; below us on the left a winding river, which, ornamented with many trees, reflected her light partially, and opposite a bank of wood and rock like the former, but in deep shade. This scene continued several miles, and, with the moon playing through the thick foliage that overhung our lane, it is difficult to conceive a more enchanting effect.

The second day was through one of those rich, varied countries we admired between Doncaster and Rotherham, without great features, but always pleasing from variety of objects and richness of landscape, though the most difficult of any to describe. But we were approaching classic ground. We slept at the foot of a mountain,[1] which we crossed the next day, which separates Bulgaria from Romania (the ancient Thrace), and which, though now debased by the name of Bal. Kan, is no less a personage than the ancient Hæmus. Few scenes can equal the beauty of this ascent, which is, however, very rapid and *escarpé*, presenting at every turn the richest and most ornamented views over the country below, which is extremely uneven and varied. We sat for about half an hour on the top, imagining parks and houses formed on the different slopes, and laying out the ground very prettily, only always stipulating that it should be wheeled into England, for which we all retain a sneaking kindness. The descent on the other side was still steeper, and winded down a side of the mountain without any trees or variety, but deep, gravelly ravines worn away by the torrents in winter. It was noonday, and you can have no conception of the heat.

The next day we arrived in the plain on the banks of a broad torrent now called the Maritza, which accompanied us all the way to Adrianople; this river, which is now almost an unknown stream, was the Hebrus, so famous for the unfortunate story of Orpheus,

[1] The Shipka Pass.

when it carried down his head and lyre, after the Bacchanals in these mountains had torn him to pieces.

We did not see any Bacchanals, or hear any poets singing on its banks; but we did not wonder at its being a favourite haunt of the former when we found at Adrianople some of the finest wine ever tasted, for which all this district is famous. How Orpheus came to wander on its banks I do not know, for I should as soon think of trotting along the Ayre and Calder navigation for any poetical beauties I could find.

Adrianople is a large old town with a great many ruins, but evidently Turkish ones, except an old wall which bounds the peninsula between the Maritza and Tangia, another small river and which may have been the original boundary of the ancient town. At Adrianople are two large mosques which we went to see. These buildings are great ornaments to the town, and are, as you know, their churches. The principal one at Adrianople is very magnificent. You enter first a large court about 180 feet square, round which runs a row of cloisters supported by pillars, and roofed in small domes; the court flagged with white marble, and with a white marble fountain in the centre. Before you is the mosque, an immense and light circular building with a large cupola, surmounted with a glittering gilt crescent. The portico was supported by six columns, each of a single piece of granite about thirty feet high, and the two ends of the front were bounded by high minarés. These are immense columns, like the Monument at London, with three small galleries on the outside from which at stated hours the priests call the people to prayers, bells never being used here. There are four minarés round the church at equal distances; their tops are short spires covered with tin, or gilt, and adorned with gilt crescents. The inside of the mosque is octagon, about one hundred feet diameter, and the dome is supported by eight arches and as many pillars. If (according to our ideas) there is little architecture in these, which are painted exceedingly gay in grotesque fresco, yet from the size of the mosque and the liveliness of the colours the *ensemble* has the most pleasing effect, as you will suppose when I tell you it reminded us of Ranelagh. The floor is matted, and as the Turks always sit upon it, the effect is not spoiled by pews, benches, etc.

On entering we took off our shoes and saw the whole of it with much less molestation than I have frequently experienced in Roman Catholic churches, though we were only attended by our Turkish janissary and had no permissions or anything of the sort. They even made us taste of a fountain which there is in the centre of the church for the purposes of ablutions, etc., and of which we found the water excellent. So misrepresented are they with regard to their intolerance and the insults put upon Christians. Indeed, so far from ever having been ill treated, I must say we have everywhere met with the greatest goodwill from them, and they seem a very ignorant but a very harmless people. Once or twice a child or two has saluted us with the gentle appellation of *jawr*, that is *devil*; but could any men in England travel in a Turkish or other foreign dress without ten times the insult? They are very curious, particularly about your arms, which they themselves are never without, and we seldom came to a village without having them all looked over by the people that flocked round us. A knife of mine, with several blades and instruments, was a great object of curiosity. You never meet a Turk, even after the plough, without pistols or a great sword in his girdle, which makes him look very formidable. The inns all over Turkey are such as you have no idea of. The Turks always sleep in their clothes, and you never find other beds than a mat carpet, spread generally out of doors at this time of the year.

We were thirteen days in riding from Bucharest; generally travelled from two or three in the morning till ten or eleven, and lay by during the day, when the heat was intense. The fatigue is, to be sure, very great, especially from Adrianople, after which the country continues bare and uninteresting the whole way. For a few of the last stages from Silivria the road goes along the Sea of Marmora (the Propontis), but its forms, though good, want accompanying orna-ments. All our fatigues, however, were at length repaid by arriving at Pera, the *faubourgs* of Con-stantinople, where we all live now, and from which I have written most of this letter. You have no doubt read a great deal about the situation of Constantinople, and know the raptures in which it is generally described. I employ my draughtsman all day in taking views of it, and I assure you I think it baffles almost as much his pencil as my pen. It really is a wonderful thing, and what I do not suppose is equalled by any view in the world. I will describe it as it appears on entering the Bosphorus from the Sea of Marmora.

Before you runs the Bosphorus, an arm of the sea about a mile and a half broad, whose varied edges are covered with villages, orchards, and Turkish burying-grounds, the most picturesque of objects, which I will soon describe, and bounded with rich and bold hills. On your right is the village of Scutari, in Asia, beautifully situated at the foot of these rich hills, and opposite, on your left, the canal of Constantinople, about half a mile or a mile broad, covered with vessels, and narrowing as it recedes into the land. Along the eastern side of this stand Pera and Galata on a high promontory covered with buildings to the water edge, and nearer you on the opposite shore.

The whole point between the Sea of Marmora and the canal is covered with Constantinople. It, like all Turkish towns, owes infinite beauty to the number of trees scattered through it, besides orchards and gardens. Their burying-grounds are the prettiest things in the world: they are large spaces not spoiled by glaring mausoleums and monuments, but shadowed with large and gloomy groves of the most beautiful cypress. On the point of the promontory on your left, surrounded by high walls, rises the palace and gardens of the Seraglio, a large, scattered, irregular building glittering with domes and crescents embosomed in wood. Behind it, higher up, the glittering domes and minarés of Santa Sophia, and the mosque of Sultan Achmet. Along the water, to the western end of the seven towers, runs a long, ruinous wall, the ancient boundary and fortification in the time of Constantine. On the top of this are innumerable kiosks or summer-houses, behind which, on its seven hills, glittering with minarés and crescents, and shaded by beautiful trees, rises the town, which covers the edges of the sea and the canal for five or six miles. On all sides of you the sea is covered with boats and other vessels, and whichever way you turn the scene is enchantment.

Towards the west opens the Sea of Marmora, the Asiatic coast, now on your left, covered with hamlets and groves, backed with hills rising boldly from the water; Constantinople on your right; and before you the Prince's Islands, which are mountains of the boldest and most picturesque kind, rising out of the sea, and forming with it the most beautiful background imaginable. On a clear day you see, beyond these, a range of high mountains in Asia, towards Brusa and Olympus. Eastward the Bosphorus winds between its rich, high shores, presenting a succession of scenery only found on its banks, and scarcely to be described. Northward runs the canal (a broad arm of the sea), whose banks are covered with Constantinople on one side and Pera on the other; on the right with the shady cypress groves near Pera, on the left with the beautiful point of the Seraglio; and the distance formed by high hills at the end of the canal.

Now, to take off a little from all these raptures, I must describe the inside of this Elysium. Imagine, then, the whole town built (both it and Pera) of old wood houses, the streets about the breadth everywhere of Water Lane, York, or, if they rise sometimes to Little Alice Lane, it is not above two streets in the place. Of course there is not a carriage or even a chair in the place, the pavement worse than I can describe, covered with filth and numbers of dogs, which, by their religion, they never kill, and which belong to nobody, but lie as they can, and are often starving in the streets. The most singular thing is that, notwithstanding their numbers and the excessive heat of the air, yet mad dogs are unknown here, which puzzles the naturalists not a little. You often see twenty lying together, and at night are obliged to walk with a great stick, for they will not get up otherwise till trod upon, and perhaps bite you for your pains. Besides, you can't see them unless your servant happens to have a flambeau, for lamps are unknown.

Fires here are common to a degree. The very night of our arrival there was one in Galata consumed above a thousand houses, and, two nights after, another destroyed about three hundred, which was spoken of as nothing. When these are frequent they are said to arise from the people's being discontented with the government; but in winter, when they use their charcoal stoves, it happens almost every other night. The plague, their other great scourge, has now let them alone for above these two years, and they are perfectly free. There were reports of it where we passed in Bulgaria and Adrianople, but, I believe, without foundation, though we often were in rooms that had been smoked to purify them.

About other dangers (whether the manners are changed or not) I do not know; but certain it is we find none, and walk about the streets amongst the Turks in our own dress just as quietly as we should in London. I have been ruining myself in shawls and embroidered handkerchiefs, which they make here admirably, and if you smell anything on this letter I must tell you it's perfumed, as is all my paper, with otto of roses, of which I have cargoes. The only remains of antiquity at Constantinople are the old wall I have mentioned, some old windows, porches, and buttresses which remain in it and are part of the palace of the later Greek Emperors, and a stadium entire, which was the place where races were run. It is now called the Ahmeidan, and there are in it two large entire obelisks which have served to mark the goal. One of these is an entire stone of about fifty feet in height by about five at the bottom. It is Egyptian. On the pedestal bas-reliefs, but much damaged. It dates from the lower Greek Empire. There is also a high old pillar built by Trajan, which has been of the finest workmanship, but of which the outside has been so often damaged with fire that few traces of its beauty remain.

Santa Sophia we have not yet seen, though I hope to be able to add an account of it in a letter to my mother, or aunt, before this goes off, as it is some days to wait for the post. We live in a small, uncomfortable inn kept by Italians here, for Liston, who is fitting up the palace, had no room for us till his furniture arrived, which it has not yet thought proper to do, being either detained at Smyrna by the winds, or lost. With him we found some very pleasant, intelligent men, and having a general invitation to his house at all hours, our time passes agreeably enough. We generally rise at five or six when we mean to make any excursions to Constantinople or elsewhere; in the heat of the day we keep as quiet as possible, which you will believe when I tell you the glass stands every day at eighty-seven to ninety in the shade, a regular heat of which you can have no idea. In the evening we again lounge out, though there is no walking with any comfort in these streets—the only walk is through them to the Campo dei Morti, a large burying-ground overlooking the Bosphorus and the Propontis, from which the evening views are charming. *Au reste*, the heat is so violent that both Stockdale and I threw ourselves into fevers in coming here, owing to *coups de soleil*, but, God be thanked, I am and have been some days quite well, and he is very near so, though the heat has a little prolonged his illness. Before the end of this month the great heats are over, and we are arranging our plans for a tour of Greece and the Islands.

You may look upon me now as returning home, having got to the greatest distance I shall ever be from you, and when I get into Italy I shall feel next door to you myself. The heat here in the night is scarce ever less than eighty-one or two, and about ten or eleven in the day often reaches ninety. After that time there is generally a cool breeze from the sea, till the heats again return after sunset. They have, however, here ice in plenty, for which they bring the snow from Mount Olympus, near Brusa, in Asia, not the Grecian Olympus. One of their great luxuries is the iced sherbet, made here in quantities, and sold in every street in Constantinople.

As I mean to write another letter to one of you by this post, I shall not now say more in this than that I hope my long proses have in some measure entertained you; when I do begin to travel you see what you are to expect, and on my return the comments by word of mouth will be full as copious as the text. The English courier has arrived; no letters, but bad news about Ostend, which I suppose is the reason of it. You, too, will think me disposed of, as we were thirteen days from Bucharest here instead of nine, and, arriving when the post had just gone, could not write for above a fortnight. This must teach you patience about my letters. My fellow-travellers, Stockdale and Wilbraham, desire their kindest remembrances. Best loves, and Greece for ever. Huzza! God bless you!

Believe me ever your affectionate brother,

J. B. S. MORRITT.

August 2.

CHAPTER IV

CONSTANTINOPLE

WHEN Morritt reached Constantinople the Sultan Selim III. had been reigning about five years. He was disposed to friendship with the French Republic rather than with either Austria or Russia or their allies; and this was only natural, since Russia had extorted from his father the humiliating treaty of Kainardji, which gave up the Crimea, in 1774; and he himself had been at war with Austria and Russia combined. His army was disastrously defeated by Suwarrow in 1789, and, after the accession of Leopold II., he made peace with the Austrians, through the mediation of Prussia, at Sistova in August 1791.

The war with Russia continued until pressure from Great Britain and Prussia brought about the peace of Jassy in January 1792, by which Russia gained Oczakow and the territory between the rivers Bug and Dniester, on which Odessa was built. On the one hand, therefore, he had a feeling of animosity against Austria and Russia, and on the other he regarded France as likely to prove a powerful ally. Already, while Morritt was still at Constantinople, the French armies of the North had cleared the French frontier and all Belgium, and were advancing upon the Rhine; and the invasion of Italy was beginning. French officers and French workmen were welcomed at Constantinople. A company of artillery which was coming to the Sultan from Toulon at this time was blockaded by the British fleet, and only a part reached Constantinople by land. This friendly attitude towards France continued till Napoleon invaded Egypt in 1798; nor did the Sultan take any overt action against the French until after their defeat at the battle of the Nile. Hence it was that the ports of the Ægean were still open to French men-of-war, and remained so until the seas were cleared by Nelson's victory. It is evident that Morritt ran no small risk of capture by French ships on the voyages described in the two following chapters, though he makes light of the danger to avoid alarming his family at Rokeby.

PERA, CONSTANTINOPLE,
August 7, 1794.

DEAR MOTHER,

I can't help writing another letter, though I know it will go off by the same post as the one to my sister; but naturally, liking a prose, and travelling not diminishing that propensity, I must talk, though at the distance of two thousand miles and more, and I only hope you will find I have something to say. As I have given Anne a long description of Constantinople, indeed, such as I cannot enlarge on till I show you my drawings, I shall not add any more about its situation. I will, however, add something on our manner of living and the appearance and demeanour of the different people that compose this Babel, as far as they have fallen under my observation.

Of the inside of the Turkish houses you see nothing at all; they chiefly inhabit Constantinople, though there are several in Pera and Galata. Of their ideas and manners, by all that we can make out, I take the "Arabian Nights' Entertainments" to give the most exact and minute description. Of their indolence, which you have so often read of, the accounts are not exaggerated. They are fond of news, and, notwith-standing the little part they can any of them take in State affairs, are great *talking* politicians, as we are told. In Pera and Constantinople are innumerable coffee-houses, where they drink sherbet, coffee, ices, etc., and you see them sitting with their long pipes at the door of these, motionless from morning till night. Those who are in office about the Seraglio, whose

names and offices are sufficiently detailed in a thousand
publications you have met with in England, generally
ride through the streets of Constantinople on horses
or mules with bridles embossed with gold or silver
and immense housings more or less rich according to
the quality of the station. Two or three slaves, sometimes twelve or fifteen, run before and on each side of
these horses, to which you always give way. Indeed,
to folks who like staring about them, as you know
some people do, there is certainly a risk of being run
over, for a Turk is much too great a man to speak to
you, and if you do not see him a good shove is the
only notice of his approach.

The Pashas or commanders of provinces and the
public officers are almost the only people you ever see
mounted or any way distinguished by dress or appearance from the multitude. These very often carry
purses full of money on their horses, and distribute it
as presents to any one whose appearance they like by
handfuls. A chaplain of Sir Robert Ainslie's, who
was here looking one day at the Grand Signor as he
passed, was called to him and given a handful
of above seventy ducats as a present. We have
not had any such good luck, but have heard of
it from Englishmen here as no uncommon thing; you
must never refuse it, for as to any delicacy or honour,
the Turks, who have none of it themselves, could
never comprehend it in others. The people here
pay no regular taxes of any sort, the coffers of the
Grand Signor being filled by the presents and extor-
tions of the Pashas and by seizing the confiscated
property of the rich Greek or American merchants
when found out, which is no inconsiderable source of
revenue. There are many here, we are told, who
possess very considerable riches, but their appearance and that of their houses, so far from displaying
it, are studiously calculated to avoid its being suspected. It is a curious circumstance, and what we
have hardly an idea of, though very common here, for

a Greek or American subject of the Porte engaged in trade to pay a considerable sum—as much as 5,000 piastres, about £350—for a protection from any foreign Ambassador which secures his property from his own government.

On particular days, too, I believe the Grand Signor receives presents in state from his loving subjects. These are very common all over the East still, and very ancient, being mentioned in the Bible, and very frequently noticed by Homer. A visit is never made to a great Turk without reciprocal presents being exchanged, and a visit to a Pasha, we have been told, does not cost less than £100, though you receive as much, for they by no means want generosity. I find in my journal one note on *Pashas* communicated by a very intelligent Greek here, who is interpreter (Dragoman) to the Embassy. You know these in England are as frequently called *Bashas*, which is a totally different word. Basha is a Turkish word, and means no more than Sir or Mr.—indeed, not so much, as it is generally used if speaking to an inferior. The other he apprehends to be Arabic, and originally Persian, in which language *Pa* signifies foot and *Shah* sovereign, the *Foot of the Sovereign* being no bad designation of his viceroys, which these are.

There are few, if any, manufactures at Constantinople, or any active merchants, except among the Greeks and foreigners, notwithstanding the astonishing advantages of their situation, which unite on the shores of the Black Sea the finest productions of the East to those of Europe and the Mediterranean. The bazaars or shops at Constantinople are excellently managed for convenience. They are in several long streets in a central part of the town, arched over in many parts with stone, and everywhere so shaded with penthouses that you may find it cool even here, which is no easy matter. Here the shops for every article are classed all together on each side of the streets in open booths, with great shop-boards, on

which the master of the shop sits cross-legged ready
to help you to what you want.   The number of these
shops is very great, and the appearance of some rows
of them quite splendid, particularly those where they
sell embroidered handkerchiefs and veils.   In these we
shall ruin ourselves, to a certainty, for they are as
cheap as possible, and the beauty of the embroidery
a temptation beyond what we can withstand.

Almost at every turn as you walk along you find,
too, a shop where they sell sherbet.   This is made of
raisins, sugar, and water, which they give you in a
large cup, into which they put snow from Mount
Olympus.   It is sold everywhere, and makes the drink
very agreeable when you are heated with walking.
This is, I fancy, their favourite substitute for wine,
as they have no malt liquors or ciders, which I think
is strange under such a prohibition.   To do them
justice, however, I have seen several who were not
the least scrupulous about it.

The wines of the country near Adrianople are
incomparable, and here the Ambassador treats us
with some wine from Troy, which accounts fully
for the spirit with which the Ten Years' War was
carried on.   A measure near Adrianople containing
about two bottles costs about fourpence of our money.
Fruit, too, of all sorts is sold here in a profusion you
have no notion of.   A pound and a half of grapes
costs a penny, and everything else in proportion.

Notwithstanding the bad management of the interior
of Constantinople, there is a very strict and numerous
watch kept up throughout the town, which interferes
on every disturbance; yet from the building of the
town, the cut-throat corners and alleys through every
part of it, and the total want of lights, it is often,
I have heard, a scene of assassination and robbery,
not so much, however, in the footpad way as in that
of housebreaking.   This is sometimes so bad that
since we have been here the servants at the English
Ambassador's have been obliged to keep guard

all night sometimes from apprehensions of a band of robbers in the neighbourhood. You will not wonder at this when I tell you that amongst the soldiery here no other discipline is kept up than that of merely attending parade once or twice a week. At night in quarters and at any other time no notice or inquiry is made amongst them, so that it is no great wonder if they are rather banditti than anything else.

Private and summary punishments are still the mode under this government. The janissaries, *bostangis* (gardeners), and all the Court officers are favoured (though not so frequently as formerly) with private exhibitions of the bow-string. They have sometimes at Constantinople executions in the very streets, if a baker is convicted of selling false weights of bread; and many other crimes of the same nature are punished by beheading, and the carcases are left for days in the streets. Indeed, nothing is removed from the streets here by the Turks; dead dogs, cats, and filth of all sorts remain till carried away by eagles, hawks, and a large kind of white-bellied vulture, of all which there are numbers constantly flying about over the town, which are held in such regard that you would be very ill treated by the common people if seen to kill one. You will agree, too, that they merit certainly great regard, as they are the only scavengers of the town. Of the eagles you see multitudes, which at first astonished us a good deal; the vultures, which are still more common, the Turks call *ak babas* or *white daddies.*

In the provinces, where rebellion is not unfrequent, their mode of quelling it is to send down a Pasha with a certain number of soldiers, who, if strong enough, takes off as many heads and inflicts as many other punishments as he pleases. *Par exemple*, there had been one near Adrianople this spring, and in the south of Bulgaria and in this neighbourhood we passed by nine gentlemen impaled, not

counting heads, which abounded, and which we concluded, like Catharine Hayes's justices, had had bodies
to them.   These had all been the affairs of about six
weeks, for there were none when Liston passed. Only
one of these, who was a great ringleader, had suffered
alive the punishment of impaling. Of the Greeks
I shall say more when I know more of them; they
are a very different race from the Turks, and with
every similarity of dress have a totally different
appearance.

Their women are the only ones who here have
any liberty, the Armenians being almost as strict
with their wives as the Turks. All you see of either
when you meet them in the streets is their eyes and
nose, a handkerchief being tied round their heads as
high, or sometimes over, their nose, and another
covering their forehead and eyebrows. Their whole
person is muffled in a long cloth gown made very
loose, the shape almost of a nun's in a Roman Catholic
country, which hides their shape entirely. When the
Turkish women are permitted to go out you see them
in great parties in boats and the walks about, often
amusing themselves like children with escarpolettes
or merry-go-rounds, but always totally secluded from
the society of men; nor would a Turk pay the least
attention, or speak even to his wife, if he met her in
the street. By all these restrictions, the prohibition
of wine, the discouragement of arts and commerce,
Mahomet certainly meant to make his followers a
nation of warriors; but what with their bad government and their want of ingenuity and improvement
even in the art of war, which they are most addicted
to, they are as much behind the Europeans in it as
in everything else. A Turk has no idea of society
out of doors, and at home I have been told by the
Grecian and Frank ladies here who had any acquaintance with the Turkish women that from their education
and way of life there were very few who were anything better than overgrown children.

We of course live here almost entirely with the
English and Corps Diplomatique, to many of whom
we had letters from Vienna, and amongst whom we
have found some very pleasant people. When we
have no other engagements we dine always with the
English Ambassador, who has been extremely civil,
and at whose house we have met a very pleasant
society.

Most of the Corps Diplomatique reside during the
heat of the summer at Buyuk Déré, a village on the
Bosphorus about sixteen miles off. To this we went
some days ago with Liston, and were presented to
the other Ministers by him.

You cannot form an idea of the beauties of this
canal, of which I hope to bring you some drawings
which will do it more justice than my description. Its
banks are cultivated and peopled. There are two or
three palaces of the Sultan and his sister along its
banks. The Turkish buildings are more in the taste
of the Chinese than of our architecture; they are
built of wood in general, and much ornamented with
painting and gilding.

In the women's apartments all the windows are
latticed, and landscapes or grotesque designs painted
on the lattice-work; the whole, though irregular,
looking gay and clean; and though sometimes too
gaudy, yet they certainly add to the scene, mixed as
they are with trees and gardens, and adorned with
domes and crescents. At one place there is a very
fine large building, which is a palace of the Sultan's
sister, and at one end of it a small building consisting
of about three or four rooms as plain as possible,
which are her husband's apartments; for when a
subject here marries a lady of the blood-royal this is
always the etiquette, and she remains quite the head
of the house. In reality it is often the policy of the
Porte to give their ladies in marriage to subjects who
are too rich or considerable, as they can't refuse the
honour and are almost ruined by the presents they

make, and the expense they are at on these occasions. The lady in question is married to the Capoudan Pasha or High Admiral.

Nearer the Euxine are some old towers which have served to guard the passage, and now ornament the banks they once defended, and beyond Buyuk Déré two built as modern fortifications by Baron de Tott, which I am told would not be bad defences if the Turks understood them, but their strength remains to be proved by the Empress's Euxine fleet. The Asiatic one is in the situation where stood an ancient temple of Jupiter *Urius*, "the giver of prosperous winds," which is mentioned by Barthélemy in his "Voyages d'Anacharsis," of which, however, there are now no traces, I believe; but we mean i possible to have a look at the situation. Buyuk Déré is a pretty village with a long quay upon the Bosphorus, in a very pretty part of it, where it is rather more broad. We only stayed one day, which was of course merely employed in visiting Ambassadors, and—would you believe it?—a *ball* here in the dog-days. I own I did not dance many dances, as you can have no idea of the heat. It was given by the Russian Ambassador, who, I fancy, thought he was at Petersburg. I had letters to him from some friends at Vienna, and he has been so civil as to offer us quarters in his country house, which we mean soon to accept, and see from thence the environs of Buyuk Déré towards the Black Sea.

We have not as yet examined the neighbourhood as we wish; for poor Stockdale has been by no means well, and has hardly stirred out at all from a very bad fever, and subsequent weakness, of which, thank God, he is almost entirely well. It was owing to the heat and fatigue of the latter part of our journey. I was rather ill for the day or two after my arrival, but recovered immediately, almost, and am once more as strong as a horse. The heat is already a good deal lessened, the thermometer being only about eighty-five from above ninety, and it generally subsides towards the end of this month, so our tour promises to be very pleasant and well timed; for winter does not begin till December. I wish it was as well timed in other respects, but we have learnt that the English squadron is leaving the Archipelago, and if the French, who have three frigates there, remain masters of these seas, our trip to the Islands will be impracticable, and we shall be confined to a land tour of Troy, Thessaly, Attica, Greece, and the Morea, which I understand will be by no means impracticable. No armed vessel enters the Dardanelles, so we are safe as far as Troy by sea. The number of French is here very great, and that of their friends still greater, the Porte taking no open part in acknowledging or favouring them, but rather inclining that way till very lately. They sport here cockades and red caps, and have a tree of liberty in the yard of their Ambassador, who is not, however, openly acknowledged by the Porte. They dance their carmagnole round this on any good news, and to-morrow we expect to see a most superb exhibition of this kind, as it is their famous tenth of August.

We have not yet been able to see the inside of Santa Sophia, so I must defer this subject, and the Seraglio if we can see it, to my next letter. The Seven Towers, which seems a large fortress surrounded by the old walls of the city, is equally shut up; that is, though one might manage to get in, it would be by no means so clear you could get out. This is the western extremity of the city along the sea; beyond it, retiring from the shore, the walls are beautiful; they are triple, extremely ruined, and covered with vines, figs, ivy, and a profusion of greens and cypress groves: along them is a long line of towers equally broken, and covered with green, presenting each a perfect ruin for a picture, and still more set off by the many beautiful foregrounds provided by the orchards and burying-groves of some neighbouring villages. We this morning, August 9, crossed over to Asia, to a point west of Scutari, where stands a miserable village, the remains of the ancient Chalcedon. A few old foundations and bits of wall are all that is left of it. A little to the east on another point stand the relics of an old Seraglio, which is at this moment pulling down.

The gardens are large, full of shady walks of cypress, the finest I ever saw, and oriental planes, which are beautiful; they command charming points of view towards Constantinople and Pera across the water. Further east still, and opposite Pera, is the village of Scutari, on a bold, high shore backed with ye Asiatic hills. I have got from my draughtsman a very good view of the bay, village, and points of Chalcedon, from near the old Seraglio.

Our last courier brought us a great deal of bad public news, and no letters from England, owing, I suppose, to the evacuation of Ostend. Since that we have had nothing but reports of good tidings, though I fear nothing authentic enough to raise our spirits. I long for another post, that I may hear something about you; I am sorry when I think how long an interval, too, will pass between your receiving my last intelligence from Bucharest, and these letters, but it could not be helped, so you must be patient at these distances. Wilbraham stays with us here still, and as he is waiting for a servant his brother is sending him from Vienna (his own having behaved so as to be turned away), he will accompany us to Troy and perhaps farther. The farther the better, I still say, as the more I know him the more I like him, and our tour here has been very pleasant and nonsensical the whole way, the party having agreed at Vienna to be as great fools as they possibly could, which those who know our talents will own to be a good deal. In short, we should be by no means what you would call good travelling company, as our tongues were scarcely still for a moment the whole month.

Now as to my own business, with which I must treat you. My money is at present in very good plight, seeing I possess about £400; but I am so apprehensive of any extra expense for escorts or vessels, that I will be much obliged to you to lodge in my banker's hands, to be forwarded to his correspondent at Constantinople for me, a couple of hundred pounds, which I would not draw on, but for fear of looking foolish on finding my pockets empty. Afterwards, when Ward has received my rents, he shall send a few more which will last me as far as Naples, I hope; if what I have does not prove sufficient, as I hope it will.

It will when this arrives be almost hunting season in England. Tell George he must get Sling into order, and that he must go often out with the hounds, whether they throw off far or near, for I must have him made a thorough hunter, and run no longer risks of breaking my neck. In the spring he must break in my young roans, and tell Anne (that in the list of squirish commissions no four-footed beast may be forgotten) I beg Rover may not be made fat and idle, but, if he discovers those propensities, may be sent out a-sporting with the gamekeeper.

Adieu, my dear mother, and believe me ever

Sincerely and affectionately yours,

J. B. S. MORRITT.

CONSTANTINOPLE,
August 20, 1794.

DEAR AUNT,

I write still from Constantinople, and, not having directed a letter to you for a long time, I will this, though I suppose, except by the difference of a day or two, it is much the same whether they are addressed to you or the *Rookabites*, as I have no doubt but such elaborate compositions are communicated for the benefit of the whole party. I do not believe my letter will get over more than one sheet this time, as I have almost said all I have to say about Constantinople in my two last letters. However, I am not yet quite at a stand, so I will give you a history of our motions since I last wrote, including that of my sights and observations. As they are rather in an irregular order, you will consider them as a part of my journal, where I put down things as I see them.

At Chalcedon, which is opposite part of Constantinople, and which we visited in a morning's sail some days after I wrote, there is nothing remaining of its ancient grandeur (for it had once considerable commerce) except an extent of orchard and garden over the promontory where most of the town stood, a small village retaining the name of Chalchi, and great masses here and there of old ruined walls or foundations which have fallen into the sea. There were here and there marble shafts of columns in the walls of the houses or by the shore, as in many villages about this place, but they seemed chiefly either Turkish or of the lower Greek Empire. A little to the east of Chalchi, between it and Scutari, is an old Seraglio, called that of Sultan *Mourat* (Amurath). It was the palace the Grand Signor occupied before he resided at that of Constantinople. The workmen are now pulling it down, and so, the whole being open, I got a view of the inside, both of the gardens and palace. The first consist, however, of nothing but long avenues and clumps of cypress, which, however beautiful, are gloomy without the mixture of livelier greens, and the palace is a cluster of low, ill-proportioned rooms, with a profusion of beautiful marble. The doorcases, windows, fireplaces were all ornamented with it, and there were marble fountains in many of the rooms. All these the workmen were taking up, and with true Turkish indifference demolishing, by express order of the Sultan, who did not choose that other people should have what had served to adorn a royal palace. One could not help regretting the fine pieces of marble thus sacrificed to his stupid pride. On all this shore the views are beautiful; it is broken into bays by the different points of Scutari, Chalchi, and others, and I think I have already mentioned that the shores of Asia are here much richer, bolder, and more varied than those of Europe.

A few days after our sail we made a party for one day to see the Princes Islands in the Propontis, which are about twelve miles distant on the Asiatic coast. There are four of them, which go by the names of Proté, Antigone, Chalké, and Prinkipos, of which the two last are the most considerable. They are all entirely inhabited by Greeks, who have here two or three large monasteries, which receive strangers. We, however, only staying to dinner, took our chance at the inn, such as it was, and did not avail ourselves of their hospitality. We passed by the two first of these islands, which are little more than bare hills, and landed at Chalké. It has its name from an ancient Greek word, Burgh will tell you, meaning brass or copper, and the remains, not only of copper ore but of ancient works, are still perceivable here in part of the island, though they do not seem to have been great. It is about five miles in circumference, and the walk round it is perhaps as beautiful as any in the world. Every turn shows you a new prospect, and the eye, sometimes wandering over an extensive sea, sometimes over the high mountains of Bithynia and the shores of Asia, at others confined to the narrow canals which separate the islands from each other, and the beautiful little creeks that adorn them, is never wearied with this inexhaustible variety.

The island itself is covered with underwood, and in parts with some large trees, which in general, however, it rather wants. That of Prinkipos, which is larger, and lies between it and part of the Asiatic coast, is better furnished, and is beautiful to look *at*, though not more so to look from than the other. On these are the monasteries, which are situated as usual in the most beautiful parts of the island, without, however, containing anything worthy of particular notice. The inhabitants live chiefly by the produce of their orchards and gardens, which they sell to Constantinople, as also by their fishery. In the evening we returned late, and amused ourselves with remarking a phenomenon not uncommon in any sea, but very common here, the extremely shining light of the sea, when struck by our oars, or anywhere agitated, that seems almost like fire, and which sticks in sparkles to the oars; it is produced, as you know, by an innumerable quantity of small insects, but I had never seen it so strong. We coasted along the Asiatic shore on account of the wind and current, and were shown near Chalcedon the rock from which ladies were from time to time thrown into the sea in sacks on particular occasions, such as running away from their husbands or masters, infidelity, particularly for favours shown to a Christian, in which case also their lover is impaled.

The day after our return we went, it being Friday, the Turkish Sabbath, to see the Sultan go to mosque. He went to one in our neighbourhood on horseback, and returned by water. He is attended by about one hundred officers in the different dresses of their stations, all very fine, and some covered with gold and silver cloths, but which I can neither describe nor you understand if I did. He rides last, with incense burning round him; his horse is almost covered with cloth of gold and gilt ornaments, and when he alights a carpet is spread for him, and he is held up on each side under the arms by two officers. In about half an hour he came out again, and rode in the same kind of procession to his boat, which is rowed by about twenty men, and is covered with gold and silver. The balustrade that supports the awning is of silver, and the gilding on the oars, etc., is inconceivably rich. He has two boats of this sort, in one of which he goes, and those of his train in the other. He himself has a fine countenance, and appears well; he is not older than thirty.

Stockdale having now got perfectly stout and well with trailing about, we thought of more expeditions, and accepted an invitation we had had from the Russian Ambassador of taking up our quarters in the Russian palace at Buyuk Déré, of which you know the geography from my former letters. As I described the beauties of the canal (Bosphorus) in them, I will add nothing, though again, if possible, more gratified by them than ever. On the narrowest part of it, about eight miles from Constantinople, are two old castles; which, however, would serve but little the purposes of defence, and are more adapted to what they are likewise used for, that of prisons. In these, very frequently, four or five are strangled in an evening and thrown into the Bosphorus, under this mild government, without ever troubling anybody but the executioner. Near these (we found from our books and remembered with pleasure) was the place Darius marched across on a bridge of boats with 700,000 men on his Scythian expedition, as a prelude to his Grecian one. These remembrances are almost all that remain here of former times, as few monuments withstand the Turks so near Constantinople.

At Buyuk Déré our friend the Russian Minister received us very cordially and gave us for lodgings a charming saloon, and chambers at the end of his garden with a view of the bay. We were here quite our own masters, and made several trips, sometimes with him, sometimes by ourselves; for he was hospitable enough not to do the honours, but leave us to our own inventions, so we were perfectly comfortable and at liberty. Buyuk Déré is about seven miles from the opening of the Bosphorus into the Euxine, to which we made our first expedition. The shores of the Bosphorus are still bold and beautiful. On a high hill in Asia are the ruins of an old Genoese castle, built when this part of the world was in their hands. It

was in this situation that stood formerly the famous
temple of Jupiter, of which there are now, however,
no remains below it; and opposite are two new fortresses built by the Turks; and several batteries are
run up along the shore—I fancy through dread of the
Empress, who is making herself very formidable in
the Euxine, where she has now not less than twenty-
one sail of the line, and indeed many think, from the
ignorance and awkwardness of the Turks, that their
batteries would be insufficient to prevent her from
forcing the passage, if she pleased to set about it,
as it is.

Near the mouth, or rather the head, of the Bosphorus the shores are very wild. You go along under
high, black rocks, against which the water dashes with
great violence. There are no trees or verdure on
them, and their appearance, if the sea was in a storm,
must be most tremendous; the swell here is always
violent, however, and the noise of the sea breaking
amongst their different caverns is peculiarly awful
and striking. A little beyond the opening on the
European side is a small village, with a lighthouse
on a high point, corresponding to one in Asia; and
opposite it a high rock rises out of the sea, with an
old marble altar upon it, to which we scrambled. It
is called the Pillar of Pompey, but is evidently, I
think, an altar, and not the remains of a column:
that you may be of the same opinion, I draw you
the design of it here. You see it is adorned with
the ox's head, festoons, and small annulets, which
I do not believe an ornament for the lower part
of a column.[1]

On the altar was once, I understand, an old inscription, which is not now legible, partly owing to time
and partly to the modern inscriptions of simple travellers who are very fond of writing their own sweet
names; so that, in some hundred years, I should not
wonder if some learned antiquarian discovered that

---

[1] The drawing being indistinct, it is omitted. The text explains sufficiently.

the altar was inscribed to *Mr. Thomas Dickens* or any-body else of equal note. As for Pompey, he most probably had nothing at all to do with the pillar, any more than Ovid had with a tower near this place which goes by his name, and where they say he was exiled. The tower is, I am told, Genoese; and besides, Ovid's banishment was on the Danube. The rock on which the altar stands hangs over the sea, and is so steep I was obliged to take off my shoes to be able to climb it. Below the spray flies with great violence, and adds no little to its terrors.

Another of our trips from Buyuk Déré was to a place on the Asiatic side called the Giant Mountain; it is marked in the ancient maps, singularly enough, the Bed of Hercules. On landing you follow a long plain called—I do not know why—the Grand Signor's ladder, where he often comes a-pleasuring. It is adorned with some immense and beautiful plane trees, the two largest of which I measured, and though they yielded in size to one in the meadow of Buyuk Déré, their sizes were 9 yards 18 inches and 10 yards 5 inches in circumference; and when in this state the plane is one of the most picturesque trees possible. The mountain is covered with wood, and the ascent commands the most beautiful views in the world—of the canal and mountains round. At the top is an old mosque or Mahommetan chapel, in the yard of which we were gravely shown a long bank, like a grave, 20 yards in length, said to be the tomb of a giant from which the mountain has its name. For fear, too, that the giant should not appear large enough, it seems only half of him is buried here, and the rest, equally long, is interred at Scutari. At the end of the town of Buyuk Déré, too, is a beautiful plain, which it takes its name from, meaning "great meadow," and where all the world ride and walk.

To describe all these scenes would but tire you; so wait till you see my drawings, which I have in abun-dance. I must write over another sheet, I find, not having half done ; so rest yourself a moment, and I go on with my story.

After having spent some days in this charming spot, and in the pleasantest manner, amongst the diplomatic people, from whom we received great civility, we returned to Constantinople. In a walk we made there the other morning we saw the famous mosque of Santa Sophia. The outside has nothing remarkable, and is heavier, and I think inferior, to that of many of the other mosques, as it was rather a patchwork between the form of the old Greek church and that of a mosque, according to their taste. The inside is large, and its great ornament is a very fine dome. The measures of all these I have not now, but will send them in another letter. The dome is not so large, by any means, as that of St. Paul's ; but it is a very wonderful effort, when we consider that it was built about the year 540.

The chief feature in this church, however, is certainly not so much the symmetry or beauty of the building as the richness of its ornaments and the beauty of its columns. Of these there are numbers, each of an entire piece of verd antique marble. The lower ones are about 20 feet, the higher about 15 feet, in height ; and I fancy the same quantity of that marble does not now exist anywhere. The floors, both below and in the galleries, are entirely of marble, with which also the walls are overlaid, excepting the roofs, which are ill-painted, after the Turkish taste. The dome, however, has been beautiful. It is adorned in mosaic with a composition resembling glass, but much harder, in which is a sheet of leaf-gold that gives it the appearance of the most beautiful gilding. In parts it has been broken and disfigured, to gratify their taste for destruction or supply the pockets of the men who show the building, and who sell pieces of it. I bought some, and mean to set one of the largest pieces in a ring, as it takes a very good polish. In one of the windows we remarked a large slab of transparent white marble, which is also very rare.

The architecture is that of the lower Greek Empire, and is not very fine, and what chiefly takes off from the effect of the marble is the dirty manner in which they keep it; for if washed and clean I know few things that would be so beautiful. I have much more to say, but news comes that the packets are closing, so if I do not send my letter it will not go off for a fortnight. Adieu. Love to you all, and do not be impatient, for on Wednesday we set off (*with Wilbraham still*) for a tour in Asia, to Nicomedia, Brusa, Mount Olympus, Smyrna, Ephesus, Miletus, Halicarnassus, Rhodes, Cos, Chios, Samos, Lesbos, and all the coast to the Troad: so you may not hear again for a month or six weeks. When you do it will, you see, be a brimming letter, so console yourselves, and believe me

Your affectionate nephew,
J. B. S. MORRITT.

SMYRNA,
September 29, 1794.

DEAR AUNT,

    I have, notwithstanding my last long letter, still something to tell you about Constantinople, which I therefore send to you, though Anne stands the next on my list. At the same time that we saw Santa Sophia, we walked to see some other lions in Constantinople. Having a janissary with us, we were admitted (paying, that is to say, a piastre or two) to enter the Seraglio. This building, which with its gardens covers entirely the promontory it stands upon, is walled completely off from the town, and the wall is so high and so situated that there is no point from whence you command the least view of the inside of the palace. It is, indeed, a little town by itself rather than a single building, consisting of a suite of courts one within another, inhabited by the servants and attendants of the palace, who here are the great men of the Empire. We were not admitted

beyond the first court, so can only speak of it as a
large area surrounded by low, heavy buildings of
which we did not see the inside, except the mint,
where we were admitted. We were here shown, as a
great curiosity, several stamps of different sizes for
the different coins, and some were struck off before
us, but though very curious for them, yet to any one
who had seen the same as we had done elsewhere,
they appeared exceedingly behindhand, as indeed they
are in everything that requires any knowledge in the
arts of mechanism. Indeed our going in was rather
that we might say we had been in so remarkable a
place as the Seraglio than for any other reason, as
no one is ever admitted beyond this court, and there
is very little remarkable in it. Indeed, the Seraglio
with its gardens, like all their other piles of building,
is seen to infinite advantage as an object from the
water, and on the outside, but makes certainly but a
poor figure within. A little way from it is a large
subterraneous place where there is now a manufactory of silk-spinners. It is a great area about
two hundred yards square, vaulted and supported by
above three hundred columns, as we were told by
a gentleman that has published on Constantinople.
This immense structure is still about thirty-five or
forty feet in height, though the ground at the bottom
is on a very different level from what it originally has
been. It was built by Justinian, or one of the later
Emperors, as a cistern to supply the whole city with
water, and aqueducts for that purpose made from the
mountains near, communicating with it. The Turks
have also built several other aqueducts since, so that
I suppose the use of the cistern has ceased; but in a
dry season like this they are now often reduced to
great straits for water, as the springs and fountains, of
which they have numbers everywhere, were almost
all dried up, and the want of water so great that it was
carried about the streets in leather vessels on horses,
and sold.

We saw the aqueducts on another tour we made to Belgrade, the beautiful village of which Lady M. W. Montague talks so much. Near the village of Bourgas, about an hour's ride from Constantinople, the narrow and romantic little valley it stands in is crossed by a high and still perfect aqueduct built by Justinian. Of this I have drawings, and in de Guys, a book that gives some accounts of these countries, there is the plan and elevation of it at length. He speaks of it as a superior work of this nature to any that now remain elsewhere. Soliman II. repaired it, a work in which he employed Greek architects. It is of a double row of arches one above the other, and has this singularity, that between the larger arches the architect has pierced the piers with lesser arches at three different heights so well that they, without diminishing the strength of the structure, add a great lightness to its appearance, and save a great expense in masonry. Another thing in which he says it is different from all others is that, through the upper row of arches, is pierced a passage by which you walk along the first row as over a bridge, with the second row over you. The length of this fine work is, below, 420 feet; above, where it is lengthened with lesser arches to be on a level with the water, it is 720 feet in length. There are eight great arches, four above and four below. Each of the lower ones is 47 feet in height by 53 feet in span, the upper ones 39 feet in height by 41 feet in span, and the whole aqueduct is 107 feet in height from the bottom.

Farther on, in passing through the village of Bourgas, our journey was enlivened by a Greek fair, where all the people of the village were out dancing and playing. A little way beyond Bourgas begins the extensive wood or another forest of Belgrade. The hills before you and on each side are covered with fine oak and beech, through which we rode for miles; we passed again by an old aqueduct of very solid workmanship and two rows of arches, most picturesquely overhung with bushes and embosomed in wood. On our right and before us we saw two large and very long Turkish aqueducts crossing the valleys near; for though infinitely behindhand in other respects, they pay very great attention to water-works, and, I am told, understand their theory and practice very well. They have no less than three or four very large works of this sort in this neighbour-hood, of which the water is conveyed to Constanti-nople. As you approach Belgrade the road winds through a beautiful and thick wood; a brook on the right, dammed up for a reservoir, seems here a small lake. With this in the foreground, and two rich and beautiful banks of wood for side-screens, I procured a charming view of Belgrade, a plain, pretty village rising on a bank covered with trees, and sloping down opposite one to the water. In this village the English and Dutch Ambassadors have houses, as have some of the English merchants; but the most fashionable summer resort is Buyuk Déré, of which I have said so much. This is certainly a much quieter and more retired scene, but it is not in so grand a style of scenery as the banks of the Bosphorus. Yet here a person might go in summer to retire (which is as seldom the case here as in England):

> His wayward length at noontide might he stretch
> And pore upon the brook that babbles by.

Buyuk Déré, though in a beautiful situation, is nothing but a long row of handsome houses built along a quay on the Bosphorus, and is as far removed from peace and privacy as the Strand at Scarborough or Weymouth. It is the opinion here that from the woods and standing water the situation of Belgrade is unwholesome, fevers being very common there. There may be some foundation for this, but I was told by a gentleman who lives there very much that it was chiefly owing to the want of caution with which foreigners lived in this climate, exposing themselves to the violent heat in exercise, and then sitting still during a damp evening; when every cold in this climate immediately becomes a fever. You will see I do not like to detract from the beauty of the place by telling you of its inconveniences; and I assure you, if you had seen the extensive and romantic woods, with the number of retired, sweet walks round it, you would have agreed with Lady Mary Wortley in its eulogium.

The next thing I find mentioned in my notes are the dervishes, whom I went to see just before we left the place. They are pretty numerous both in Galata and Scutari, where they have dances, and public meetings on Monday and Friday at Galata, on Tuesday and Thursday at the other. We were shown into a large room, round which sat on the mats the spectators. The middle was railed in like the circus at Astley's, and in a gallery above was some music consisting chiefly of flutes and drums. About twenty of the dervishes below sat round this inner circle, and the president recites something aloud in a singing tone, which they join in with all the mummery of prostrating themselves, etc. The music strikes up slowly, and they walk round the room some time; when the music grows brisker they take off their upper garments, and, clothed in nothing but a vest with sleeves and a very long cloth petticoat, begin the dance. The first turns round to the second, and bowing first to the president and then to him, begins to whirl round like a child making himself giddy. His petticoats with the velocity of the motion spread out and leave him exactly the figure that, if I recollect, is drawn in the religious ceremonies. The second follows his example, and in this manner the whole whirl round and round for more than half an hour with their arms extended, then prostrate themselves, walk about, and begin again. How they can by any practice bring themselves to be able to do it without falling from giddiness I cannot conceive. I am sure you will agree with me in thinking it a great religious acquirement, and not wonder when I tell you we returned to our house extremely edified and improved by it.

At Scutari they are still more determined to get to paradise, for during the dance they amuse themselves by cutting their arms and bodies with sharp knives till the blood spurts out, holding hot irons in their teeth and mouth, with many other feats of this sort. We did not see them; and as these exploits can be easily conceived, and they do not in other respects differ from what we were present at, I cannot say I much regret missing so disgusting a sight, as you will easily suppose it was.

I think I have now with great success got through the chief things that struck us during our stay at Constantinople, having little more to add upon anything we saw there but what will be best supplied from my journal some other time, with explanatory remarks by word of mouth. I only will mention one remark for Anne's benefit, as she heard considerable accounts on the subject from Miss Stanley's Italian trip, which is that scorpions are here much more common than even in Italy, so that she might have frightened herself all day long. In an evening, in the Ambassador's garden, we frequently found several under the dried bark of some old trellises. Mr. Liston himself was one day stung by one of them; but on applying oil and camphorated spirits did not suffer much from it. The largest I saw with its tail and all was not above two inches long, but I believe there are larger.

CHAPTER V

TRAVELS IN ASIA MINOR AND SAMOS

FOR his guide to the ancient sites which he visited in Asia Minor and Greece, Morritt relied chiefly on the recently published works of Richard Chandler; but he uses his own judgment and sometimes expresses a different opinion. Chandler had been sent out by the Dilettanti Society, and travelled in 1764–6. He published " Ionian Antiquities," 1769; " Inscriptiones Antiquae," 1774; and " Travels," 1775–6.

It will be seen that Morritt uses the names of Latin deities, Jupiter, Minerva, etc., instead of Zeus, Athene, etc.; but this was customary in his time, and not a mark of scrappy or superficial scholarship.

IS-MIT (NICOMEDIA),
September 3, 1794.

DEAR MOTHER,

I write to you from the Turkish town of Is-mit, once Nicomedia. . . . We took our leave of Constantinople two days ago, and set sail for this place, accompanied by Wilbraham, and a Mr. Dallaway, chaplain to Mr. Liston, who is a very agreeable addition to our party, as he is both pleasant and well-informed. We set sail with a fair wind and a delightful evening at four o'clock, and arrived that evening at the larger of the Princes Islands (which I mentioned already), called Prinkipos. The manner of travelling here, which is generally pursued and is certainly most convenient, is this. You are always attended by a janissary, with whom you are furnished by the Ambassador, as every one of the Corps

Diplomatique have a certain number whom they employ as expresses, etc., and on these occasions we make a bargain to be furnished with the necessary number of horses and conveyances through the route we mean to take; all side-steps and extra peregrinations are of course not counted. We have taken a Greek servant as an interpreter, who besides his own language speaks Turkish, Italian, and French, so we now shift for ourselves with regard to eating and drinking, which our janissary from Bucharest had cut us rather short of, and I think you would imagine that did not much suit either Wilbraham or myself. We mean to keep our Greek, therefore, the whole of our tour, though before it is finished I hope to have made a very pretty proficiency in modern Greek myself, as I find it extremely resembling the ancient language; and the principal difficulty is want of habit, especially in the pronunciation, which is totally different from our own.

We are at present much better equipped for a Turkish expedition than we were before our arrival at Constantinople, as we have procured ourselves thick quilts to sleep upon, and blankets, as the heats are now over and sleeping al fresco is not quite so delightful as it was. As to inns, I told you before you only meet with small coffee-houses, and never with any other bed than a carpet or a low sofa. You would delight in Turkey, for the seats (which are beds at night) are never so high by half as your own dressing-room sofa, with thick, broad cushions; indeed, when I return I mean to fit up the tea-room *à la kiosk*, that is, like a Turkish summer-house, for your own self, as I am sure it would suit you.

The island of Prinkipos is as beautiful as I have already described that of Chalchi, and in the same style. After sleeping there we proceeded in our boat to Nicomedia, which your maps will tell you is at the end of a long gulf of the Sea of Marmora, at the mouth of which are some small desert islands, or rather naked rocks rising out of the sea. The whole of the coast of Asia, of which you never lose sight, is very bold and fine, but more particularly in the Gulf of Is-mit. On your left hand, near the point as you enter it, are the ruins of a large ancient fortress and castle, not far from which is the obscure village of Gheibizé, once Libissa, where Hannibal finished his life. There are several remains of old towns on or near the shores of the gulf, but nothing, as we have heard, remarkable. Opposite Nicomedia the gulf is about two miles broad, and ends a little higher up. I can conceive few mountains bolder or more beautiful than the opposite shore, which is part of the branches of the Olympus. The hills are very high, extremely varied, and at a small distance appear rich and clothed, though I do not know how to trust anything that looks like cultivation, which is most probably only browned by the sun. The ridges are rough and steep, and the shape of the shore only excelled by the shores we had left at Constantinople.

The town is ill-built, like all Turkish towns, and yet, like them, looks beautiful on the side of a steep hill mixed with trees. There are very few remains here; the only one we have seen worth notice is the remains of an old palace, which covers the top of a small elevation, and of which a square building yet remains entire all but the roof. It is built of very large hewn stone, and floored with marble, and seems to have been a very magnificent room; it is now filled with bushes and shrubs that make it a very picturesque ruin. There is little doubt but it has been an ancient palace, and the Turks give it the name of Eski-Sera, or the old palace.

The people here are so ignorant that we could not make anything certain out from their accounts. One of them told us it was an old palace of the Sultan's, another that it was built by the Genoese. As there was nothing architectural about it we could not make it out to be antique. It had certainly been in the use of the Turks, judging by the paintings, which remained in some parts, but might nevertheless have been built long before them. I have made my draughtsman take some very good views of it, and shall read a further lecture upon it when you see them.

There is in the town also an old fountain with a Greek inscription over it, which was not to be read, however, and some old column shafts, friezes, etc., in the walls, which were antique. We are lodged here in a small room of a Greek monastery, where I am writing, and where there are six poor Greek monks living. To give you some idea of their notions of curiosities, I must tell you what just happened to us. I asked this morning if there were any medals or engraved stones ever found near here, as there often are in this part of the world; and I wished to see if there were any worth buying. I had my expectations much raised by a man's telling me that in effect he had some very curious coins; but was, as you will suppose, a little surprised when he returned to me with a handful of German halfpence. As I had never heard of Joseph or Maria Theresa among the royal race of Bithynia I did not bargain for any.

We are now proceeding by Brusa to Smyrna, and after visiting everything to be seen on the coast of Asia shall finish with the Troad; go in October and November by Cavallo and Mount Athos to Salonica; cross Macedonia and Thessaly through the vale of Tempe, etc., by land to Larissa, then by Thermopylae to Livadia, see Thebes, Boeotia, Phocis and Parnassus, and winter till February at Athens. In spring see the Morea, and cross to Sicily.—N.B. With common precautions all this can be done, and the bugbears we amuse ourselves with of robbers, etc., though founded in reality, may be very well avoided by common prudence. The Morea has hardly ever been visited except near Olympia. I know that at present it is all visitable with trouble and resolution, and I hope before I return to have seen many places we have scarce an idea of. Do you not envy me our winter's plan at Athens, where we mean to keep house, and send wine and English porter from Smyrna. I shall bring home drawings of every hill and grove in Greece; you know I am now and then an enthusiast. I assure you the comfort and satisfaction I have in my present tour, the odd scenes we meet with, the fun we have, and the pleasure I feel all day long, especially in Wilbraham's company, can only be equalled by the satisfaction I shall have in returning at the end of it. W. leaves us at the Dardanelles, as he does not mean to make the tour of Greece at present. Adieu. I am, you will easily see, in my usual good spirits; Stockdale says I am made on purpose to travel with; he and W. beg their best respects. That Anne may not call us Irishmen, to travel through Tempe to the beautiful parts of Greece so late in the year, I beg leave to add that winter here never begins till after Christmas, and the month of November is generally one of the finest in the year. Adieu.

Believe me sincerely
Your affectionate son,
J. B. S. MORRITT.

SMYRNA,
September 29, 1794.

We passed, on our road from Nicomedia, a village still called Evakli; one of the remains of antiquity in this part of the world. It was once Heraclea, and is situated on a promontory that runs out into the sea; though I believe the ancient town, or at least the citadel, stood farther off in the situation of a smaller village now called Jawr-Erakti, and inhabited by Greeks. It is on the summit of a conical hill covered with wood and backed by a high, dark purple range of crags and rock, whose bases are likewise richly clothed. This view from the sea, with the beautiful cedars of a Turkish burying-ground before it, was

so very perfect a landscape that we stopped to take
a sketch of it.   Indeed, to have an idea of colouring,
this is certainly the finest landscape country in the
world ; for though, as Gilpin observes, it is with us
that the sunsets are most beautifully adorned by the
richness and glow of the clouds that always attend
them, yet whoever has seen the sunset over these
seas or the Bay of Smyrna must own that the absence
of the clouds (though that is not always the case) is more
than compensated by the warm glow over the whole
ether, the extreme bright purple of the western hills,
and the dark and decided blue of those at a greater
distance from the illumination.   It is not here that
a sunset is improved by a Claude Lorrain's glass.
Nature has given the effect in a much superior
manner in Claude's own colouring.   Indeed, I do not
at all wonder that we are so apt to accuse Italian
masters of forced colouring, for had these scenes been
given with their full effect upon canvas, we who are
accustomed to a colder and more watery sky should,
I am sure, imagine them exaggerated.   It is not here
that "evening grey" would have been mentioned by
Milton, at least at this time of year.   I must tell you
I was stopped in my prose here by the arrival of an
English courier with a number of letters from all of
my friends, among the rest one from you, which I
assure you gave me no small pleasure.

As for politics, I hope that in some measure the
change is for the better everywhere.   The news of
Robespierre & Co. having been beheaded [1] is just
arrived here—with furious reports and histories of
counter-revolutions.   As to the decapitation, I am
happy it is so well authenticated ; for the rest, I do
not believe a word of it.   However, I think, I hope
they will establish some kind of government with
which their neighbours may be at peace.   I find here
that our fears about getting to the Islands were very
premature, as the merchants here all assure us there is

[1] On July 28—two months earlier.

not the most distant reason for apprehension, and that we may go everywhere in the boats of the country perfectly safe. There has been sent from Constantinople, in consequence of the manly and spirited remonstrances of Liston to the Porte, a squadron of Turkish vessels sufficiently strong to over-awe the French, who, by our squadron under Montgomery having sailed, are again at sea with their remaining frigates. They have, however, never attacked or annoyed passengers, and still more avoid offering an insult to the Turks at present; under their convoy, therefore, we are perfectly safe, as we have from the Porte a very strong firman or travelling order.

SMYRNA,
September 30, 1794.
(Dying with heat.)

DEAR ANNE,

Though Heaven knows whether I can possibly finish this before the post, or at least before we set out, yet, as I am determined to try though I write all night, I will begin. The courier has just brought me a long packet from Liston containing letters from you all; you can't think with what pleasure I have been devouring them. You are all excellent correspondents, for a post never comes without a tolerable parcel for me. However, though infinitely grateful for your diligence in writing, I must say I never read in my life a much more saucy and impertinent composition than your last letter, which was dated Scarborough. You have toured to a fine purpose, I must say, and I wish I was only with you half an hour to make you a little pretty behaved and sensy. Notwithstanding my gravity, however, as a tourist, and the long accounts I have to give you of my late motions, I feel much more inclined to talk nonsense if I had time and paper to throw away upon it. I have just finished a letter of prosation to my Aunt Frances in which, however, I have not told her half of what we had seen and heard, so I will go on with my story, and you may piece it together with her letter and my mother's which I wrote from Nicomedia.

After two days' journey from Nicomedia we came in the evening to Nicaea, now called Is-nik. In the plain where it stands, at the end of a large and beautiful lake, was the scene of the last great battle between Tamerlane and Bajazet, which ended in the latter being put into a cage as a canary bird, and shown about to be stared at, pretty much as we are in travelling through any place here, *i.e.* as a show of wild beasts in England. I do not recollect whether you are alarmed at thunder and lightning amongst the rest of your fears ; if you are, you would not much have enjoyed our entrée into Nicaea. The old wall is still standing, and encloses a space three times as large as the town. We passed through a hole in an old ruined tower by way of entrance. The night was excessively dark, and just before we arrived began one of the most violent storms of lightning I ever saw in my life. The light the repeated flashes threw upon these ruins had an effect which it is impossible to describe ; you can imagine it from having seen the Eidophusikon, and I wish it had been possible for Loutherbourg[1] to have been of our party.

Not, however, having the least inclination to be wet through, we were not at all sorry to arrive at our quarters for the night. In the course of it the storm continued with greater fury than ever, with slight shocks of an earthquake ; at least, this is what all my fellow-travellers vouch for. To say the truth, I was laid very snug in a corner of the room, and never opened my eyes till morning. As far as eating and sleeping go, I believe few travellers ever went on with more success.

As there are many curious remains to be seen at Nicæa, we stayed there some days. I wish you could

---

[1] Royal Academician, 1781. His Eidophusikon was a sort of diorama, showing the changing effects in calm, storm, moonlight, etc.

only have seen our lodging. It was in a deserted house belonging to a Greek. There was nothing that the least resembled furniture, either Turkish or Christian. The roof of our principal room let in the rain through so many places that we were put to our invention to find out a dry spot. Having accomplished this, and made ourselves sofas *à la Turque* with our bedding, and tables with our books, we found the necessity of caution in moving, as the floor was rotten and in pieces. Our servants cooked our dinner on a bit of packthread in one corner, and we wrote remarks like Yorick's in the other, and very curious ones they are.

The town itself is very old, and in as much decay as our château. It was famous, you know, for the council that made the Nicene, or really *Nicaean*, Creed, of which we found (as we thought we made out) some mention in the ancient inscriptions that abound here. It was, however, most flourishing, as all the cities in this part of the world were, during the time of the Roman Empire. The walls, which have been bunglingly repaired by the Turks, still remain. They were originally a beautiful and well-built work, entirely built of hewn stone, with a suite of square towers at equal distances. The Genoese, and afterwards the Turks, have almost hid or destroyed these by great fortifications in brickwork, into which they have heaped, pell-mell, broken columns, friezes, inscriptions—indeed, whatever they found that would make a wall.

When we left this place we went to Brusa, where we stayed some time. This town is now, in a manner, the capital of Asia Minor. It is also of the highest antiquity. Tradition says that it was built as early as Croesus by a king at war with him. It was in later times the residence of the Sultans before they took Constantinople, but now, though one of the largest and most populous towns of the Turks, it has few remains of antiquity. What makes it most worth notice is the great beauty of its situation. The inconceivable richness and fertility of the plain in which it stands, the different slopes and heights on which its houses and mosques are grouped, and the ruined remains of its old fortress on a high rock, made a beautiful picture when combined with Mount Olympus, which rises finely behind it, ending above in bold crags and forests without end.

This mountain, which is shaped something like Skiddaw, forming therefore, like it, one grand object, is about three times as high, and covered with forests and rocks. The lake is wanting, as the little stream that waters the valley is not of consequence in a scene where the other features are so large. We went one day to the top of Olympus. I got some views of the different parts of the ascent. *Au reste*, the tops of all hills are alike, except that this was even now covered with snow in this climate, and after so hot a summer ; and was so cold we absolutely were starving. The gods were, however, lodged like gentlemen, and we should have been very glad to have made an acquaintance with any of them, but they did not please to appear.

We were here in very classical ground. The Arganthus, a mountain opposite, was the scene of the story of Hylas, and in Ghio, a village on the end of the Gulf of Mondania, and at the foot of it, is all that remains of Cius, a city founded by Jason's companions at the time of the argonautic expedition. On this mountain games were annually celebrated in honour of Hercules and Hylas. We went afterwards to Apollonia, where we again found some inscriptions and broken remains of grandeur, though entirely in the last stage of ruin. The town is on a peninsula in the middle of a most charming lake, whose islands, covered with woods and villages, have, thank God, had no Turkish Pocklingtons [1] to improve them. A more lovely scene of the sort I never saw. The Swiss lakes, you know, have few islands, and those of ours

[1] Pocklington's Island on Derwentwater had been spoilt by recent buildings.

that have are almost spoiled. The hills round the lake are seldom very near it, so that the view in its character is rather *riant* than bold, but when we saw it, a sky that would have been a favourite with Gilpin threw such beautiful tints on the lake and islands, that they appeared everything that was lovely. I have drawings of it which explain the matter better, I hope.

The country from hence to Smyrna is a succession of mountains more extensive than I think I ever saw. In fact, the different chains of them cover the whole of Asia Minor. In consequence of this, I never saw, I think, a country so rich and grand in its distances, but there are very few really pleasing views, as the fore-ground is everywhere bad, and there is seldom even a good middle distance. The springs being everywhere dried up, nothing like verdure was to be seen excepting the trees (for the herbage was as brown as possible where there was a spare blade of it), and the country was seen under every disadvantage. We amused ourselves, however, pretty well on our journey, at Loubad, a small town on the other end of the lake of Apollonia.

We on our arrival, as the café was very bad, sent to desire lodgings at the Greek priest's. He excused himself, as it was a Greek feast, and all the villagers of the country were assembled in his house and yard; but of course we desired to be admitted to so gay a party, and attended in the evening. Imagine to your-self a large court with sheds round it, men and women of all ages dressed as I have already described the Greek dress, sitting in circles cross-legged under these, eating and drinking, children in their cradles swinging, tied to the beams of the shed; crazy bag-pipes, flutes, etc., playing the most dismal Greek tunes, which are, I must say, anything but music. Their wine was better; so we sat down cross-legged amongst them, and were very merry.

You will, of course, ask me if the praises travellers

generally favour Greek beauties with are deserved.
Indeed they are; and if you had been present with us
you would, I think, have allowed that the faces of our
village belles exceeded by far any collection in any
ball-room you had ever seen. They have all good
eyes and teeth, but their chief beauty is that of
countenance. Of this you really cannot have an idea.
It is an expression of sweetness and of intelligence
that I hardly ever saw, and varies with a delicacy and
quickness that no painter can give. I am sure, to have
an idea of a countenance being thoroughly lighted up,
you ought to have seen them; and this beauty extended itself through almost all the party. Besides
this, their appearance in their elegant dress did not
give us the least idea of peasants, and, joined to the
gracefulness of their attitudes and manners, we began
to think ourselves among gentlewomen in disguise.
The married women as a distinguishing mask wear
veils (turned back, that is to say). The girls have a
still more curious custom : amongst the tresses of their
hair they string long chains of a small silver coin
about the size of a silver penny. They marry extremely early, and with good reason, if the men have any
eyes, as a woman of twenty-four or twenty-five begins
here to grow old. The men, too, have a custom which,
I believe, is very ancient: those who are betrothed
wear a wreath of flowers on their head. Of these,
there were several who were very busy in showing us
their brides and hearing how much we admired them.

That you may trace us in your maps, we went from
thence to Jelembeh, and then to Magnisa, the ancient
Magnesia, near Mount Sipylus. It is situated just like
Brusa, but the town is not so handsome or the plain
so rich. The Sipylus, though less, is steeper than the
Olympus, and the part beyond the town is a perpendicular and high crag, too steep for trees or foliage.
The plain before it is large, and famous for the victory
over Antiochus, by which L. Scipio got the surname
of Asiaticus. Mount Tmolus and Sardis, the capital

of Lydia, and the residence of Croesus, with the Pactolus, are in sight, though at considerable distance. The Hermus, which poets tell us was so famous for its golden sands, runs also by Magnisa. It is a dirty, muddy river, and has not one claim to attention but what its gold has bought—*comme tant d'autres*, but I hoped ancient Greeks had not been so venal. I need not add that Sipylus was the country of Tantalus and Niobe. Of the phenomenon Chandler speaks of we, however, saw nothing. There are no remains at Magnisa but an old Seraglio, now nearly ruined, and the Genoese fortress. The next day we crossed a very wild range of Mount Sipylus to the plain of Smyrna. We have stayed here about a week, and received many hospitalities from the English settled here.

Chandler gives a very minute account of Smyrna and the remains there. What little there still existed of antiquity is almost destroyed now, but we were delighted with the Meles, Homer's favourite stream. It winds along in a deep and narrow valley, and is a clear, pretty rivulet. Its bed is overgrown with bushes and flowering shrubs, and over it are two ruined aqueducts. When down at the side of the stream the confined scene round is as pretty as possible, and might assist Homer in his meditations as much as any place I know. We walked along it and had views taken of its whole course. Indeed, I agree with you so much in your idea of having views of the country as well as of the buildings, that I have multiplied sketches of almost every pretty spot in it. I own I always expected more pleasure from a country than from the ancient buildings in their present ruined state, and when an author gives me a long account of old stones and rubbish without containing one remark on a country interesting on account of great actions, and the birthplace of the first men of the world, I think him perhaps a good antiquarian, but certainly not a classical traveller. My letter to my aunt F. will

tell you our plans, and future direction ; we mean to
winter at Athens.   Do not you long to be with us ?

Your affectionate brother,
J. B. S. MORRITT.

Thursday, October 11, 1794.

DEAR MOTHER,

Guess a hundred times, and you will never
imagine from whence I write to you—so I must tell
you. I am in a large cave by the sea-shore at the foot
of Mount Mycale. The sea, which washes to the
mouth of it, is at present flying with a thunderstorm,
which has prevented our setting sail, as we intended,
for Samos. At the mouth of our cave is a small creek,
in which is anchored the open boat we meant to go in.
We have now made a considerable tour from Smyrna,
and are on our return through the islands of Samos
and Scio. Our first expedition was to Ephesus. The
country as far as there is not interesting. The ridges
of Mount Coressus are high, and covered with low
shrubs, the effect of them not striking except by the
morning and evening skies, of which, in this country,
the lights are surprising. The plain beyond which
Ephesus stands is washed and has been formed by
the Cayster ; it is flat and morassy, and the river
winds along it like the Maeander, making a thousand
windings along the whole plain. This river, as well
as the Maeander, too, was famous, you know, for its
vocal swans. Of these I can't say we saw any, but
after passing it can answer at Aiasaluk for a most
excellent goose or two, which were devoured with no
small satisfaction. Such is the difference between
poetry and matter of fact.

You will see a long and accurate account in Chandler
of this place and of Ephesus, so I will only mention
what I think he omits and tell you that we stayed here
two days examining the ruins, which are very extensive, and making unsuccessful attempts to bribe the
Aga and persuade him to let us bring off the beautiful

alto-rilievo Chandler mentions over the gate at Aiasa-luck. In the ruins of Ephesus the architecture is completely destroyed and on the ground; the remains as they lie are some of them, however, magnificent, especially the large fluted columns Chandler supposes those of a temple built by Augustus. The Corinthian friezes and capitals that are scattered near are of the finest workmanship and most elegant design. We thought, too, that we discovered evident traces of two temples, one opposite the stadium, the other small and behind the town on a hill, which are not noticed by Chandler. The bases of the columns remain very evident, and the line of them is traceable. There are scattered in the same place capitals which show they were Corinthian, and of the largest remains still a great line of frieze, and cornice beautifully ornamented. These I measured, and have got the drawings of.

The gymnasium which he speaks of, behind the town, we had heard, and have found every reason to believe, was really the famous temple of Diana. There are many strong proofs, I think, of this; its size, situation with respect to the marble quarries, the marshiness of the place, every part of its character agrees with it. The ruins are immense, and the building has stood on a great extent of ground. I was also convinced that the sea had in former times come entirely round the mountain to the temple, for it stood at the head of the *sacred* port, which Chandler himself mentions from Strabo as distinct from the *city* port, and the whole plain on this side is a low morass overgrown with reeds.

The Cayster is mentioned by authors as remarkable for forming new land at its mouth, and not undeservedly, for Ephesus, which was on the shore, is now full three miles from it. The buildings, too, on this side of the hill are remarkably in favour of the idea, having been built with high vaults and a narrow terrace that is walled strongly in front, and exactly resembles a staith or small quay to land goods. The

very streets are still traceable. The building we suppose the temple still bears the very remarkable name
of Kislar Serai, the Palace of the Virgins.

The country beyond Ephesus is fine, especially when
we came to the banks of the sea, with views of Samos,
a high, black, mountainous island, separated from the
grand, rocky range of Mycale by the narrow strait of
three-quarters of a mile, so famous for the last great
triumph of Grecian liberty. The south side of Mycale,
which we afterwards rode along, is bold, high, and
craggy. Round its points we saw several eagles
skimming round in circles, and sometimes sitting on
its crags and screaming, which gave what Mr. Gilpin
would call *infinite character* to the scene. In the large
plain on the left we had the Maeander; it resembles
that of the Cayster, but is much larger, and, like it too,
has been formed by the river. Priene, once a seaport,
is now four or five miles from the shore, and Myus
still further.

The ruins of the temple at Priene are a great and
splendid heap of architectural fragments, all on the
ground; the blocks of marble are immense, and the
worked stones very elegant. The walls under it, of
which part remain, and those of the city, which do not
seem likely to fall, gave us the highest idea of the
ancient skill in masonry. After looking at the ruins,
talking over Bias and old stories, we turned across the
plain to the Maeander. The sun was now setting, the
sky in a glow with its rays, and the islands and mountains round us glorious. Opposite us was the woody
ridges and summits of Latmos, and more to the left a
high, conical mountain whose outline was everywhere
broken with crags and glittering in the parting lights
of the sun. The moon over it grew brighter as the
sun set, and when the evening came on—in memory, I
suppose, of Endymion—did the honours of Mount
Latmos gloriously.

We at last ferried over the Maeander to the ruins of
Miletus here. There is only a Turkish hut or two,

already full of their own inhabitants, not counting fleas, bugs, etc., so we made our beds under a tree and slept in open air, though now in October. I despair of giving you an idea of this climate. Its mildness and the beauty of its mornings and evenings exceed what I could have conceived. Barthélemy in " Anach- arsis " makes his hero speak of himself as "assis sur les bords du Méandre, ne pouvant se rassasier ni de cet air ni de cette lumière dont la douceur égale la purité." It cannot be more spiritedly or more justly described. The theatre at Miletus still remains pretty perfect—that is to say, the shape of it in the side of the hill, one or two of the marble seats, and the entrance ; the communications with the seats and the upper passages, though a good deal filled with dirt, are very tolerably perfect.

Among the ruins are several Turkish ones, and two palm trees, the only ones we have seen, which looked very oriental. We went on southward over Mount Latmos, which, being a charming hill for hunting, was chosen by Endymion for the scene of his amusements, and where he fell asleep for Diana's. In four hours we came to a poor village, with ruins of the famous temple of Apollo at Branchidae. Three columns are standing, two still support the architrave and frieze. They are about forty feet high, fluted, and of the most beautiful Ionic proportions. The area of the temple has been immense, and from two points of the rising ground it stands upon the sea opens. A setting sun, when we saw it, shone full on the temple ; beyond, the sea was as smooth as a mirror, and the eye wandered over the neighbouring islands, or fancied distant ones. Samos, Icaria, Patmos, Leros, Calymna, and some smaller islands near us, were all scattered over it, and you can hardly conceive a more delicious scene. The moon at night, and the sun at daybreak the day after, showed it off still more, in new lights and equal beauty.

We attempted to sleep in a miserable mud cottage,

but before midnight turned out with a legion of fleas
and vermin and again took our station in open air,
where we should have managed very well if we could
have left all our fleas behind. Yesterday we returned
in hopes of getting here time enough to sail for Samos.
We had been on the point of embarking before, where
the passage was longer ; we thank our stars some accident made us ride forwards, because the boat could not
very well get to shore, and we did not like being carried
to it, I believe, and a man happened to say the wind
was rather against us. We crossed the plain of the
Maeander, when the wind rose to a storm you can
scarce conceive. The clouds gathered over Mount
Mycale, along which they swept, casting a shade like
night ; the promontories out at sea and the whole sky
in that part were as black as ink. It was worth being
wet through to see the scene. The effect of Mount
Mycale's summits and promontories as the cloud
advanced was inconceivably grand. At last it burst
over us in such a storm of thunder and lightning as I
never in my life witnessed. The sea flew on one side
of us, the thunder roared like a cannonade, almost
deafening us with the sound among the tops of the
mountain. The lightning was forked and continual,
often followed immediately by the thunder.

Suppose every effect you can, you will never imagine
a sublimer scene. We were very wet, and took refuge
in a Greek village ; the storm lasted above five hours.
Thunder in England is a perfect popgun to it. We
were very glad of our lucky escape, for had we put
to sea there is no doubt you would have read that
disagreeable paragraph Abney talks of, as how Mr.
Morritt, a most amiable and accomplished youth, had
with such and such companions been most classically
shipwrecked and drowned off Mount Mycale. No open
boat could have stood it. This morning we rode
here where the boat is lying—being detained, have
cooked some fish and our dinner in the cave whilst
I am writing, my draughtsman taking views of and

from the cave, and the weather is cleared up. So now we have only to dine, and are within about an hour's sail of Samos, where we shall sleep to-night. Adieu till then.

I thought I had taken my leave of you, but it is now night, and the scene is still the cave. After we had dined and dismissed our horses, the Greeks here very honestly asked an enormous price for the boat, and I believe, having something of their own to do, as honestly refused to set sail till morning. Being in a pet is of no avail, so here we are till three or four o'clock, for we are grown, by miracle, very early risers. How you would laugh at us if you saw us, or perhaps be tender-hearted enough to pity us, which we don't deserve, for we shall do very well. I am writing in one corner by the light of a lanthorn, on my English writing-desk ; Stockdale and the rest, laid down on our mattresses, in another ; a fire in another part, with a collection of Greeks and our janissary smoking round it ; saddles, heaps of cotton, corn, etc., to be shipped the first opportunity : so that it is not at all a bad representation of Gil Blas' cave, and I believe we are not in much better company. The moon has risen, and shines beautifully at the mouth of it, and the scene round us is romantic to a degree. After what we have already gone through, all difficulties vanish, and I shall soon be as sound asleep as you will in your beds at Rokeby.

You see I am not tired of my tour ; a more satisfactory one you cannot conceive. Every hill I see here is interesting, and seems an old friend after what one has read about them ; I am more mad about Greece than ever, and look forward to the time, when I shall make the whole family as mad as myself by bringing drawings of every hill and dale in the country. Except when on horseback I am reading or writing all day long, and only regret the not receiving Burgh's notes, which will certainly be written in vain ; pray beg him

to direct them to Zante, and if I receive them at
Athens they may still be of some use, as I shall from
thence make a long tour to the islands and Morea.

I left off here to write doggerel to Anne, and am
now continuing my letter from Samos.

We sailed at four o'clock in the morning from the cave,
crossed the straits between Samos and the Continent,
which in its narrowest part, more to the north, is not a
mile over. We were three hours crossing in this part
below the island, and anchored in the Bay of Tigagna,
once that of Samos. The morning was again, as usual,
beautiful. We took up our quarters at Cora, a Greek
village about a mile from the shore, from which I am
writing. You would have laughed heartily if you had
seen our party yesterday setting out to visit the
temple of Juno and ruins of Samos. There are no
horses in the village, and we were mounted on mules.
The Greeks, almost as obstinate as their beasts, would
hardly be persuaded to let us saddle or bridle them,
and indeed the animals seemed much more used to a
bare back and a halter. When, with much driving
behind and leading before, we contrived to get them
out into the fields they took so many side-steps, chose
so many roads in preference to the right one, and often
entered such strong protests against going forward at
all, that we must have been an excellent spectacle to
a bystander. I was glad to hear, from Wh—'s conduct, that Mr. Pitt managed his mules better, and can
only regret that my stick could not produce so great
an effect as the Secret Committee.[1]

We got at last to the remains of the famous temple of
Juno, near a small village called Myles. The stream

---

[1] The Committee of Secrecy was appointed by the House of Commons, in
the summer of 1794, to examine the papers and books of two revolutionary
societies. The result of its reports was that Pitt brought in a bill for the
suspension of the Habeas Corpus Act. It was strongly opposed by Fox's
party, which included Whitbread ; but was passed by a large majority. The
Government prosecutions for treason which followed later in the year, and after
the date of this letter, ended in an acquittal.

of the Imbrasus runs near, and the temple is not far from the sea-shore. There is only standing one column of white marble. Its diameter is not less than six feet, without a capital, and about thirty feet in height; the base is buried in the ground almost, and the capital, which has been thrown off, lies not far from it. It stands on a large, irregular oblong space that seems raised above the rest of the plain by the ruins of the fallen temple, now covered with earth and overgrown. This temple was in Herodotus's time the largest of all antiquity. Traditionally it was first built before the Trojan war; and afterwards, when architecture was in a very early state, it seems to have been the first improvement after the Doric and before the Ionic was brought to perfection, as it is different from any I ever saw; so, as Master Jacky Curious says in his elaborate work, that you may judge for yourself, *see, here it is.*

We next persuaded our mules, with much difficulty and various modes of argument, to proceed round the end of the bay to the ruins of Samos. In these we were disappointed, as nothing is standing or hardly traceable. It stood along the shore and the side of a steep hill that rises at some distance from it. There remain some pieces of strong wall that seem to have belonged to a considerable building. The foundations of the city wall and an old tower run up the side of the hill; we could also make out the stadium, the arcade underground that formed the slope for the seats, and the communication with them. It seems to have no range of seats on the side towards the sea to which it runs parallel. We saw no other remains, though Tourneforte mentions the theatre. We afterwards walked to the top of the hill to a small Chapel of the Virgin, where there is a deep cave, at the end of which are two cisterns full of cold water from the rock, great objects of veneration to the Greeks, who are extremely superstitious now, and attribute to these fountains a thousand curious properties. We found in the chapel, and copied down, some ancient Greek inscriptions, which repaid our trouble better than the cave and fountain. We returned to our château at Cora, which is a Greek house of which the master has turned out for us. This morning some great Turks coming here seized all the mules in the village, and the wind being northerly makes it impossible to sail up the straits, so here we are for another day. I am the more sorry for it as, having seen all there is to see, I have nothing to do ; a great grievance when you have been used to doing a great deal, as we have for some time past.

All my letters from England, as well as some of yours, are so full of politics I am tempted to rejoice with you that I am not there, beset as you say by party people. I think a man at my age had better be making observations, to form his opinions upon them, than acting strongly on what he can't be master of. Everything to me seems in these times to run so much in extremes, that an acting man, especially if a young man, would not find it easy to preserve his character as a moderate one, the only honest one anywhere.

The present crisis over, the question will no longer be agitated between riot on the one side and aristocratism on the other, as it now is universally. The war will perhaps be over, in which I am convinced we are defending ourselves against cut-throats, and are allied with pickpockets. The French have knocked up the name and idea of liberty so effectually that my only hopes are to see her rise from her ashes in Poland. They had been successful, by our last news.[1] *You* asked me once (or my sister, perhaps) if I did not think they were growing democrat, *à la Française.* I firmly believe, to tell you the truth, that their being so (though with them that was pardonable) was so far from the truth that it was completely an aspersion invented by their enemies effectually to overthrow their cause. A more artful or a more wicked lie never came, I believe, from the head of an aristocrat, which

[1] See above, p. 21.

is saying as much as I can say; I only hope that they will continue as they began, and not relinquish their first principles as the French did, that there may be at least one nation you may wish well to, without disgust at their conduct. I assure you, however, my opinion of the French or the Poles may alter, as it has done with the first; my opinion of their opponents on the Continent never will. That England may get well rid both of her allies and her enemies is my prayer. *En attendant*, till things go quieter on one side, and more honestly on the other, John Bull is but ill off. I think I shall contrive, by what I see and hear, to hate both sides. So much so that I shall return as English as I set out; that I may is the sincere wish of your affectionate son,

J. B. S. Morritt.

Cora,
October 10, 1794.

Thursday, October 11, 1794.

Scene—A Cave in Mount Mycale

Nonsense *and another friend of yours writing this stuff in a corner, by a lanthorn; other folks, both* Turks *and* Christians, *asleep round them.*

Indeed, dear Anne, though strange 'tis true,
Lately my Muse has grown a slattern;
She never writes heroics now,
So take this nonsense as a pattern.

A Muse! you cry. Can she be such,
Who dogg'rel stuff in rhyme rehearses?
Indeed she is, and just as much
As when she wrote sublimer verses.

So, when a girl in beauty's bloom
Has graced a Duke's connubial clutches,
Grown old, and married to the groom,
Her Grace is still my Lady Duchess.

Her titles proved, she now goes on,
Though, faith, with little more to say
Than what by you has long been known,
And felt by me before to-day.

To wit—that wheresoe'er I wander,
Whether I'm with you or without you,
Whether by Greta or Maeander,
I talk, and write, and think about you.

A party round me jabbering Greek
Might interrupt a nicer bard ;
Stockdale's asleep—I cannot speak :
To tie my fingers would be hard.

Then say, dear Anne, in such a case,
If I can scrawl a foolish letter,
Could any mortal in my place
Employ a tiresome evening better ?

One letter finished, to my mother,
Has told you all, I think, in prose ;
And now that I've begun another
How 'twill be filled no mortal knows.

Yet 'tis a secret in our trade,
Whenever Sense is at a stand,
To call in Nonsense to our aid,
And always find her near at hand.

Come then, dear Folly, here descend,
To eke out dogg'rel rhymes so clever ;
I'm sure I send them to a friend
Who loves us both as well as ever.

By you supported I have run,
Fearless of Bugaboos and frights ;
Have often had a world of fun,
And seen a thousand curious sights.

The tour to Greece so very dreadful,
It even made my Colonel tremble,
When once of you I had a head full,
Was nothing to a man so nimble.

Militia captains all the war
Convinced me danger was a sham;
With you, dear nymph, I laughed at fear,
So off I came, and here I am.

Then till we're tired of one another,
Folly, we'll both together trudge it,
Make with our tour a deal of pother,
And come to England with the Budget.

There seated by some Yorkshire fires,
We'll talk as every traveller's trade is;
You'll pass for wisdom with the squires,
And I for learning with the ladies.

Then the adventures of our cave—
Lord, how they'll make the natives stare!
Anne shall herself for once look grave,
And think us better where we are.

'Tis true, I own, we might be better,
Than seated in this cave of sorrow;
Yet we can write a nonsense letter,
So hope for better things to-morrow.

We yawn—dear Folly, let us free her,
And fearing she should do so too,
Remember we shall some time see her,
So wisely drop the subject now.

VATHI, SAMOS,
October 14, 1794.

The above, really written entirely in an Asiatic cave
under Mount Mycale, show to what a height genius

may be carried in any situation, however disagreeable. After having given such a loose to my imagination, I shall not gallop away over any more paper in rhyme, but condescend to write some observations in prose.

I am now in the port of Vathi, in the island of Samos, waiting till to-morrow morning to cross again into Asia Minor. We came here from Cora to-day, a cavalcade on mules, the most stupid and disagreeable devils that ever were mounted—*nous voilà*, however. You will imagine how we jumped, just as we arrived, on the appearance of a Venetian consul, who spoke to us in broken English. He has taken very good care of us in procuring us a lodging for to-night and a boat for to-morrow, and we have just been hauling down a Venetian flag from a staff on his roof, and hoisting the Union Jack, which he had in his house, with three cheers ; so now the Greeks are properly informed of our arrival. His wife we found a nice ninny-nonny hoddy-doddy old girl about seventy, who was born of English parents at Smyrna, and of course held a long prose with us in English.

To us who, thank Heaven, are tolerably national, these adventures are rather pleasant, I assure you ; and I think you who have never been out of England do not know the beauty of the English language, nor how pretty a sound it has on these occasions. I have since been bargaining for some coins found here with a Greek, who, *à l'ordinaire*, asked a guinea and a half, and took five shillings. I flatter myself I have got a bargain, and am extremely delighted with my wonderful collection. I dare say if anybody that knew anything about the matter saw it, I should find it had as pretty a set of trash as a gentleman need have. I certainly have some that would admit of a very learned dispute whether they were the Jupiter Tonans or the Venus of Paphos.

From Vathi we set sail to the ruins of Claros, once the famous oracle of Apollo. We arrived late, but in time to walk over the ruins, which are very old, Claros having been almost emptied to people Ephesus so early as Alexander. We discovered the cave of the oracle, **or**, of course, supposed we did, but though our intellects were most delightfully feasted, our carcases fared but very ill. There is nothing here but an unwholesome, damp cave, to which we preferred our boat.

As to your own account of your journey, you do not tell me anything of Fountain's Abbey, which I have never seen, and want to hear something sensy about, as all the masters and misses I ever asked about it could tell me no more than that, like your walk of onions, it was a sweet place. I suppose, by the description you give of the Pocklingtonisms about it, that the blue gates and Queen Elizabeth maintain their ground ; if they wish still to keep up this style of beauty, I hope when Queen Elizabeth grows old she will be replaced by a statue of Miss Lawrence in her black satin and slippers, which, besides being equally Gothic ornament, will have the merit of being a family thing. Apropos of Miss Lawrence (for she puts me in mind of Richmond Races, and they of York), I expect in your next a full, true, and particular account of the latter, a list of all the horses, etc., and everything that could put me in mind of England, and Yorkshire in particular ; for, as a native of the county, I retain a dash of vermin, you know, about horse-racing, though not so much as you, I do believe. In two days from hence, I hope to write Abney an account of the flourishing state of his possessions in Scio, where we go next. As for this place, it was consecrated to Bacchus, and the birth-place of Anacreon ; would you believe that, notwithstanding very accurate researches (made for the advancement of learning, and totally without ideas of following Anacreon's example), we have not been able to get a drop of wine or even brandy in the whole place ? We walked, however, to the ruined temple of Bacchus, which is still seen near here, and I only hope, like the Englishman who addressed Jupiter in the capitol, that if ever he gets the better of Mahomet again, he'll remember we took notice of him in his adversity.

We have just had a curious adventure with the Turks, which I must tell you. It is now evening (for my letter has been interrupted for a walk to the ruins of Teos). This is a small town, with an old fortification round it; as the Turks have a garrison here they keep about as great a fuss with it as if it was Breda or Berg-op-Zoom, and understand about as much of the matter as little Robert. Our poor painter, when the gates were locked, happened to be on the wrong side. In great dismay at finding himself shut out he came to the gate and jabbered German by wholesale; we sent to the porter, the keys were carried to the Aga (the Commandant here); we applied to him, but as he was a great officer, he would not risk opening the gates to the enemy. In vain we talked of our firman from the Porte; there was only one way of opening the gate, a bribe, and to this we had some objections. To complete the history, the poor fellow on the outside, in an amazing fright about robbers if he stayed out, very quietly finished the dispute by climbing over the wall these warriors made such a fuss about, and is just come in grinning. If the Turks find out he is an Austrian, I should not be astonished if they took him up after this as a spy of the Emperor's. A number of them round us are smoking their pipes and are in some amazement at seeing him here; I believe they rather think, by the potcrooks I am now making, that I brought him in by magic.

I hope by the time this gets to England you will be

expecting at least Henry's return from his Flanders campaigns ; I long almost as much to hear his histories as I do to talk about my own, which, for a traveller, is saying a great deal. His tour to the Continent will be a good deal shorter than mine, but the French are not such agreeable travelling company as Stockdale and Wilbraham; so I think the sooner he gets back the better. There are many French at Smyrna, settled as merchants, who sport the cockade, and two frigates in the harbour, to the no little annoyance of our trade there. Why no English ones are sent to protect it when our fleet is superior everywhere else, is one of those secrets that I believe nobody can understand, for no English vessel can without the greatest risk enter the harbour. The sailors in the French vessels all wear the cockade or *bonnet rouge*, and amuse us with national airs all day long ; however, they are now very orderly and well behaved there, thanks to Mr. Liston, who bullied the Turks till they checked them. The English vessels have twice or thrice lately escaped their clutches, and made them quite outrageous about it. They had about a month ago received their new colours, which was some trifling alteration in the flag, and, instead of cruising, were in harbour dancing round the tree of liberty and celebrating a grand national fête. Just at that moment arrived safe an English merchant ship they had been in quest of for a fortnight, and dropped anchor just before them. So much for the news of this quarter of the world. With you, I suppose, frights and fears of internal com- motions being over, an invasion is hourly expected, as it was before, when the French were in Holland. If they get to Richmond or Catterick, I beg you will write me word immediately.

I now finish my letter from Chismé, a small town on the edge of the sea, opposite Scio, for which we are going to set off immediately almost. I have been riding this morning from near Vourla, and thinking of you the whole way. I felicitated myself heartily,

I assure you, that Rokeby was not in the climate of
Asia ; we have travelled for hours through lanes of
such beautiful myrtle yesterday and to-day that I am
sure if they fell in your way there would not be a
window in the whole house without a bush in it.
I shall to-morrow write Abney a long account of his
farm here, and tell him how his fences and game are
situated, whether he has many vagrants, and all
information which one justice ought to communicate
to another on these occasions. I fear his neighbourhood here is almost as thin of gentlefolks as that of
Linley and Measham ; however, there are fewer hare-
hunting parsons and attorneys, and the shrubbery
walk is much superior, so I don't know whether I
shan't counsel a removal. We have for half an hour
been making puns, and flatter ourselves that by good
pronunciation it will make no bad story for Miss Dering
that when I was in this part of Asia several Greek
ladies came over from Scio to *Chismé*.

Yours very sincerely and affectionately,

J. B. S. MORRITT.

CHISMÉ,
October 18, 1794.

CHAPTER VI

The Troad and the Site of the Homeric Troy: the Islands of Chios and Lesbos

Morritt visited the Troad with a book by Lechevalier in his hand. Lechevalier (called Chevalier in his letters) had been secretary in the years 1784–6 to Count Choiseul-Gouffier, the French Ambassador at Constantinople. His researches in the Troad attracted much notice in England as well as on the Continent; and Morritt adopts with enthusiasm the theory that the Homeric Troy was on the heights of Bali Dagh, near Bunarbashi. The question had been discussed at intervals for some 2,000 years. The natural belief that the Greek colony of Ilium Novum stood on the site of the Homeric Ilium had been disputed as early as 200 B.C., when Demetrius of Scepsis argued that the true site was at a place called the "village of the Ilians" further inland, from some idea, apparently ill-founded, that the sea had receded since the Homeric age. This site is in a marsh and has little to recommend it, and most writers of the Roman Empire and afterwards, until 1784, reverted to the Ilium Novum (*i.e.* the hill known as Hissarlik) as the true site. Lechevalier's arguments for the site near Bunarbashi were the commanding position, and the two springs, hot and cold, mentioned in the Iliad, which he thought that he had found at that spot. His view was almost universally adopted for the next hundred years, so that Morritt cannot be accused of hasty conversion.

But since the discoveries from Schliemann's famous excavations in 1871–9 at Hissarlik, confirmed as they seem to have been by still more thorough investigations, especially those of Dörpfeld, most scholars have returned to the old belief that the sites of Old Troy

and New Troy were the same. It must, of course,
be assumed that the Homeric descriptions were
written with accurate knowledge of the local features :
for there is nothing to discuss if this is not assumed.
Objections may be raised to either theory, and
advocates of each may sometimes have overstrained
the correspondence in minute details ; but the objections to the Bunarbashi site, which Morritt describes,
are by far the stronger—for instance, its distance from
the sea-coast ; nor has the spade revealed any pottery
or other remains which would suit the Homeric
period. On the other hand, the proof from the two
springs, on which Morritt's letters lay so much stress,
seems to be now discounted. Mr. Leaf, one of the most
learned Homeric scholars, who has visited the Troad
more than once, writes in a book on Troy published
in 1912 : "It is no longer possible to use this as
evidence ; no such combination of hot and cold springs
now exists in the plain. All the sources have been
tested : some are warmer than others ; but the
difference is in no case great, and nowhere are two
springs of perceptibly different temperature near one
another." Morritt himself, as will be seen, confesses
to being rather disappointed by the amount of warmth
in the so-called hot spring. It may safely be said
that the more recent and more complete excavations
and discoveries tend to confirm Schliemann's choice
of Hissarlik ; but it is never wise to dogmatise on any
antiquarian subject. Sir Richard Jebb, in his " Homer,"
written after Schliemann's researches, still adhered to
Bunarbashi and rejected Hissarlik ; though it may
perhaps be questioned whether he would have done
so after the more recent spade-work of Dörpfeld and
others, and with the light which has been thrown
upon Homeric history and Homeric art not only by
the discoveries at Mycenae and Tiryns, but more
especially by the recent work of Sir Arthur Evans
and others in Crete.

KOUM-KALEH,
November 12, 1794.

DEAR AUNT,
      I write to you at last from the heart of Homer's
country, from the shore of the Troad. The Simois

runs across the plain near us, and we are surrounded with the monuments of his heroes. You will imagine it, of course, rather difficult to talk of anything else. However, I have a good deal of prose before I get so far, and must give up at least this sheet to bring up my account of our tour so far. I left off my story, I think, in the island of Samos. We sailed next to Claros, now Zille. It is on the sea-shore, and was famous for an oracle of Apollo. We landed in the evening, and found no reception but a large, solitary, damp cave, with a spring in it. Not a hut is now standing, though the walls are still traceable, and contain a ruined theatre scooped in the hill-side, which has been built of brown stone ; many columns of porphyry, now completely crumbled away into earth and small stones by exposure to the weather; and the foundations of an immense temple. On a hill near is a fountain with marble steps into it, where Chandler supposes the oracle to have been. I refer you to his account of it, which is accurate, but I doubt very much the placing of the oracle. Besides the cave I have already mentioned, we saw among the ruins of this temple a large subterraneous hole of which the mouth is in the centre of the foundations which remain. This induced us to suppose, I think with some reason, that this temple, like that at Delphi, had been built over the oracular cavern, and there appear to be subterraneous communications under the whole.

The situation has been delightful. It covered the top of a broad, flat promontory whose bays on each side made two secure ports ; high rocks lift it above the sea, and the little valley of the Halys, behind it, is a pleasant, quiet scene, well wooded and fertile. We had the luck to be here when the sun was setting, and enjoyed it with the addition of the beautiful forms of this vast bay, bounded southwards by the cliffs of Mycale and Samos, and northwards by the peninsula opposite Scio. I have already mentioned the beautiful

colours of the evening here, and the effect of them
over the islands ; you really cannot conceive anything
more beautiful. I told Anne in my last letter the
accidents of our voyage.

We slept on the shore here, and coasted the day
after by the situation of Lebedos, which, however, is
uncertain as well as that of Colophon. A calm drove
us again to the necessity of sleeping on the shore
under some rocks, and the next day we arrived at the
port of Teos. The situation of Teos was on the
isthmus of a high promontory, in a rich plain with
hills on each side and the sea before and behind it—
in front, to the walls ; behind, at the distance of about
two miles, where was the port, Gerae, now Segi Geck.
Chandler describes it, and so accurately that I can add
nothing to his account except that the trees on it are
almost all covered with a vine, which the time of the
year did not show to him with the same advantage ;
but I could not help thinking their festoons, loaded
with grapes, a classical as well as a picturesque
ornament to a ruined temple of Bacchus. We then
crossed the passes of Mount Mimus, of which shrubs are
the only ornament, to Chismé, and embarked for Scio.

You will, I know, partake our pleasure when I tell
you we here found an English merchantman in the
harbour, whose captain invited us constantly on board
to treat us with roast beef, potatoes, and porter, articles
all unknown to this part of the world. In Scio the
modern Greeks are seen to the best advantage ; they
are less molested by the Turks, enter much into trade,
and are richer, easier, and more flourishing than in
any part of the Empire. The country for some miles
from Scio is covered with houses, and having been
built by the Genoese, they are of stone, and much
superior to any we had seen. They have each a large
orangery behind them, so the valley has the air of a
perfect garden. The mountains, however, which rise
behind it are barren and ugly, for the island, at least
this side, is little more than one continued high range

of brown rock, on which what little verdure it might have had was destroyed by the heat of the weather.

We then sailed to Chismé and to Smyrna by land. As we went exactly Chandler's route, I refer you to him, for he is very exact, and I shall fill my paper better than by telling you what you know already. What little remained of Homer's school (as it is called) in the island of Scio is now totally destroyed, for the goddess and her lions, which he talks about, in the centre is nothing more than a bit of stone about two feet high, all broken, rising from a flat, square area, into which form the top of a low rock is chiselled. His living beauties, however, are not the least impaired, for we happened to see all Scio walking on the shore one fine Sunday evening, and a more handsome assemblage of girls I never saw in my life. Every young woman is a beauty; but, in revenge, no woman is young after twenty. I do not know whether you, however, would allow them pretty; for in spite of very fine natural complexions they have a rage for paint, still more generally than with us or our mad neighbours, for not even a servant-maid stirs without it. Another oddity is their wearing over their shoulders a coloured garment stiffened with wood, or bone, in the exact shape of a bell-hoop; their arms come through the pocket-holes, and give them very much the air of a turtle on its hind legs. They are just as "familiar" as they were in Chandler's time, though, without being very prudish or censorious, he might have called it by a stronger term. However, notwithstanding the oddity of their appearance, it is impossible not to remark that they are one of the most beautiful sets of women in the world, and I never saw a ball-room that compared with the quay at Scio.

We only stayed a few days at Smyrna, and, having bargained for horses to the Dardanelles, sallied out again with our light troops, much of the baggage and heavy armour being sent off to wait our arrival at

Athens. The weather had now broken up, and some rains had made the grass spring, and the weather cooler. You can't think the relief it was to us to see a grass field, for we had not beheld such an object for months. It was now quite a second spring, the weather clear, open, and cool. In this delightful way we crossed the plains of the Hermus and Caicus, at the ends of which the irregular and varied gulfs and promontories afforded us delightful sea views. Your maps will show you how uneven a coast Asia is. This, with a western aspect, makes the evening scenes always delightful, and when in almost every one of these bays we recollect the situation of a Grecian colony, how much it strikes you to pass through Ionia for days, and scarcely see a few miserable villages! North of Smyrna, however, the case is better. The country as far as Ida is in the hands of Kara Osman, one of the most powerful Agas of the Empire. His possessions are hereditary, and partly by his own sense, partly by that of his ancestors, he has introduced a cultivation and plenty throughout them very different from the southern part of the country. He has very greatly protected the Greeks and Franks in this country, so that everything is on a better footing. We remarked a number of villages along these valleys, and twenty or thirty ploughs at work, a sight we had not seen for a long time. At a small village in the plain of the Caicus I found some inscriptions, and, inquiring where they came from, we were directed to the shore. We here found a few architectural remains, seemingly those of an Ionic temple, though no foundations or appearance of a town, and a broken colossal trunk that by its proportions seemed that of a Hercules.

We went up the valley next to Pergamus, still Bergamo. You remember how famous this city was in the later times of Greece, under the descendants of Attalus, and the Empire of Rome. All the remains here in any perfection are either Christian or Roman.

The common sewers, through which a small river is directed, run under the whole of the town, and are an arched vault about thirty feet high, and near as many broad. This great and useful work was a favourite one with the Romans in all their towns, and was a greater addition to their comfortable living than the ornaments of their predecessors. We here saw a large theatre, of which the two side-wings and the scoop of the hill, with arches at the top, still remain ; these are more or less perfect, but in every town the same. This was built of good solid brown stone; the Grecian ones we had seen were all of marble. There are here great ruins of the Church of St. John the Evangelist, established in the early ages of Christianity. It is a large brick building without a roof, stripped of all its ornaments but a frieze from some ancient building inserted in the wall. It is bowed at the end where the shrine was, and on each side of it are two detached rotundas about ten yards across, and thirty high, with a cupola roof. These have probably served as chapter-houses, etc. That you may have an idea of the present enlightened state of Christianity here, a Greek told me that the church had been built above four thousand years ; and that a small mosque near it had fallen down every time the Turks attempted to build it, not the least finding out that the church might have exerted its magic powers to much better purpose in keeping up its own walls than in destroying those of its rival. We were here, too, agreeably surprised with many remains we had not heard of.

In a dale behind the present town the two hills which form its side are scooped out into an amphitheatre, of which some of the seats still remain. The circle of the amphitheatre is continued round by high arches, and a strong wall of stone work as high as the rest of the hill; on the top of these are some arches of an arcade that has run all round as communications for the seats, and retreat in case of rain.

These are each about thirty feet high, as I should judge by the eye, and are built, as well as the wall, in the most solid manner.   Below a stream of water was admitted under long vaults, in which we were able to remark the contrivance to stop the stream with flood-gates in order to float the amphitheatre for the amusements of the Naumachia, or sham sea-fights. There are lesser arches to carry off the water at a certain height, and the same contrivance to stop the stream above when they emptied and cleared the theatre.

Behind the town is a very high, conical hill, on which has been the citadel and a great part of the ancient city.   This, having been since used by the Genoese and Turks, is now one hodge-podge of fine remains jumbled pell-mell into walls and fortifications. Of the ancient walls and citadels, a few of the lower courses of stone and the foundations remain, very distinguishable from the buildings raised upon them. Amongst the numbers of foundations, we distinguished some of baths, and saw quantities of broken Doric friezes and columns lying over the whole hill.   A causeway of ancient work remains in part up to the castle, and is in many places formed of rows of ancient marble columns laid across and covered with earth.   Many of these the whimsical engineers that placed them have bored into cannon, and raised the causeway into a battery.   I should think, however, if fired, they would do much more harm to their neighbours than to the enemy.

When we left Bergamo we crossed the plain northward, and leaving it, embarked for Lesbos opposite Mitylene.   At the little town where we embarked, and afterwards in Lesbos and the Troad, we had an opportunity of seeing more of the higher sort of Turks, and in a manner which, for their honour, I must mention.

Being ill-lodged, we sent our servant to the Aga, or governor, desiring him to inform us of a better place. He instantly offered to receive us in the most hospitable manner, gave us a room, ordered us a good dinner to be dressed in his harem, provided us by inquiring of our servants our usual breakfast, and never thought of any return but what, in the custom of the country, we pleased to give his servants. In Lesbos we one day sent to beg at a country house a room to eat in; we received the same civility. The dinner was immediately dressed; the master even had the attention to send us some excellent Cyprus wine, and pressed us earnestly to spend the evening and night there, and to walk about where we pleased. These we thought singular adventures, but having since repeated the experiment with the same success, I begin to think there are gentlemen in all nations.

These Agas live very comfortably. Their houses are large, good, and well adapted to the climate. They are chiefly of wood, painted, roofed like the Chinese, very deep, and with large, open porticoes, sometimes all round. They have many horses, are fond of shooting and hawking, and have often, with their agricultural servants, not less than three or four hundred attendants.

Before we get to Lesbos you will ask me what is become of Cuma, the capital of ancient Aeolia. Its situation—and we hear nothing more exists—is a small village called Chandilar. Mitylene has scarce had a better fate. Its two ports mentioned in Strabo, and the present town of the same name, convinced us of its situation, but nothing remains of the birthplace of Sappho except a few broken columns scattered in the Turkish burying-grounds as gravestones, and the marks of foundations in a hill near it. No traces of public buildings or temples, unless a hollow scoop in the hill, much like a gravel-pit, was the theatre, as I imagined from its form and situation, though Stockdale says he can make out better theatres near Acomb.

We crossed the island of Lesbos in hopes of finding remains of its other cities. The country on the south is one continued forest of olives, which grow almost without cultivation, except, where the ground is steep, keeping the earth with low walls round the roots, and which are a great article of trade to all this part of the world. Intermixed with other trees, the hills, which are steep and craggy, have a picturesque appearance, and in two places the sea, running in through narrow straits, spreads like a lake into an immense and beautiful basin, surrounded by these hills, and perfectly land-locked. At the head of one of these ports was the ancient Pyrrha; nothing remains of its glory but some broken columns and capitals in a field, probably part of its ruins. Methymna is now called Thymnia, but I heard there were no traces of antiquity. The north of the island is a barren rock, and the villages on it are situated on its crags in the most fantastic manner.

There is a very ancient custom in Lesbos still, which derives from their Grecian ancestors there, and which I tell you as an advocate for petticoat independence. When any one dies, his estate descends to his eldest daughter, a singularity which I don't believe exists in any other country in the world.

On quitting Lesbos we sailed to the southern part of Mount Ida, and landed near the village of Narla, where our horses were to meet us at about three in the morning, after being becalmed. We lay down round a fire of sticks on the shore till they came, and then crossed Ida to the ruins of Alexandria Troas. We were near the situation of the ancient Gargara, and for two days crossed one of the most romantic countries I ever saw. The southern branches of Ida are beautiful, rocky points and deep dells covered with wood of all sorts, and when you are satiated with them, uneven plains open out on each side in the most agreeable manner. I cannot give you a better idea of them, though you will say I am partial, than by telling

you they put me much in mind of the country between
Richmond and Kirby Hill, especially the look-out over
the plains.

At Alexandria we found the walls much more ruined
than Chevalier represents them. There are some
foundations of temples, though stripped of their ornaments, and the ruins of a theatre and stadium. The
principal remain, and which he mentions, is a large
square building of coarse granite. Its front consists
of three arches, the middle one larger than the other
two ; a low row of arches, which on one side are open,
run all round the other three sides. The front has
been adorned with a fine cornice with ova and den-
telles. You will see that Chandler and Chevalier dis-
agree about this building—the first calling it a gymnasium, the other baths. It seems to me very likely
that the gymnasium might contain baths, but I am not
acquainted enough with ruins to talk about it. I can
only say that, seen through the beautiful trees which
now cover the ground of the city, it seemed as picturesque a ruin as I could imagine. I have accurate
drawings of both the inside and the out.

We rode to some warm baths near, though all the
marble sarcophagi near them mentioned by Chevalier
have long been taken away to adorn fountains for the
Turks or serve as cannon-ball at the Dardanelles. We
then rode towards Troy, and slept just by the monument of Aesyetes, in the house of the Captain Pasha,
which Chevalier mentions.

The next day we crossed the Scamander, the Simois,
and the plain of Troy in a heavy shower, when, as I
saw nothing, I say nothing ; for we hurried to the Dardanelles, about twenty miles higher up the Hellespont,
and it rained the whole way. Yesterday being also a
disagreeable day, we stayed there in the house of a
Jew who is English Consul, and only saw the Turkish
castle, some large cannon, and a manufactory of coarse
earthenware. There is another castle opposite, the
straits being only about a mile broad. Above it we

this morning perceived a small artificial barrow, exactly resembling those in the Troad. The cities of Madytus and Kœlos still exist above it in the villages of Maith and Kœlia; this, then, was the situation of the Cynossema, the promontory where Hecuba was buried. Surely this is a strong corroboration of the reality of the other tombs. You see I am already half mad, and begin to conjecture, but I have not been over the Troad yet, and you will have much more to-morrow.

We this morning ran up the Hellespont to discover the situation of Abydos. There are no remains but some small pieces of old wall; traces of regular slopes in the hill-side, and a ground covered with stones, leave no room to doubt of its situation. The narrowest point where Xerxes passed with his army is a little higher up the strait. If I had been a Grecian I should have looked for the place where he came back. This was also the place, you know, so famous for the pretty story of Leander. Sestos is not immediately opposite Abydos, but a little more up the stream. After taking drawings of the straits, both up and down, we ran down with a charming wind to Koum Kaleh, a Turkish village and castle at the mouth of the Hellespont, an hour and a half, where we now are. This is the exact situation of the Grecian camp; the Simois runs near it; the Sigean promontory and the tombs of Achilles and Patroclus are a mile off towards the Aegean. But all this to-morrow when I have seen them. You see I am half crazy; would you believe it? I am writing now, at near midnight, and my friends have been snoring round me these three hours? Good-night.

BUNARBASHI,
November 12.

I now begin with great pleasure to tell you what we have seen in the Troad. The plain, at the part where we slept last night, is about three miles broad. Its broadest part may be five, its length fourteen, from above Bunarbashi, from promontory to promontory. It is flat and fertile, but near the sea and the banks of the Simois is in many places marshy and covered with reeds and osiers. We set out first in an eastward direction, and, crossing the Simois, rode to the pro-montory of Rhoeteum and the tomb of Ajax. The Simois is here a broad, rapid torrent full of mud and sand, evidently extremely variable, as in summer it is often dry and in winter very considerable, much at present, in size and character, like the Tees about Middleton. The plain ends in a long, low range of hills running from the Hellespont towards Ida, and changing their direction eastward about the middle of the plain.

On the promontory is another conical barrow. The top of this has been dug away, and there now appear in it great semi-circular walls that seem to have served as foundations. A low semi-circular arch is open at the side, into which we crept. It goes into the centre of the monument, and is a long vault almost filled up. This is exactly similar to all the sepulchres we had seen, and shows at least that this is a monument for a single person, and not a heap of earth thrown up in the later wars over a number. It is remarkable that Strabo mentions the monument of Ajax as having been violated by Mark Antony, and also the existence of a small shrine consecrated to him on the promontory. The foundations we saw might be those of this shrine, but I cannot, I own, entertain a doubt of the existence of his tomb, as it exactly resembles the other tombs, is situated precisely where ancient authors place it, and has evidently been opened. We got from hence a drawing of the coast and station of the Grecians. We then crossed southward over the low ranges of hills, which here put forward into the plain. We soon after came to the valley of Thymbra, now called Thymbrek. It is much less than that we had left, and runs east-ward from it.

In a Turkish burying-ground and village, on the

banks of the stream that runs down it, we saw a great
number of columns, some architectural ornaments, and
an inscription too much defaced to be made out.   These
are the remains of a temple near, of which we could
not discover the exact site.   Chevalier mentions more
about it, and supposes it that of Apollo Thymbrius,
with much appearance of reason from inscriptions he
found there.   Northwards, near Chiblak, a Turkish
village, we were a good deal surprised by finding a
hill covered with remains of buildings, apparently of
considerable extent, and several shafts of columns
nearly half buried in the earth, but still standing.
They are of a grey granite, but stripped of their
capitals and architecture.   I should not be surprised if
this had been the original situation of the remains we
had just seen in Thymbrek.   At least, these have not
been mentioned in any book of the Troad I have seen.
We found a buried altar or pedestal, with part of an
inscription in Greek.   We stayed above an hour to
get a spade and pickaxe, and hoped by clearing it
to find out the name of the place.   It was after all,
however, too much broken to make anything of, but
from the mention of Julius Caesar we found it was of
a later date.

We soon after came into the valley of the Simois
again.   Bunarbashi was opposite us on the other
side.   The valley here is really very fine ; the hills
that rise round it, and on which some small villages
and Bunarbashi are situated, are green, cultivated
and ornamented with trees.   Those on the left are the
beautiful hills of Callicolone mentioned in Homer ;
they have not in the least lost their character.   We at
last crossed the Simois again, and by a short and easy
ascent came to Bunarbashi.   We mean to visit its
tombs and the sources of the Scamander to-morrow.
At present I can only say that its situation in every
respect is a probable one for that of ancient Troy, and
is in itself a very pleasing one.   Chevalier's Scamander
rises a little below it out of a grove of beautiful trees,

and out of our windows on the other side we see the barrows of the Trojan chiefs, one of which he supposes Hector's.

We are here again well lodged in a Turkish gentleman's house, who has received us very civilly, and you will not wonder that I have set a negotiation on foot for permission to open these tombs. I dare not hope to succeed, but there is at least no harm in trying. You see how much we are at home among the Turks. I assure you I shall never believe in dangers again. Do not you envy me in such circumstances the pleasure of fancying myself at the Scaean gate and seeing everything round me correspond with Homer's own account of it? Nothing can, I think, be more accurate than he is in the description of this country, and it is by no means difficult to trace most of the scenes in the Iliad.

Independent of the pleasure our tour has already afforded us, the gaining a clear idea of this country is, I think, worth almost the whole tour, besides the visionary satisfaction that a person who, like me, is mounted on a pretty unmerciful hobby-horse must feel in treading over the steps of old favourites. To-morrow we sleep at the Sigean promontory, now Yeni Shehr, and I shall have to add an account of the Scamander and the other tombs. If Chevalier deceives me about the first, with his story of the warm spring and old channel, I am sorry to say I shall be cruelly disappointed. I have as yet, however, no reason to suspect him, except a natural fearfulness in trusting a French author. If not more agreeably detained by the tombs here, I shall tell you more of this to-morrow. In the meantime, good-night.

YENI SHEHR, THE SIGEAN PROMONTORY,
November 13.

I now shall finish my history of the Troad, which is justly your due, as Chevalier's book, which you once lent me, was as great an incentive to my touring as

any I had read.   I am sure you will be delighted to
hear from me the very strongest confirmation of his
truth in essentials, and that I have no longer any doubt
about the situation of Troy or the geography of Homer.
We were this morning so full of the Scaean gate and
sources of the Scamander that though it afterwards
lay in our road our first sally was down to the springs.
They gush from under a hill below the house where
we slept, surrounded with willows, poplars, and
beeches.

The warm spring rises at some distance from the
others.   It had rained violently all night; there is but
a small spring, and its waters, received into a large
basin, are exposed so to the cold.   In such circumstances Chevalier ought not to be blamed if we did not
find its waters so warm as we expected.   In the part
of the basin where they rose they were much warmer;
and we were told that in frost they were very sensibly
heated.   Their temperature at present was about the
heat of Bristol.   This was sufficient to convince us
that if the stream in question ever had joined the
Simois, it had at least the properties of the Scamander.

We next rode to the hill behind Bunarbashi.   I saw
a hill covered with stones and grey-wethers, but
could not make out many of the foundations he
mentions.   We were told by the Turks there had
been some remains there, and I believe I saw some
traces.   Above Bunarbashi, near a mile on the
highest part of the hill, are four tombs, exactly like
the others, which he supposes with reason to be those
of the Trojan heroes.   They were thus on a con-
spicuous point exposed to the view and respect of the
whole plain, as the Grecians were to the Hellespont.
Beyond these the hill finishes on three sides in an
abrupt precipice, the Simois winding below entirely
round it, hemmed in by rocks in a beautiful defile.

We must agree with Chevalier that Troy could not
exist higher up the Simois than this; and so the
Scamander and Troy must be sought for lower down

than this, for it is not possible that a long range of mountains and defiles should really exist between the camp and the city, unmentioned by Homer, who always places his battles in the plain, and who would have certainly varied his battles with all the circumstances of a mountainous country if such had existed. But below this point the Simois receives no streams but the Thymbrius, near its mouth, which is sufficiently marked by the name of Thymbrek. Chevalier therefore showed his judgment in searching for an old bed to some other stream.

When we descended the hill we passed again by the sources of the Scamander; and after taking a view of the situation of its sources went on along the west side of the plain, near its course. We observed on the ground we at first passed over great traces of building, and I should not at all wonder if the city had existed on this side more in the plain than Chevalier supposes. The hot springs and the Scaean Gate are, I have no doubt, where he places them; but supposing the city not to have existed so high as the precipices I have mentioned, the circumstances of Hector's flight round the city, which he does not, I think, get cleverly over, remain in this case possible; and the monuments were out of the walls and behind the city—as he himself acknowledges, more customary with the ancients—and there was certainly no reason for burying Hector within the walls, having a twelve days' truce to do it in unmolested by the Greeks.

I have, however, no doubt of the situation of the Scaean Gate; the hill of wild fig trees, though now not so covered, is near it. The heights above Troy command a most extensive view of the plain, as far as the Sigean promontory and the Hellespont. As for the Scamander, it now is certainly not so beautiful a stream as Chevalier would have you suppose it is, except that its waters are very clear and pure, even in this extremely wet weather, agreeing strikingly with Homer's account that it admitted no increase from floods or diminution from drought, which is the very contrary with the other streams in the plain. It winds for a long way through an extensive marsh, not unlike Cradock's Bottoms near Rokeby. At the end of these, below the tomb of Aesyetes, it runs off in its present channel to the sea. This is as evidently artificial as possible—the course straight and the banks thrown up. We rode to the beginning of this, and perceived immediately evident marks of a channel running into the Simois. It is now dry, but is perfectly traceable, and leaves no doubt, I think, of the stream having originally run in this direction. Perhaps the stopping of it may in part have occasioned the marsh. The Scamander in size contains about the same quantity of water as the Foss, perhaps more; but it is more uniform in its depth, and a much stronger stream; it is everywhere clear, a quality Homer notices in a thousand places.

We then rode on to the Greek village of Yeni Shehr, where we now are, on the Sigean promontory. This you know was the station of Achilles—his tomb, with that of Antilochus and Patroclus, is very near here, towards the shore. We were disappointed in our hopes of opening the tombs at Bunarbashi. The Aga gave us leave to work, indeed; but as he ran a risk in so doing, would only let us try in the night, and would not furnish us with more than two men for fear of committing himself; he could only give us permission for one night; and on such terms it is easy to conceive we should not have been able to make much progress in a structure of earth and great stones, which these are. We gave it up on this account, and came away.

The weather has now broken up, and I fear the winter has set in. It has for several days been little but constant rains and stormy weather. This is very much against us, who in a day or two are to sail for Lemnos and Greece. To-morrow we go if possible to Tenedos, and hoped to stay no longer than to see the island, and immediately set off for Lemnos.

November 14.

I continue my letter from the Sigean promontory, where we have the ill-luck of being detained by the south wind. Patience is an excellent recipe for anybody that has to do with wind and weather, so here we are in a dirty room full of fleas still. We shall have the amusement, if we please, of showing our learning by deciphering the Sigean inscription, which, as well as the basso-rilievo Chandler mentions, is in the church here. The Greeks, who are as superstitious as Chevalier represents them in supposing these stones remedies for the ague, are obstinate about preserving them to the last degree.

Firmans have been repeatedly given by the Porte to different people to empower them to take the inscription stone, but the superstition of the Greeks has even resisted the will of the Porte. The famous Hassan Pasha attempted to carry it off, but the Greeks told him that before he did he must take off the head of every man. As he was a Turkish Pasha, permitted by the Porte, I only wonder he did not take them at their word; and perhaps they almost deserved it for their stupid resistance, for in their hands the stones are only wearing out by patients rolling on them for the ague.

Theirs, however, is not the only instance of these sort of remains being kept here from mere spirit of stupidity, as at Bunarbashi we saw a broken basso-rilievo of two figures, not ill-executed, which an Englishman had brought from Alexandria Troas, and which the Aga here refused to let him carry off, though he offered four or five guineas for the permission. It now lies in a dirty garden, with the carved side downwards. The Englishman deserved his disappointment for being so stupid as not to ship it directly for Tenedos and the islands, which he

might have done from the shore, and put it beyond
the reach of Agas.

You, who are probably now shivering over a large
coal fire, will think my description of a pretty country,
if we happen to see one in Thessaly, the work of fancy
at this time of the year; but I beg to observe that we in
all probability shall see it in the highest advantage with
the colours of autumn. For at present the trees have
not begun to turn here, and have hardly lost a leaf
yet, notwithstanding high wind; and as the rain has
made all the grass spring, we shall, I hope, see
Tempe in full beauty, if we can but contrive to get
a fine gleam to see it in.

> Believe me
> Most affectionately yours,
> J. B. S. MORRITT.

MONTE SANTO, CARES,
December 6, 1794.

DEAR ANNE,

I very probably shall not at present write above
five lines, but a beginning is always something. From
my date you will have some difficulty in finding out
where we are. In old times this was Mount Athos. I
have yesterday and to-day thought so often about you,
and so often wished I had you trotting by my side on
Asphodel, that though I can only scrawl while the
horses are getting ready, yet I cannot help scribbling
to you. You no doubt feel infinitely obliged to me
for my kind wishes, and think yourself as well trotting
round the banks of the Tees. For my part, I am again
in one of my crazy fits, and am delighted with the
country round me. You, I dare say, recollect a good
deal of what you have heard me say about Switzerland and its beauties. Put it all together, with the
richness and luxuriance of a warmer climate, and more
habitations, and you will not exaggerate those of
Mount Athos. You will, however, before I tell you
what we have seen here, be perhaps not sorry to know

how we got here. As Mr. Vellum observes that in business there is nothing like method, I will for once in my life, at least, follow his advice, and begin where I left off; though I can't say our mode of travelling at all suits so methodical an account of it.

My account, then, shall be twofold: firstly, how we got to Monte Santo; and secondly, what we have seen there. For though I know you are a little maddish yourself, yet it ill becomes the dignity of a travelled man to tell his story so confusedly. After we left the Troad, and paid due honour to its heroes, we sailed to Tenedos. It is a small island cultivated with vineyards, and with more cultivation than we often have seen in Turkey. Some small villages, and a little town with a harbour and an old Turkish fortress, is all we saw there, so that as we were detained six or seven days we began to be heartily tired of our stay there. Our different grievances were at any other time ridiculous enough. We had hired a boat to sail for Lemnos the first fair wind, and, after waiting some days for one, were ready to embark with the wind in our favour when a French frigate came and dropped anchor at the mouth of the harbour. As we heard she would have certain intelligence of our motions from her spies here, we thought it rather prudent to stay on shore, not having the least desire to finish our tour by a trip to France at present. The next day she proceeded on her road, and when we thought her at a tolerable distance we set out. Our boatman in the evening anchored off the island, for as it's a considerable distance, and Lemnos a dangerous shore, they never leave Tenedos till after midnight, that they may not arrive in the dark.

Imagine us, then, tossing in an inconvenient little bark, with no place to creep into but a hole at the end where Stockdale and I could just lay down in case of rain. As the devil would have it a heavy storm just then came on; the wind blew with such violence that we every instant expected out boat to slip or break her cable and drive out to sea. We had the most

violent thunder and lightning, and blessed ourselves
not a little that we had not persuaded our boatmen,
as we had endeavoured to do, to cross at once. We
tossed about all night, and in the morning the wind
blew directly from Lemnos, and we sneaked back
again to Tenedos after as pleasant a twenty-four hours'
jaunt as we could desire. We at last, however, got
over; the distance is about thirty miles to the island,
and about twenty more along the south coast of it to
the port where we stopped. This you may be sure
we did not accomplish without keeping a very sharp
look-out after the French frigate.

At Lemnos we stayed some days. The island is
very curious; a high point in the middle of it has been
a volcano, and the whole island is a heap of pointed
crags and stone. The south coast is a chain of
rocky promontories and points standing as small
islands in the water, that have a very fantastic appearance. There is hardly a single tree on the whole
island, and they even fetch their firing from Mount
Athos. We found no antiquities here, and should not
have stayed except for fair winds.

To give you some idea of this happy government,
we called upon the Aga, who before had not been very
civil to our servant, whom we had sent, and desired,
when we had drunk our coffee in form, he would
permit us to hire a house. He very soon ordered us
to be received into one, and, as we had asked him, sent
a man the next day to order us mules and show us
whatever we wished to see in the country. The mule-
teers made a price with our servant for their cattle,
which, unfortunately for them, coming to the ears of
our guide, he gave them a hearty thrashing, seized their
mules, and said he had the Aga's orders not to let us
pay for anything. He would not even accept anything
himself, so we travelled, *à la Turque*, at other folks'
expense. The Aga had been piqued by some Englishman passing here who had not called on him; but
after our visit was determined to do the honours.

We found him very busy building a large frigate, and on inquiring what it was for, were told it was destined for the Grand Signor at Constantinople; this Aga, it seems, had in the course of his life got very rich, and the Court, *à l'ordinaire*, sent with their compliments to behead him. He very naturally made a few objections to the scheme, and proposed instead to build them a ship. As the offer was accepted he kept his head on his shoulders, and his ship is easily built here, for he employs the Greeks, and I dare say pays them little or nothing.

We at last got away from Lemnos. Mount Athos which you see from it, is one of the grandest single objects I ever saw. It rises in a high, conical form directly from the sea, and as you here don't see the continuation of the land, the end of the promontory, being towards the island, is very striking. The mountain is extremely high, and, rising immediately from the water with no surrounding objects, seems still higher. We had a passage of above sixty miles, for we ran a long way up the coast, and were above twenty-four hours on the water. We had thought of going to Thasos, but it was a good deal out of our way, and we heard that there were pirates from Cavallo in these seas. We were becalmed and had a very slow passage, but saw no danger. We arrived at shore about three in the morning, and landed in a harbour near a great Greek monastery here. Everybody was fast asleep, so we stopped in a poor open summer-house, under which was a fountain. We thought ourselves very uncomfortable, and sat down muffled up in our great-coats to wait for morning. Through the broken boards of our summer-house we saw a chip fire, and heard a groan or two. This was very terrible, you will say, and we thought it pretty much so when we walked down, for we found the boatmen of a small skiff in the harbour, who had that very morning fallen in with pirates, been stripped to their shirts and trousers, and two of them were severely wounded

with ball. We now thought ourselves very well off
ashore, and our summer-house improved very much
upon second thoughts. As soon as it was light our
eyes were amused with one of the finest countries I
had ever seen. All the mountain is covered with
Greek convents, of which there are not less than
twenty scattered over its sides in the most picturesque
points of view you can conceive. One of these, embosomed in wood, was above us at a little distance
from the shore. Its turrets and high, battlemented
walls, mixed with tall, thick cypresses and surrounded
with wood, had an air completely monastic; farther
up the hill was another, equally venerable. The bank
on which they stand is uneven in the extreme, covered
with wood, and now with all the beauty of autumn
colouring.

As, besides the greatest profusion of oaks, chestnuts,
and oriental planes, the mountain is covered with
shrubs and evergreens, you can hardly conceive
anything so rich and varied. We stayed one day
at this monastery, and saw with wonder the comfort
in which they live here. In the courtyard of the
monastery is a thick orchard of oranges and lemons,
now full of the finest fruit I ever ate. They gave us
some very good wine, and I can really say these were
the first convents I ever thought did any good in the
world, but in this inhospitable place an institution
that receives strangers, and where every passenger
that calls of every sort has a right to a loaf of bread,
is really a very useful establishment. We rode from
hence about twelve miles towards the point of Mount
Athos. After gaining the top of the hill above the
convent, the road lays westward along the side of a
slope, terminated to the left by the sea, and in front
by the summit of the mountain; on this slope, which
waves in every direction, the road winds at one
instant through thick and beautiful woods, at another
along lawns or open fields, commanding, besides this
lovely foreground, views of the sea and the different

islands of Thasos, Samothrace, Imbros, and Lemnos, or the coast of Macedonia, with a high range of distant mountains.

Athos itself, before us, is a still more magnificent object; its sides, which are covered with wood, terminate in a high, pointed crag, of an amazing height, which catches the lights of the sun, and reflects it in the softest and most brilliant colouring, both in the morning and evening. I have no hesitation in saying that, accustomed as I have been to beautiful scenery, this surpasses any I had ever seen, for the details of it were everywhere as lovely as the *ensemble*. At every step clear springs, rising out of beds of verdure, dash across the road; at every step you pass trees covered with ivy, every one of which would make a picture; several villages, monasteries, and other decent houses, surrounded each by tufts of trees, or rising out of banks of wood, are seen in the most picturesque points of view; the sea below forms a thousand bays, over which the trees hang on the water edge; the mountain itself, more uneven than I ever saw, gives you a fresh view at every turn. By this means the scene unites every beauty of the wildest and grandest sort to those of the finest and most fertile countries. The retired scenes of rock and wood are as perfect as the effect of the grand prospects of the country and the islands, and the forest is at the same time full of the finest trees, now in their greatest beauty, and a thick bed of shrubs and flowers. The grass, which had just sprung from the late rains, had the verdure of spring, and the weather was as warm as it is with us in the beginning of September.

Delighted with the scene, we arrived at Cares, and lodged in another small monastery. From it we returned eastward again: the road ascends the ridge of the promontory; the southern side of it terminates also in the sea, and is covered, if possible, with still thicker foliage. The change of the leaf gave these banks a richness I had no notion of, and the evergreen oak mixed with them, here an immense forest tree, is so light a green as not to have the wintry effect of our firs and spruce. The road winds, as if on purpose, first on one side of the ridge and then on the other, as if to give us the full view of both seas ; sometimes it continues along the top with a valley on each side, open to the two seas. We stared and talked till we had exhausted every bit of our admiration, and were obliged to stare in silence. The southern view, including also some small islands, is bounded by the high ridge of the opposite promontory of Cape Falso. Its woods are still richer than the other, and the view in general is more confined. It has not such variety of objects, but some old, large monasteries placed among its woods, of which you see the turrets and battlements among the trees, seem the very temples of solitude and retirement. If I talk romantically you must lay it to the account of the place, for I can't describe it in other terms.

We descended a steep zigzag for a little way, to a large monastery below. When we were at it, we looked round on an amphitheatre covered with wood ; through the middle of it runs a clear torrent, in most parts hid by the shrubs and trees that hang over it. On one side on the slope the monastery stands, a plain, large, venerable pile, made more so by the cypresses and large trees that rise amongst its walls. We were admitted into a large, clean, and comfortable room, and for the first half-hour were fixed at the window, and agreed very cordially in pitying all you poor people that stay at home ; I have no hesitation in preferring it to everything I ever saw, even in Switzerland, and will never again suppose I have seen the finest thing in the world, for there is no limit to beauties of this sort. The view of a double sea, adorned to such a degree with islands and shores, was what I had not a notion of. The variety of these islands is another beauty. Thasos, a very mountainous island, wooded and cultivated.   Samothrace, a high, craggy, barren mountain, with the boldest outline rising from the water.   Imbros and Lemnos low and broken lines.

Now I have described our lodgings and situation, I will our company.   Imagine one thing more dirty, sycophantish, and ignorant than another, you will have a faint idea of a Greek papa.   This is the title of their priests.   One or two of the superiors look sometimes rather cleaner, but are all equally ignorant. In one of the convents we were so popular that a papa proposed to attend *my lordi* as cook, and another told Stockdale we were all much too young to travel together, and proposed to attend us to take care of the party.   I was highly flattered with the compliment, but we rather objected to a Greek travelling tutor.

CHAPTER VII

FROM ATHOS AND SALONICA THROUGH THESSALY AND BOEOTIA : ATHENS

I FINISHED this part of my letter at different times and places in my road here, and am now comfortably settled in an Englishman's house, who is our Consul here. I will, however, as usual, go on with my story. The last great monastery I have mentioned was that of St. George, where they pretend to show the tomb of their patron ; we paid, of course, high reverence to them as Englishmen. The country eastward, after a short and romantic ride through a wood of oak, with fine rocks and torrents, grows less beautiful ; the isthmus that joins Athos to the Continent is a low neck of land not more than three-quarters of a mile across. It was here Xerxes cut a road through for his navy, but, notwithstanding the fuss the " old ancients " make about him, the Duke of Bridgewater is certainly a much greater workman. There are now little or no remains of his ditch ; in the part we crossed it was not traceable, but I thought there was some appearance of it near the seas.

From hence to Salonica is a tiresome journey of three days. Our first design was to have visited Amphipolis, but, besides there being some risk, we could not discover that there were any remains would repay our trouble in those parts. At Thasos are many, but you conceive we had no great desire to go there. We went, on these accounts, directly to

Salonica, and passed a country by much the worst and most inhospitable I have found in Turkey.

The few miserable villages we passed through are entirely inhabited by Greeks or Jews. The Greeks here have the power in their hands, and exercise it in so rascally a manner that we inquired after Turks as eagerly as we should elsewhere after Englishmen. What makes the people worse is, that in consideration of their working mines of iron and silver, of which there are many here, their enormities are connived at, and even protected, by the Porte. Everything you have to buy or order in these villages is a signal for the whole body to unite in cheating you. No redress from a Greek Aga; he only cheats higher than the rest. I assure you the Turks are so much more honourable a race that I believe, if ever this country was in the hands of the Greeks and Russians, it would be hardly livable. The country being here unsafe, from banditti, we had everywhere escorts from two to seven men, armed with muskets and pistols. With this formidable force, and our own arms, we passed very quietly. After a tiresome journey we got safe here, where we found a very hospitable reception at an English merchant's, and are refitting to go on through Larissa and Thermopylae to Athens. The road, we find, is very practicable, and so we can execute our whole scheme. To-morrow we mean to make a short trip in Macedonia, and then, after seeing Salonica, we shall set out.

After our perils by land and water, however, we are safe here, and likely to continue so, and I hope my next letter will be from Athens, if I do not, however, write another from hence by this post to my mother. All my letters, as we were long in getting here, have gone forward to Athens; and as the last post from England seems to have missed here, we are quite in the dark here about what you are all doing. Great reports are circulating, however, about a separate peace of the Prussians and Austrians with France; but merchants' news is generally a trade trick, as the peace raises or lowers the sale of cotton.

I am just now writing a good deal in a way you would if you were here, with a pretty little child of the Consul's on my knee, as witness her mark. So, you see, I am improved by my travels; but my little friend is so pretty, and talks such nice Greek, that I have been amused with talking to her.

The French are here, as in every other port of the Levant, in great numbers, and of all sorts. All, however, except one or two, have quitted their cockades. Society is in these places a curious and not unpleasant medley. You hear as many languages at once as you see men, and at present as many opinions as languages. What I have most inquired of, as having no bad opportunity, was the effects of the Revolution in the provincial towns of France, from which the *émigrés* had escaped at different times. The private history of it is, I think, both more interesting and more dreadful than the public, which is little more than the news of Paris. The sufferers, too, are more to be pitied, as they are not of the detestable class of aristocrats whose crimes and infamy raised the spirit in their country, but merchants and people of the middle rank of life, the most virtuous in every country, and the most exposed to plunder in their own.

I was much pleased with an expression of a poor young man here, whose father is imprisoned at Marseilles, without accusation, for he has had no part in the government of either side. He said, " Il n'y a contre nous, que l'honnêteté, et les richesses—crimes chez le gouvernement révolutionnaire." Another object of still more interest here is a poor young lady, whose father has been guillotined by these brutes, obliged, with horror in her heart, to wear the cockade amongst her black ribbons, that she may not expose the rest of her relations to the same fate. I have just seen her walking about with a party of them, and I own I almost joined with Edmund Burke in regretting the Age of

Chivalry. The higher sort of them, however, are here less scrupulous of declaring their sentiments at this distance from their enemies; and of those who wear the cockade there are scarce any who do not execrate the present government, though they temporise to save their property. One or two of them have given us letters, and assisted us at different times, with more liberality than we expected; but envy, hatred, and malice are considerably weakened by their long journey from their headquarters at Paris, and before men here they begin to feel as men.

We have been walking over the town here; it is very poor and dirty, even in comparison with Smyrna and Constantinople.

Adieu, and believe me, as usual, your affectionate brother,

J. B. S. MORRITT.

SALONICA,
December 17, 1794.

DEAR MOTHER,

I write still from Salonica, though we very soon mean now to continue our journey to Athens; indeed, you will wonder, after my letter to Anne, that we should still be here. We have been making so many inquiries about the road, and have been obliged to dawdle so much, that we are still here. We are, however, at last in a moving condition, and talk of setting off to-morrow or the day after. Two days after I wrote to Anne we set off on an expedition I told her of to Pella. It is a ride of about twenty miles from Salonica, across a large flat Bannat-like plain, covered at this time of the year with marshes and water, which put me very often in mind of the dear country from Cambridge to Ely. About half-way we crossed the Axius, an extremely broad river, at least now, over a wood bridge, which, being in a most crazy condition, we thought proper to lead our horses across. The river is, as I said, considerable, not less than four hundred yards over, and one of the most rapid. Of all the towns I have yet seen built by the ancients, Pella is certainly placed in the worst situation; at least in winter. The present village of the name is at some distance from the ancient situation.

We were lodged here in the house of the Turkish governor, and were received with their usual hospitality. We rode down to the ruins, at about a mile from the village. The town was situated at the end of a marsh, and almost in it. At present nothing remains but a square old wall in ruins, which may have been anything; another with a strong, clear spring in the middle, which is warm in winter, a few traces of the city wall, and some catacombs. Every other trace of antiquity has been destroyed by time and the Turks, or sunk in the marsh. We wondered less at it when we saw the place, as it is little more than a quagmire in winter. We stayed a day here, and issued a proclamation for medals by the town crier, and got several, particularly of Philip and Alexander. The greatest curiosity here is a number of small heads found all over the ancient situation in ploughing or digging, which I have not heard of anywhere else. They are small and made of hardened clay, most of them women's heads, with a great variety of ancient head-dresses. We only found amongst them one whole figure of a man in armour, ill-made enough, and found above sixty heads, so it put me very much in mind of your island of sheep's heads. One or two of them were well preserved and finished, and seemed to be taken from very pretty originals. What these can have been I am not antiquarian enough to say, or why they are only found at Pella.

I cannot make out that there was any temple here where such offerings were deposited, as I thought at first probable, in a temple of Aesculapius or Apollo, for cures performed. They are found in great numbers, and seem most of them Roman. I have bought, too, a little bust in alto-rilievo on a square bronze medallion, of which the work is not bad, and is well preserved. Don't tell anybody, as it will depreciate my collection, but it cost me twopence, and is certainly no worse than that. The figure seems a Diana with a quiver at her back; the drapery is Roman, I believe. In our return home we were very near stopped by the swelling of a torrent, and our servant, who, being a Frenchman, is a little *Gasconishly* inclined, chose to ride into it; by which means he came in for a good ducking, and returned as wise as he went in.

LEVADIA or LEBADEA,
January 3, 1795.

MY DEAR MOTHER,

I write to you again as I promised you in my letter from Salonica; we are, as you will see, pretty well advanced on our road to Athens, from which I shall send you this letter, and I hope you will find in it some specimens of the genuine Attic salt : if the first part happens to be dull, you must also remember it was begun in Boeotia. You will be anxious, no doubt, to hear what we have seen in the interesting country we have crossed, and though I cannot say we have met with many remains, yet, as our account of situation will remind you of places you have read of, it cannot but interest you as it has done us. We left Salonica at last and crossed the gulf to a village opposite, cutting off a tedious land journey at this time of the year, over the swampy plains of Macedonia. The principal town here now is St. Catherina, a small place where the Aga lives who commands most of that district. We took strong letters of recommendation, and a dozen bottles of rum still stronger, which were very graciously received, and we were furnished with meat and lodging while we stayed and horses when we went, at the expense of the town.

The town is just on the beginning of that part of Macedonia which rises towards Olympus. This mountain, or, rather, this chain of mountains, is high, and of a bold outline, now covered with snow, and resembling the Swiss hills, but long before the bottom it was perfectly free from it. We coasted the sea eastward along the foot of the mountain, and were at last stopped by a large overflowed plain at the mouth of the Peneus, and crossed some high ridges of Olympus into the famous Vale of Tempe. Will you believe that we crossed it and arrived upon the opposite mountain, Ossa, before we knew where we were, and should not have found out if a Greek merchant at the town where we slept had not informed us ? Don't think us stupid, but believe me Tempe is (now at least) by no means handsomer than many dales about Rokeby, and not so handsome as some. It does not therefore follow that the ancients have told lies ; but the woods which they celebrate it for are now almost all destroyed. The valley itself is pretty, but the hills on each side are bare and barren. The river, which in summer is very clear, was now muddy and overflowed ; and in this climate it must be a wonderful charm, when the heat is so great as to dry up all the springs round it. The evergreens, bowers, etc., we did not see, and can only say that it has several fine trees, some groves, and many pretty villages on its banks, but is not at all the superior scene we expected, and far inferior to Athos or Mount Ida. Below, as ancient authors describe, the river runs in a deep gorge between the two mountains, which both rise over it perpendicularly in immense rocks. By this we should have entered the valley, but the overflowing of the river prevented us. The next day we arrived at Larissa. Thessaly is a singular country, and exactly what ancient authors describe it.

Immense plains of the greatest and most surprising fertility, separated by chains of mountains of the greatest barrenness and boldness, and which, as Barthélemy so well observes, presented such natural boundaries to its first inhabitants that Thessaly consisted of almost as many nations as it contained valleys. The country, however, is nowhere picturesque, except just in the passes of the mountains, as it everywhere wants trees, and has an air not unlike the beautiful plains of Cambridge and Huntingdon. The modern Larissa is a large Turkish town, neat and clean, built along the banks of the Peneus, over which it has a bridge of stone arches. The ancient town was considerably higher up the river. As we mean to cross this part of Greece again at a better season of the year, we were deterred by a rainy day from visiting the ancient situation. We crossed Thessaly southwards, and slept the night, after leaving Larissa at Pharsalia, still called Pharsala. The plain of the famous battle lays below it, for it is situated on the slope of a hill, with the citadel on its top. The walls of the citadel remain in many parts, and you see in the fortress large cisterns to supply the garrison with water. The plain, you will not be surprised to hear, is like all other plains, and more interesting to see than to describe. In the mosque-wall we saw here a bas-relief which I should have been glad to carry off. It represents an Augur with the divining rod in his hand, seated and holding conversation with a bird (I believe a raven) perched on an atlas before him.

This is the country of Achilles. About six miles from Pharsala, we passed the ruins of a large town I believe to be Phthia; at least it is on a river which answers the character of the Apidanus, and is evidently ancient. It has no remains but the wall, which in parts is pretty perfect. We afterwards passed the remains of some less remarkable towns at Thaumaci, Hypata, and Lamia, all situated in Mount Othrys, through the passes of which we came into the valley of the Spercheius. Oeta, which is on the other side of the valley, is a most magnificent object, I think the most so of any mountain we have seen. It now was capped with snow, but in the valley the leaves

were on the trees, and it looked like a summer view.
The gulf of Malia and the view of Euboea are good in
this descent, but as you approach the plain it looks
barren, swampy, and covered with marshes. The
day after we crossed it, and in two hours came to
Thermopylae. From the mud brought down by the
Spercheius, the sea is now much filled up in this part,
and the marshes at the entrance of the defile would be
no longer impassable. The road, however, is the same.
At the entrance of the pass it is about ten or twelve
yards across, and continues so for a short way. A
steep but low rock overhangs it the whole way.
Beyond this the road opens, and the hills on the right
slope gradually up towards Oeta.

It was here the Grecians had their camp, and here
the Spartans retired with the body of Leonidas, and
died defending it. The hot springs from which it
had its name gush out at every step, and a low hill
near the entrance of the pass was that, I believe, to
which the Spartans retired, and where their tombs
were erected afterwards. The hot springs are
sulphurous, and taste a good deal like Harrogate
water. Beyond them the road is again very narrow,
and the hills over it are steep and covered with wood.
On part of them is a guard-house, established to
prevent robberies, of which I will by and by tell you
the system in these parts. We gave them, however,
every chance, for we stopped to draw the view, and
afterwards lost our road, and wandered up the
mountain. We slept at Pountonitza, once Opus, the
capital of the Locri Opuntii. Since that we crossed
into Boeotia, passed the little village of Chaeronea,
which I detest even more than Pharsalia; we next
paid our devoirs to Trophonius at Lebadea, and called
upon Pindar and Epaminondas at Thebes, whom we
mean to visit again; so shall now only send their
best respects. *Nous voilà* at Athens, and here I could
go on for ever, like Father Shandy at Auxerre.

I assure you it is well worth the whole tour for the

moment you are here and look round you : the world seems just to have rolled back some thousand years, and you are in the midst of all you have read about. Was it not for meeting a Turk or two under the temple of Theseus or the citadel, you would be tempted to think it really was so. I will not cram into the end of a letter, however, what I have to say about Athens, but after I have finished my sheet shall begin another to Anne containing particulars. Our mode of travelling in this country is this : We took from St. Catherina a janissary belonging to the Pasha of Joannina in Epirus, at the recommendation of the Aga of St. Catherina.   The robbers that infest the whole of this country are almost all subjects of the Pasha of Joannina, who connives at them and shares the profits. They are Albanian Turks, and differ in language, dress, and manners from the others, whom they despise. They are a very lawless, desperate gang, with much the same virtues and honour, however, among them as that of Captain Rolando in " Gil Blas." They are, many of them, perfectly independent in some districts, live on divided plunder, stand by each other faithfully, and set at defiance both the power of the Sultan and of their Pashas. In other parts the Pashas themselves support and are supported by them, and Ali Pasha, of Joannina, has so numerous a Court and such power over his subjects that he may be considered as a perfectly separate government from the Sultan, who acts entirely under his direction here, to avoid an open rupture, which would show only his own weakness and the strength of his antagonist. The Pashas of Scutari have had a perpetual war with the Porte for four or five generations, and are still unhurt, and as formidable as ever. The Pasha of Joannina is still more powerful, and, though not in name, is in reality commander of almost all Greece, for he has seized by his guards all the passes of the mountains, and, under pretence of guarding, stops, plunders, or murders any passenger he pleases. With one of his janissaries, and ourselves disguised in Turkish dresses as janissaries likewise, we passed perfectly safe, but the least ostentation or appearance of riches would have exposed us very much. In summer the way we have come is almost impassable, but now the robbers are much dispersed and cannot so easily keep the field, so that, with a good deal of caution and inquiry, we have been able to come. You shall hear more about our friends the Albanians when we have seen Joannina, which is in a manner their capital, and where we mean to pay a visit to Ali Pasha.

On arriving here we had hoped to find all our letters from England, as everything that came for us to Constantinople was to be forwarded here to us through Smyrna or Salonica. Our packets from Salonica, which had been sent off before our arrival there, have somehow miscarried, and at Smyrna the plague, which had begun when we left it, has declared itself with violence; everything is of course shut up, and God knows what has become either of our letters or the greatest part of our goods and chattels which we left there, and which I suppose are still lying in the warehouse of the English Consul. We are here, then, without anything but just our bedding and travelling clothes, with a few of our books; we know little or nothing about England or you, and have some uneasiness about Wilbraham, whom we left at Smyrna. If he stayed long he is in no danger, as he is in the house of an Englishman, who understands well enough how to prevent the plague from entering, but he will very probably be shut up till it ceases, which may not be for many months. We got away just in time, or should very probably have had the same fate; he is particularly unfortunate if it is so, as the plague is scarce ever known to break out in the winter, and the deaths that happened while we were there were ascribed to fevers, etc. At present, however, the plague rages there certainly, and as I have not heard from him, I can only hope he followed our example, and left the place in time.

The only news we have heard about England is that she is left to finish the war alone, and that all her faithful allies have made peace. At least, she won't pay any more subsidies to His Majesty of Sardinia, or be cheated by the King of Prussia; the war will, I hope, be a naval one, and *alors nous verrons*. I never fail drinking her good health, and Rule Britannia, for I think we are in a much fairer way without such allies than with them. With all this stuff, however, I don't know one particular, so you will possibly laugh at my intelligence and stare at my opinions. I am anxious beyond measure to hear something about you all, but I will at least take care, if possible, that you shall not have the same anxiety about me, as I will write constantly; but don't be surprised if some of my letters are long in coming, as they have to pass through a curious sort of post before they arrive at England.

We have taken a house here, and mean to stay some weeks, both to see Athens more perfectly and to wait for the spring before we again open the campaign. The two last days are almost the only cold ones we have experienced, and they have been so clear and fine that the cold only makes walking pleasanter. When the wind is in the north the air is frosty, and snow appears on the hills; if it changes southwards, the weather is like our April or May, and you can have no idea of anything so pleasant. The soil of Attica is the driest imaginable; the olives which still cover it are here perfectly evergreen, and are now in as full leaf as in summer.

You will imagine the mildness of the climate when I tell you that a vine in the yard of the English Consul's house, where I am writing, has not yet lost its leaves, and that almost everybody we have met brought us little bits of ice, as a great curiosity, which you will imagine is not a very great one to us. There is, in fact, no winter here, and a sky always pure and healthy makes Athens the finest situation I ever saw. The proverbial fogs of Boeotia we were witnesses of, and the climate is so different in Attica that I immediately, in my own mind, justified ancient writers, who notice the difference, which I had before imagined fanciful from their very great vicinity. The hills which separate them shelter Attica to the north. The soil is uncommonly dry after the heaviest showers, the air is always clear; and were I to choose my winter's residence, I would certainly prefer Athens to any place I ever was at.

You see narcissi and stocks in flower everywhere, and oranges or lemons in every garden in the town. The country, covered with olives in leaf, has quite a summer aspect, and the view of the bay and islands of Salamis and Egina is delightful. We walk out every day, and you will envy me when I tell you that our morning's walk has to-day been to the famous Academy, still called " Academia." Two low, small hills, commanding the view of Athens, the Piraeus, and the whole country, have been the situation of these famous walks. I do not wonder at Plato's choosing such a situation for his lectures; it is one of the prettiest in the country. There remains nothing ancient but the name.

We recollected in our return that the tombs of the Athenians killed in battle were on each side the road to the Academy, and you will be glad to hear that in looking attentively about we saw in the fields a low semi-column, such as they placed over their tombs, inscribed with the name of an Athenian, *Theodotus*, and which I have no doubt is one of them. Those of Marathon were buried on the spot they fought on, but afterwards the Athenians always brought their dead here, and the road to the Academy and to the Piraeus was the place where they were buried. We found one or two of these semi-columns without inscriptions, most likely from time. The most of them have

been taken away to adorn Turkish burying-grounds,
or stuck pell-mell into the walls of any building that
happens to be near.

Believe me,

Most sincerely,

Your affectionate son,

J. B. S. MORRITT.

ATHENS,
January 11.

ATHENS,
January 18 to 22, 1795.

DEAR ANNE,

I begin a letter to you, as I promised my mother
I would, with some account of our proceedings at and
about Athens. I will first preface it, however, by
telling you we have been made very happy by receiving this evening some news of you, as a letter
of my mother's has contrived to reach us, though of
so old a date as September 24.

Her letter brought us the most pleasing account of
Henry's conduct and health. I have heard nothing
from him, at which I am not, however, surprised, for
it is not an easy matter to correspond when we are
both of us in motion. I fear his motions have lately
been neither so voluntary nor so unmolested as
mine ; however, I hope they have been as safe. If
the allied troops have gone on with their system of
being beat, he might have had a chance of making
a tour through Holland at His Majesty's expense, as
he had through Flanders.

The French here are in great glee at some news
they have of the English under the Duke of York
having received a terrible check. We hear no particulars now, and when we do they are hardly ever
to be depended on, as a Frenchman's imagination is
not the least active weapon of the *fiers républicains*.
I only trust in God that our dear Henry, if not in
England before, has at least not been involved in
the disasters of the army. We hear more and more

that peace is declared, only exclusive of England, and if so, our land forces at least, and he among the rest, will, I hope, when you receive this, be most of them safe and well in old England, if our worthy allies have really had the conscience to include Holland, though they give up Flanders.

I can imagine a charming party at Colton Lodge when we all get back again, for as Henry has learnt to smoke of the Dutchmen for his health, we have learnt it of the Turks from civility. The first thing that is offered us on entering a Turk's house is a long pipe and a dish of coffee, and I often wish you could see us sitting in form with our legs crossed (*à la* Cath. Stanley), on a sofa, making the agreeable to an Aga. Don't let Christopher hear of it, as I mean to surprise him some day by a complete Turkish smoking apparatus. I am, indeed, at this instant of writing to you, such a figure that I do not believe you would know me if you saw me. My English dresses having quite done all that could be expected from them, I am at this moment *à la Turque*, and have been for some weeks.

I shall alarm you by telling you that your shawl makes me a magnificent turban ; but don't be afraid I shall pass it at the custom-house by swearing to it as part of my dress. A fine ermine pelisse, with my other long robes, makes a very smart Turk of me, and I strut about the streets of Athens with great effect.

To leave off this nonsense and tell you something about what we have seen : We came into Attica across the Asopus and Mount Parnes, which separate it from Boeotia. The mountain is almost entirely rock, and in general uninteresting, but its branches towards Attica are covered with firs, broken into dells, and resemble strikingly some of the scenes about the Tees and Greta. A ruined ancient fortress covers the top of an insulated rock that stands up grotesquely in the middle of one of these dells and caught our attention from the irregularity of its situation, which hardly admits a pathway up to it. From this the plain continues to Athens, which we saw in the descent, and which is about ten miles distant. The plain is cultivated and, as formerly, covered with olives. They grow here in the greatest abundance, and their oil is still famous. The plain is large, dry, and not too dead a flat; several hills rise out of it on all sides, rocky and steep, but not very high.

We soon had a full view of Athens, the approach to which throws your mind quite back to ancient times The first object that strikes you on approaching the town from every side is the citadel. Its present walls, built by the Venetians on the ancient foundations, enclose the top of a high insulated rock, containing eight or ten acres. Over these domineer the remains of the temple of Minerva, of which the front is entire and most of the other pillars standing, from the side by which we came; the smaller pillars of another little temple (of Erechtheus) are also seen in the citadel. The road, about a mile from Athens, passes a small hill, where was the famous Academy; beyond these we could see the whole town, which is still considerable, and the remains and monuments round it. Its situation, independent of beauty, is the driest and best chosen I can conceive, sloping every way from the rocks of the citadel and covering the sides of some other low hills near, in a clear climate and a gravelly soil. The object which, next to the citadel, embellishes it most is the little [so-called] temple of Theseus on a low, green hill at the end of the town. It is absolutely entire, and is at present a modern Greek church. The only changes it has undergone is in roofing the inside, which was in the ancient temple, I believe, open, and the unroofing of the portico between the pillars and the body of the temple, where the people assisted at the sacrifices.

These make no alteration in its form; it is oblong, built entirely of marble. It is, I believe, about sixty

feet in length and half that in width, and at the end of
the entrance are two columns supporting a beautiful
frieze in basso-rilievo.   The sculptures representing
the combats of Theseus with the Amazons, and different
circumstances of his life, are, I believe, as well as those
in the citadel, the work of Phidias.   The heads of all
are mutilated, and it must have taken some pains to
destroy them so much.   Indeed, I hear they were
destroyed prior to the Turks, in the barbarous ages
of Christianity, and by order of the Greek Emperors,
who, adopting the zeal of the iconoclasts, broke them
as idolatrous ; and, indeed, the Turks, though they
repair nothing, generally don't give themselves much
trouble to destroy things placed so high as these are,
which seems rather to have required the animation of
bigotry, as well as the blindness of barbarism.   Would
you believe, however, that the Turks have lately been
breaking up part of the white marble flags that surround the temple, merely to burn into lime, because it
is nearer at hand than most other limestone ?

We walk about constantly here ; at first we lodged
with the Consul, who is poor and a Greek, two circumstances which together always make a man a scoundrel.
Finding we were cheated by everybody we employed,
we left him and took a house of our own, so we are
now Athenians.   Our stay is made more satisfactory
by the acquaintance of a Frenchman established here
for the last eight years.   He is a painter, and, having
been employed much by Choiseul-Gouffier,[1] has added
to his talents a great knowledge of architecture and
connoisseurship, with some acquaintance with antiquities.   He has dug much about Attica and found many
valuable marbles and remains since his stay here, and
he has given us much information about the antiquities
worth seeing in the country.

He lately dug in the plain of Marathon, and in a
small island, now surrounded by a marsh, discovered
several ashes and small tiles, on which were inscribed

[1] French Ambassador at Constantinople 1784-92.

in Greek, "Of an Athenian." Such is the situation in which were buried the conquerors of Darius. A small hillock, consisting of larger bricks and stronger masonry, was the tomb, probably, of the generals Callimachus or Stesilas, who fell in the action. What makes this remarkable is that the tombs of Marathon were unknown till he discovered them by accident in searching for statues, having found three busts of Hadrian, Antoninus, and L. Verus buried in another part of the plain. As he knew Chevalier and Choiseul, I inquired about the urn and Minerva, etc., found in the tomb of Achilles. The Comte Choiseul gave him at Constantinople the broken pieces of copper which had been really found there, and of which one piece, resembling a spear-head, was to be, no doubt, the spear of Achilles. Another, with something like grapes on it, was the famous urn Bacchus gave Thetis, etc., etc.

On cleaning them completely and putting them together, it appeared they all together formed a single figure. The spear-head became a female figure whose two feet, being joined and pointed with a spike below, had a slight resemblance. The boiling of part of the copper in the fire had swelled little knots of rust and verdigris, which were made into bunches of grapes. A flat plate of copper supported by two horses, into which her feet were fixed, was the car of Minerva; *au reste*, the figure was antique and curious enough. On her head is a verde Ionic capital, and on her shoulders are two sphinxes. This I describe from a cast he made of it, and mean to employ him to make one for me, as it certainly was found in this tomb, and he conjectures it to have been the remains of the mad ceremonies which Caracalla, in imitation of Alexander, paid there. Round it was found much charcoal, mixed with ashes of victims and some apparently human bones. He has opened a tomb near Athens, described by Pausanias as that of the Amazon Antiope, mistress of Theseus. He found here also ashes, and in it, and in some others which he searched, small vases resembling Etruscan, with only the outlines of the figures roughly marked in red on a white ground. They were usually a part of the offering to the dead on these occasions, and either did or were supposed to contain the tears of their friends. These searches, however, leave no doubt of the barrows in all this country being really tombs. We have several times paid Minerva a visit in the citadel, and, indeed, go up there almost every day.

In the way after passing through the town you mount along the north side of the rock towards the Propylaea, which are at the west end of it. Above, on the left, a small cave about four feet deep is the famous grotto of Pan. The Propylaea, or Gateway to the Citadel, is beautiful, though built up between its pillars by shabby buildings and Venetian fortifications. As I shall procure plans, it is not worth giving you a very particular description of these buildings. Of their effect I shall say that they are entirely built of large blocks of marble. As you enter you have the remains of a portico of six Doric columns in front, of a great size. Two square wings project on each side, adorned with Doric columns facing inwards, and in front with pilasters and a Doric frieze. Over the square gateways in the portico the top is composed of single blocks of marble of an immense size. To see the different parts of it you are obliged to walk to every different corner of it, as, besides many of the pillars being gone, the rest are so built up as to produce no effect. We could judge, however, of what it had been, and the chaste and simple architecture, with the nobleness of the design, distinguish so sufficiently the age and hands that built it.

Having passed this on the right, below is a large theatre ; but the front of the temple of Minerva, rising over some miserable huts built before it, immediately strikes you. It is much on the plan of the temple of Theseus, but far larger, and with more columns. I mean to bring home if possible not only drawings but models of all these remains, as our French acquaintance models very well, and has already finished part of it upon the exact proportions. The building is Doric, and the outward colonnade has consisted of forty-six columns. In the front the colonnade is double; and over the portico before the pediment still remain some mutilated figures, of which the drapery and limbs have been of the most exquisite workmanship. Between the triglyphs the alto-rilievos are on this side almost entirely defaced. Above the inner row of pillars and round the whole body of the temple runs a row of alto-rilievos. The sides are not entire, for, a bomb thrown by the Venetians having fired a powder magazine here, the explosion destroyed the roof, and threw down great part of the colonnade on each side. Most of the marble pavement, of the finest white marble, remains. The walls within, of which great part remains, were also of white marble, and have been covered by the later Greeks with Christian saints and angels, luckily now almost washed out by the rain.

In the middle of this fine building the Turks have built a small, shabby mosque, and even that set awry towards Mecca, to look still worse. The back part is the same as the other, but only with one row of columns; of the second row there is only one remaining. Over the remaining columns on the south side the alto-rilievos are less defaced. They represent the combat of the Centaurs and Lapithae, and in each department is represented a Centaur with his antagonist. Fifteen remain, and in these nothing can exceed the variety and imagination of the attitudes, or the brilliancy and exactness of the execution. You cannot really conceive the life and spirit with which every figure is designed, though there is scarce one unbroken in some manner. I wish I may be able to bring you some as specimens. In the ruins below are laid a thousand other basso-rilievos, some of which I probably shall procure.

I left off here last night, and, having been employed all the morning in the citadel, can at last add with some pleasure that my negotiations have succeeded with the commandant of the castle, and that to-morrow will I hope put me in possession of one at least, if not more, of the alto-rilievos of Phidias which are over the grand colonnade. I shall also try to bring off some of the basso-rilievos below which are broken parts of the interior frieze, and which are of the same hand. Do not you think I shall make a pretty addition to the marbles at Rokeby? I dare hardly be too sure of my prize yet, and tremble lest he should still change his mind. However, the moment I have them I shall take the precaution to ship them for some of the Islands, and as this letter will not be closed till after to-morrow you shall hear how I go on. I leave you to imagine the beauty of such a building entirely of white marble; and the regret we had in seeing the flags which remain, and the large square blocks, which have been thrown down by the powder, broken in pieces to make paltry, ugly gravestones in a Turkish burying-ground, or miserable ornaments for their doorways.

Near the temple of Minerva is another small one of Erechtheus, still very perfect. It is an oblong Ionic building, with pillars only at the two ends. The Ionic ornaments are continued over the two sides; but without columns. It has been divided into two, and contained the shrines of Minerva Polias and of Erechtheus. The little square on the left side was the shrine of Pandrosos, the young lady who did not peep into Erechtheus's cradle when her sisters were so curious as to open it. The square on the right, I am assured by our French acquaintance, has been nothing more than a large portico serving as entrance. We could not examine it as we wished, for the Turks have now some magazines there, and we only examined the outside of it. The entrance, however, has, I believe, been there; for the pillars in front at this end are raised on a high wall of marble, and have no steps up to them, so have not served as a portico. There is a little staircase descending into the temple through the shrines of Pandrosos. This little shrine is so perfect that the very ceiling still remains. It consists of single marble blocks, which lie across the whole roof, and are worked so admirably within that I have seen few ornaments of stucco in England so light and finished. In the wall are four female figures, instead of pillars, of the most beautiful design; they are colossal, each about seven feet high, and, having been elevated some height from the ground, are not delicately carved, but boldly touched to effect; the drapery, however, is exquisite. Their arms are broken, their noses and eyes much defaced, and they are built up in a shabby, rough wall; but originally the spaces between them have been open, and they supported the roof. These, if you talk learnedly, you must call the Caryatides. The pillars are all Ionic, but the capitals extremely ornamented, and the scroll round the whole seems worked in filigree, from the delicacy and lightness it is carved with. I never saw the Ionic order more beautiful, and begin really to think the ancient Grecians were inspired by some genius of elegance and taste that has since given over business, for we do not make any more of these kind of miracles now. We spend whole mornings in the citadel, and have now been here a fortnight without a moment of ennui (*i.e.* since we got a house of our own).

We have a thousand other things to see in the neighbourhood, but cannot satiate ourselves with admiring those in the town. How much more wonderful it is when we recollect that these buildings were chiefly made by a people whose whole territory is not so large as half Yorkshire, and built, under Pericles at least, in the time of an unsuccessful war! I shall never talk at the Quarter Sessions about a county bridge as long as I live. When I read my letter over I don't know whether it will entertain you. On paper a pillar is a pillar, and there is no conveying to your mind the effect they produce upon mine; you may therefore find it very dull reading about what I have seen with great pleasure, and my head is so full of all these things that I can talk of nothing else, for I have read of nothing else, heard of nothing else, and seen nothing else worth talking about. In short, my whole mind is entirely in Athens, and all my ideas are gone back some two thousand years, so I shall perhaps not be so amusing, though more instructive company than I generally am. With this apology I go on with my story.

We walked out some days ago to the stadium, which is still to be seen at some distance from the modern town, though close to the wall of the ancient. Our house is towards the north side of Athens; going out eastward we passed the situation of the famous Lycaeum, of which a few old stones are the doubtful remains. On the left is Mount Hymettus, below which, across the Ilissus, is the stadium. It is a long space scooped in the hill, which is raised round it to a level for the seats, and except being, I think, larger, has nothing more remarkable than many we had seen. Near the end is a subterraneous arched passage through which it is said the unsuccessful candidates escaped the hisses of the people. Perhaps it served as an entrance to the performers also, separate from that of the rest. The bridge over the Ilissus has been a pretty strong piece of masonry, now entirely broken; not however, I should think, from the violence of the stream, for could you imagine that the famed Ilissus even now in winter contains generally not one drop of water? I believe a small stream runs underground under the bed of it as it rises up nearer the sea, but really, except for an hour after the melting of snows, the ditch in the west pasture is much more considerable, and I do not believe a minnow will live in it. "The fields that cool Ilissus laves" are therefore much cooler than it, and it is much as true in poetry as "Maeander's amber waves," which are muddier than any horsepond; I could certainly make a better river with a gravy spoon, and I'll back Robert against the God Ilissus for making a stream at any time.

Turning back from the stadium along the narrow gutter down which the river Ilissus should run, we remarked a few stones, once the ruined temple of Ceres; a little island that should be where I believe were the Ilissiad Muses; and near the town the more majestic remains, which some call Hadrian's Pillars, some the temple of Jupiter Olympius. Whatever they were, you will like better to hear what we saw than what we think about them. There has been here, then, a large building with three front rows of columns at least. Twelve of these only remain now, nine in three rows at one end and three in a line with one of the rows at the other. They are Corinthian, and of an immense height. This you will suppose when I tell you that my head reaches no higher than the base, and that they are (as Wheler measured) seventeen feet nine inches round, or five feet eleven inches diameter. We then came into the city (after remarking the immense terrace raised before these columns and supported by strong masonry), through a little Corinthian gateway built by Hadrian, and with the inscription on it mentioned by several authors. On one side is written, towards the town: "This is Athens, once the city of Theseus"; on the other, "This is the city of Hadrian, and not of Theseus." I tell you what you may read in fifty books—however, I tell you what I see; so I at least have the merit of letting you know other people don't tell lies.

Turning through the town northwards we called in our road on our French friend Monsieur Fauvel. He lives in a deserted convent of Capucins, in the wall of which is the little rotunda of Lysicrates, called

foolishly the lanthorn of Demosthenes. It is surrounded by Corinthian columns and cupolaed, and it
has supported a tripod, won by Lysicrates and his
tribe in the Athenian contests of music, and consecrated as usual in a little building of marble. It is
now built up in white mortared walls, but has been very
elegant. Round the frieze are represented Bacchus
and his fauns turning the Tyrrhenian mariners into
dolphins, and the sculpture is of the best kind. The
figures are about a foot high, and delicately treated.
We looked over the statues, medals, and drawings
Fauvel is surrounded with, and returned home by the
little tower of the winds. I will not, however, describe
more buildings; they shall be for another letter, as
I am sure they must tire you.

It is very pleasant to walk the streets here. Over
almost every door is an antique statue or basso-rilievo,
more or less good though all much broken, so that you
are in a perfect gallery of marbles in these lands.
Some we steal, some we buy, and our court is much
adorned with them. I am grown, too, a great medal-
list, and my collection increases fast, as I have above
two hundred, and shall soon, I hope, have as many
thousands. I buy the silver ones often under the
price of the silver, and the copper ones for halfpence.
At this rate I have got some good ones, and mean to
keep them for the alleviation of Sir Dilberry's visits,
as they will be as good playthings as the furniture and
pictures for half an hour before dinner. Don't you
think the whole family much indebted to me; I am
sure you are sensible of the obligation. The con-
jecturing on defaced medals is very ingenious, and
I begin to grow quite a connoisseur. Thus employed,
guess with what spirit our tour goes on; I really fear
I shall never get out of Greece. Our house, to be sure,
is not so good as Rokeby, but what signifies a house
here, where I am now really writing at ten o'clock at
night without a fire, with half my clothes off because
they were too hot, though our windows and door are

half an inch open at every chink. This is the case whenever the south wind blows, and the weather is really like May. We live here most luxuriously in other respects, and our larder contains hares, wood-cocks, and wild ducks in abundance. We had two days ago eighteen woodcocks together, some of which fell by our own hands on a shooting-party. Amongst our other delicacies I must mention the famous honey of Hymettus, which is better than I can describe or you imagine easily, without I could enclose you some. We are very well with the Turks here, and particularly with the governor of the town, who has called on us, sent us game, made coursing-parties for us, offered us dogs, horses, etc., and is a very jolly, hearty fellow. We often go and smoke a pipe there, and are on the best of terms. I shall really grow a Mussulman. If they are ignorant it is the fault of their government and religion, but I shall always say I never saw a better disposed or manlier people. Their air, from the highest to the lowest, is that of lords and masters, as they are, and their civility has something dignified and hearty in it, as from man to man ; while I really have English blood enough in me almost to kick a Greek for the fawning servility he thinks politeness. They salute you by putting their hand to their heart ; and I should not have mentioned this trifle but that, as some of them do it, it has the most graceful air in the world.

The Greeks are, you will see, in *très mauvaise odeur* with us ; and I would much rather hear that the Turks were improving their government than hear that the Empress had driven them out, for I am sure, if left to the Greeks in their present state, the country would not be passable. We have just breakfasted, and are meditating a walk to the citadel, where our Greek attendant is gone to meet the workmen, and is, I hope, hammering down the Centaurs and Lapithae, like Charles's mayor and aldermen in the "School for Scandal." Nothing like making hay when the sun shines, and when the commandant has felt the pleasure of having our sequins for a few days, I think we shall bargain for a good deal of the old temple.

Thank my mother for the advice she sent me from the Archbishop. I shall be proud to answer His Grace's learned questions anent Grecian antiquities, and to give Miss Markham any hints in my power on the varieties of Grecian dress, of which I shall bring a pattern from the Islands. I must observe, however, that the English ladies were very accurate in the shape of it, though the *belles Grecques* are much less exposed than my Lady Charlotte.

I am wanted by the Centaurs and Lapithae. Good-bye for a moment. Scruples of conscience had arisen in the mind of the old scoundrel at the citadel; that is to say, he did not think we had offered him enough. We have, however, rather smoothed over his difficulties, and are to have the marble the first opportunity we can find to send it off from Athens. I, only being sensible of the extreme awkwardness of Grecian workmen, tremble lest it should be entirely broken to pieces on taking it out; if any accident happens to it I shall be quite crazy, as now there is nothing damaged but the faces and one of the hands. If I get it safe I shall be quite happy, and long to show it you at Rokeby.

Yours,

J. B. S. MORRITT.

CHAPTER VIII

THROUGH THE MOREA, INCLUDING THE TERRITORY OF THE MAINOTES IN LACONIA

TRIPOLIZZA, MOREA,
March 26, 1795.

DEAR FRANCES,

I write to you once more from the very centre of the Peloponnesus, and with a pleasure you have scarce an idea of. My head is full of what we see and hear, and so I will try to make you in some measure a partaker of our tour, and shall recall you so much to ancient times that you will possibly think me dreaming, and that I see things as they were a thousand years ago, when I talk of towns and places which you have considered as ancient names, vanished entirely in the course of time.

We set out from Athens on the 19th, and, passing by Eleusis, slept at Megara. There we found a little statue, half buried in the ground, which we dug up. You will laugh at me when I tell you that it had no head, and its arms were broken; however, it was a female figure, and the drapery and attitude pleased me so much that I took the trouble of packing it off on a mule for Corinth, and so to Zante. If I can get it well restored in Italy, it will figure in the Rokeby collection; and its greatest charm perhaps will be that I found it myself. At least, it was not expensive; for, giving half a crown to a priest that belonged to a chapel near it, we pretended to have a firman, and carried it off from the Greeks in triumph.

We went by land to Corinth; but not by the famous Scironian rocks, of which the road is now entirely destroyed. On the isthmus, after passing a tedious range of mountains, we rode along admiring the beauty of the two seas, and afterwards coasting the western one. The attempts to cut the isthmus are still traceable, and one or two canals have been formed, but stopped by the rocks. The Grecians, for want of powder to blast these, have not been so good canalists as His Grace of Bridgwater, who would, I think, have succeeded. Nothing surpasses the situation of Corinth, and the extent of the ancient buildings shows that it has been a favourite one of the ancients. It is certainly the most considerable ancient town we have seen, and its walls, altogether, cannot have been less than ten or twelve miles in circuit. At present it is a small place, backed by the high rock of the Acropolis, and sloping gently into a plain covered with corn.

We stayed here three days at a Greek's house who is protected by the English, and met with great attention from the Aga, as usual. We saw the ruin Chandler mentions, and supposes the Sisypheum. It has eleven Doric columns, and is so exactly on the plan of a temple that I really think the opinion of the country much more probable, that it was the temple of Neptune. Near it are remains of some antique baths, and a fountain. Burgh will tell you how much this agrees with Pausanias.

The castle we did not visit, as the Turks are shy of permitting you. It is Venetian, and we had less regret as we were assured there was not a trace of antiquity. Pirene now is almost dry above, but the spring by which the waters descend in the town remains, stripped, however, of its ancient ornaments. The water was formerly famous; it is even now the best I ever drank, and has the lightness of Bath water, but is cold, and as pure as possible. We visited Sicyon the second day of our stay. It is a poor village, called Basilico. The plain that leads to it is as fertile as can be, and the ground under the olive grove so covered with beautiful flowers that it accounts for the descriptions of ancient poets, and the enthusiasm with which they speak of spring. Ours sometimes copy them so exactly that when we feel March winds and April showers we are apt to think they rather wrote from their fireside (when poets have firesides) than from the pleasing plains of Yorkshire, or Teviotdale, where nature gives them flatly the lie till towards the beginning of May. Sicyon is on a large plain, raised like a platform, by a long breastwork of rock, above the plain, which runs along the sea-shore.

We found in being some sepulchres in the rock, the destroyed foundations of two temples, the theatre stripped of its stonework, the stadium, and a large brick building, which, from the goodness of the masonry, I believe Roman, but of the use of which I am absolutely ignorant. It is built more like a house of one story than anything else, and runs round three sides of a court, the windows looking into it. It is possibly of a later date. We found in the peasants' houses a quantity of ancient coins of Sicyon and Corinth, and discovered a fountain distilling from a cave near the gate, mentioned by Pausanias. The day after we rode to Cenchreae, the port of Corinth on the eastern side; we found it entirely ruined, though still a port. A few foundations are scarce worth mentioning, but on the opposite side of the bay we had the pleasure of finding a salt spring mentioned by Pausanias, and called the bath of Helen. Nothing can exceed his exactness; and Paterson's book of post roads is not a better guide in England than he is in Greece. Under his guidance, the next day we left Corinth. I ought to add, however, upon the salt spring one remark, that it seems a great confirmation of the gulf of Lepanto being higher than that of Sarone, into which it runs, no doubt, by this channel. It is slightly warm in winter only, but this may proceed from the ground it springs from here.

We passed in our road from Corinth by the situation of Cleonae ; here are two small barrows mentioned as tombs by Pausanias. He then passes to the cave of the Nemean lion, a mile and a half from Nemea. Chandler places this, I do not know why, beyond Nemea. I can assure you, however, that in this very place in the hills, at this distance from Nemea, we found a deep, large cave, remarkable as there was an artificial niche beside it in the rock that had contained a statue or tablet, and another a little above it. This leaves me, I own, no doubt but that this was the cave supposed the lion's, and that it had attracted since the veneration of the people. We then, on leaving the mountains, recollected Mycenae. A country labourer led us to the place. You remember Mycenae has not been in being since its destruction by the Argives two thousand years ago ; and has hardly flourished since Agamemnon. Owing to this entire desertion, the place has changed very little since Pausanias. We found in the walls a gate he mentions. It is composed of enormous stones, as are the walls beyond, and over it we found with pleasure a basso-rilievo of two lions, supporting a plain column. They are rudely carved, which you will certainly not wonder at when you recollect that they were supposed the work of the Cyclopes, and that they and the walls were of the days of Proetus and Danaus. The pillar is curious from the state of architecture in that time. Without a base, extremely short, a capital plainer than common Doric, and for entablature it supports an ornament ; in this form perhaps you will call the bottom of this a base, but it is so disproportioned it is rather a pedestal. The breastwork of the hill on which the citadel has stood is of the same massive work, and of the same hands.

A little beyond this is a very extraordinary ruin. We had observed twice in our way the foundations of buildings similar to that at Orchomenos, which I supposed the famous treasury.[1] They are little

---

[1] Now known as the " bee-hive " tombs.

rotundas entered by a single doorway, and seem all to
be ruined by the falling in of earth. The plan of them
is as follows:

The passage part of this building is covered by one
immense stone. I had already noticed the size of that
at Orchomenos, which was of marble. We soon after
came to one of these entire; an entrance was in the side
of a kind of barrow, and was almost choked by the
top part having fallen. We crept under and found
ourselves in a large rotunda, built of immense stones,
and ending above in a kind of point. The size of the
stone over the entrance was beyond anything we had
seen; it was in length about thirty feet, in thickness
four feet, and in breadth full sixteen feet. As it was in
a very uneven situation, the machines the ancients
must have used to remove this immense mass exceed
all belief. The area within is about fifteen paces
diameter. Without, it is an earthen barrow, and over
the entrance it is held up by a wall; both sides come
forward. Some, I hear, who have seen it, suppose it
the tomb of Agamemnon, which was here. One
remarkable circumstance makes us doubt it. The
treasuries of Atreus and his sons were here in
Pausanias's time, and were subterraneous; I have no
doubt besides of their being the same building which
we saw at Orchomenos, and so they confirm one
another. However, you will say they may be both
tombs. If they are, they are the only tombs I have
seen into which an entrance was left, unless they had
been opened. The tombs of Ajax, Achilles, Hector,
and all in the Troad are plain barrows without any
entrance but where they had been opened; therefore,
I am really inclined to believe them the treasuries of
Minyas at one place, and of Atreus and the Aloidae in
the other. However, as I tell you facts as well as
opinions, you and Burgh may talk over the matter
and settle it for us, as we are not very certain, and
have not yet made up our minds. We slept at Argos
that night. There is (you will see) little there, but

I wonder Chandler, who inquired, said there were no
traces of the theatre, as we who, meaning to return,
paid but slight attention to it, this time saw it on the
road to Tripolizza yesterday, almost immediately on
turning the end of the houses.

Directly after, from the foot of a hill, a rapid river
gushes out in several parts. It has three beds, the
largest about eight yards over; but being of an even
depth, and flowing with the greatest rapidity, it dis-
charges as much water as the Tees at least. This is
the Erasinus, which rises at Stymphalus in Arcadia, is
absorbed, and springs afresh here from subterraneous
channels; from thence, a little way on the left, is
Lerna, and the situation of the marsh of the dragon,
etc.; but, as Hercules dried it up, it is no wonder that
we did not see it. We then crossed the Parthenius,
a long, tedious hill, and descended into the plain of
Tripolizza, between Tegea and Mantinea. It is a
Turkish town, not upon the site of any other, and
therefore has no antiquities except the stones it has
stripped from Tegea, which the Turks chip and whiten
so that inscriptions and basso-rilievos vanish for ever.
This is the capital of the Morea, which is governed
by a Pasha of three tails, who has married the
Sultan's sister, and who resides here; he is, of course,
a very great man, and we have stayed here to-day to
get his protection, without which our firmans from
the Porte would here be little regarded.

To-morrow we visit the ruins of Tegea. It is now
the Ramazan of the Turks, in which they eat at
night, and therefore sleep in the day. For this reason
we can't visit him till the evening. However, I hear
he is a very good sort of man, as all the great Turks
are that we have seen, and I dare say we shall be
very well received. We last night visited an Aga
here, who received us with the greatest kindness.
We had letters from the Aga of Corinth, and he has
desired us to consider ourselves as his strangers, and
to apply to him while we shall stay. We find the

Morea even better, instead of worse, than the rest of European Turkey, and have hitherto travelled with the greatest security.

We have at last been to the Pasha's. As this is the grandest ceremony of the sort, I will give you some account of it, that you may imagine the style of an ancient Satrap. We called in the morning on his Greek dragoman or interpreter; he is in effect one of the rulers, as he has the ear of the Pasha, and during favour (which is often during their want of him) everything he does is well done. He is a fine-looking, middle-aged man with a most venerable beard. He hears and adjusts all complaints, and we found him surrounded by villagers and ignorant people, and were struck with the patience and readiness with which he got through his business. He is well informed on many subjects. He appointed an hour in the evening to be presented to the Pasha.

We went in the evening, and found an immense and mean-looking range of buildings round a large court, which was the Pasha's palace. The court was lighted very well by pans of blazing tar set up on poles. We found an amazing number of Turks of all ranks walking in a dirty gallery behind the house, open, with sheds like a booth, to the court. We went to the dragoman's office attended by ours, for his only speaks Greek and Turkish. While we were here a Turkish buffoon came in to make us laugh, as he did the Pasha, and danced, imitating lameness, etc., with a thousand grimacings and face-makings of this same style. The dragoman gives him, and almost all the lower people of the house, money every week, and the other greater officers do the same ; this is the way a Pasha's servants are paid. After coffee and pipes we went to the Kiaya, or second under the Pasha. He received us in a large room sofa'd round with a red carpet of cloth. On entering his, or indeed any room, you take off your slippers, and walk in short

yellow-leather socks, which are a part of a Turkish
dress. We here found our friend the Aga we had
been with before, sat down, and drank our coffee,
which is brought always. Our dragomans and all
the people that attend on the Kiaya stood while we
stayed. We then returned to the dragoman's again
to wait till the Pasha was ready. It is sometimes a
mark of his dignity to make you wait a long time.

We at last were introduced, and took our seats on
the low sofa, everybody besides standing in the room.
Two boys brought us round a very fine covered vase
of china and a spoon; we concluded the sweetmeats
must be excellent, but unfortunately it was nothing
but a little pounded sugar. The sweetmeats, we
supposed, had been changed by the boys that have
the serving them, and taken for themselves. We then
had coffee; our dragoman presented our firmans, and
he assured us of his protection, and that we might go
safely throughout the Morea. In fact, he is an old,
superannuated hoddy-doddy animal, and we were very
much obliged to the dragoman for our passports. We
waited for them in the dragoman's room, and were
amused by some other Turks, who came and played
the buffoon in their taste, and one who is kept in the
house for the valuable talent of playing cup-and-ball.
Indeed, the Pasha has in his dependence at least a
thousand men, who have each their different offices,
of course most of them equally laborious.

We are delayed at Tripolizza day after day for want
of horses and different excuses, so I shall hold a little
more prose with you. We have visited the ruins of
Tegea and Mantinea, where, however, we found
nothing worth seeing. We had some satisfaction in
riding over the famous plain, the scene of the victory
and death of Epaminondas, but the tombs, forests,
and trophies of antiquity have long been stripped
from it. Of Mantinea, the foundations and lower parts
of the wall remain; it is about three miles round, and
almost circular. Tegea is covered with earth, and,

though marbles are found, in digging above ground there is scarce anything. The country is extremely destitute of wood here, and the mountains are bare and ugly; so the poetical beauties of Arcadia, if ever it had any, are now much vanished, at least on this side. Mount Maenalus is at the north end of the valley, and the country towards Cyllene is as high and rough as Switzerland. The "mild Arcadians ever blooming" do not give me the most pastoral ideas in the world, and I am by no means in danger of setting up a shepherd's establishment and languishing for the Phyllidas on the banks of the Alpheus.

We have dedicated our time here to making inquiries about the rest of our tour in the Morea, and have found with great pleasure that there are along the whole south side of it many remains which have, many of them, never been visited by travellers, deterred once by real danger, and afterwards by the bad repute of the neighbourhood. There is, however, as we find on approaching it, little or no risk, and the country, excepting the province of Maina, is perfectly safe. This is south of Sparta, and includes the two promontories of Malea and Taenarum. It is inhabited by Greeks, the real descendants of the Lacedemonians, and they have in this corner resisted all the efforts of the Turks, to whom they pay neither tribute nor obedience, and who dare not approach the country. They are all robbers, or rather, pirates, and infest these seas with small armed boats, which pillage all the small craft from port to port.

In their country a total stranger is sure to be stripped of everything he has, though they seldom murder; but we understand that by applying at Calamata, a town near them, we may get such protection as to be able to visit anything to be seen there in perfect safety, as they acknowledge the guards of these chiefs, and never molest them. I heard there are many curious remains there, from some of the natives of the country whom we have met; and I hope we shall find it practicable to go there, as we shall have the honour of being certainly the first who have gone.

My mother, I remember, mentioned in one of her letters the walls of Tiryns near Argos; we mean to go there on our way to the Isles. In the meantime I can tell you that they certainly exist as much as ever, and that they are in the place the ancients assign them. An Englishman we have met in our tour, and know very well, wrote a letter some days since mentioning them, and adding that they were still one of the wonders of the world. This will convince you, as many other circumstances have us, of the superficial manner Chandler saw this country in. He strikes me as a college fellow turned fresh out of Magdalen to a difficult and somewhat fatiguing voyage, for which he was as unfit as could be; and though very good at an inscription, was sure to go in the beaten track, and be bugbeared by every story of danger and every Turk that pleased to take the trouble.

As we have pretty well got over the bugaboos—which in authors are often an excuse for not seeing so much as they ought, in some ignorance of the manners, and in many fear of the Turks—I think we shall see what is to be seen here, which is the more important to do, as these parts are not the least known or mentioned by modern authors; and one great advantage of travelling is seeing what one cannot read about.

We hear of nothing but successes of the French: Amsterdam taken, etc. As the Turks always judge of nations by their success, they are all sansculottes. The Greeks, for this reason, are all on the other side; and after what I have said of their honesty and conduct, I am sure you will rejoice in so honourable a set of allies. They are much of a piece with some other of our continental friends, only they are not subsidised. You will be surprised at a Turk's being a sansculotte, but the reason is not very paradoxical. There is a great deal of equality amongst them, for the Sultan is sole master of every life and fortune in his dominions. The rest, therefore, are all more or less free with respect to one another, and approach the French a good deal—for having only one ruler is the next thing to having none at all, and complete anarchy is more like complete despotism than extremes usually are.

I believe Hood, the gallant captain that sailed for Anne's cotton, and who since made so happy a figure in cruising for *commissaires* into Toulon harbour, is commandant of the small squadron sent to keep the French in awe at Smyrna. I have the greatest hopes that I shall meet him in the Isles; you will feel what pleasure we shall have at shaking an English acquaintance, especially a sailor, by the hand in this part of the world; though to have a perfect idea of it you must be absent from England as long as we have.

We have great obligations to this squadron. It has blockaded two of the French frigates at Smyrna, in which harbour they swing amicably with ours, side by side, and do not make any more cruises. A third is at Chismé, an awkward little bay opposite Scio, where they must amuse themselves in a barren country, and one that did not produce a dinner sufficient for our travelling party. Their enemy, the English frigate, is at Scio, opposite, where our men and officers must be as agreeably situated as at any place in the Levant. We left an English merchantman there blocked up, who received us on board with the utmost hospitality, and where we passed more than one happy evening. The captain, like a true John Bull, on the arrival of the English ships, hoisted his colours, fired his guns, and sallied forth to Smyrna in full triumph.

We are in no danger therefore now of falling into the hands of the Carmagnoles in our voyages, and we shall take a boat respectable enough to overawe the corsairs of the country. We shall hear nothing more of you now till we arrive at Zante, where we have desired our letters may be kept; so we hope you keep well, and are not in danger of falling into the hands of General Pichegru. (So far Tripolizza. March 29.)

CARITINA,
April 1.

We are stopped in our road at an Aga's to-day, partly by rain, partly for want of horses, as the Turkish post is not so well served as that on the North Road in England. Yesterday we visited Megalo-polis, the famous city of Epaminondas. We found few remains, but were gratified with tracing the exactness of Pausanias's description of the situation, and the hills in and about it. We found the theatre curious, as being the largest of ancient Greece. It is a grand semicircle, as they all are, measuring in area from horn to horn 174 feet, by about 87 feet in depth. The slope on which the seats ranged was scarce less than 60 feet in height, measuring along the slope. The marble of Megalopolis has been the most beau-tiful possible—a deep red with white veins, which, when fresh, must have had a charming appearance.

I retract all the abuse I bestowed on Arcadia, which is all to be laid to the account of the side next Argolis. The country at Leondari is as beautiful as any we have seen. The Alpheus, a clear, fine stream, its banks beautifully adorned, and the valleys bounded by high mountains, and covered with wood and verdure. The country from Leondari here puts us often in mind of that between Rotherham and Sheffield, and we more than once thought ourselves in England. The little river Helisson, on which Megalopolis stands, has a beautiful course. The Alpheus, near Caritina, quits the valley, and runs in a deep, narrow bed, hemmed in by two romantic rocks: above the one to the south rises Mount Lyceus, and above the other a high point with the town and fortress of Caritina. These are modern and shabby. Over the Alpheus is a very high old ivied bridge, in a most romantic place, of which, if the rain does not continue, my painter shall take a drawing. It is the only river I have seen that can compare with those of northern climates; and all the others, almost, are torrents in winter, and gravel-beds in summer.

The large ones in Asia are muddy and filthy; and we thought often how much the ancient poets would have said if they had had to celebrate the rivers of Scotland or the lakes. Arcadia is, however, really charming; and if the Vale of Tempe had been half as pretty, we should not have been so much disappointed. Both countries are infested and dangerous, but the precautions we take free us from all anxiety. The robbers are chiefly in league with the Agas, and we take the strongest recommendations. From Tripolizza our letters to the Bey of Calamata (the suspicious party) suggest that he is to conduct us where we want to go with a suitable escort, and that if the least misfortune happens to us or our baggage, his head will not be thought a sufficient reparation.

Love to you all, and believe me most affectionately
Yours,
J. B. S. MORRITT.

KITRIS, MAINA,
April 18, 1795.

DEAR ANNE,
We have at last got into a country which, for your consolation, everybody before we came here, both Turks and Greeks, told me was impassable, and that we run the risks of true Englishmen in attempting to see it. If I see any danger of not getting out of it, it is not from banditti, but from the hospitality and goodness of its inhabitants, and we really have

thoughts of domiciliating, and staying in Maina. We are in the territory of Sparta, and have found the descendants of the ancient Spartans the terror of all their neighbours, and free in the midst of slavery. I am sure you will think me romancing, especially when I tell you that I write to you from the house of a Spartan lady to whom we brought recommendations; that we have lived here since yesterday, to-day being Easter Sunday, and have found a reception from her, and manners so different from all we have seen, and so charming, that we begin to think ourselves in the enchanted tower of some fair princess, and stare about us with all the surprise of knights errant not yet used to adventures.

You will like to know how we arrived here, however, though I can hardly turn my ideas back from my present situation, as we are quite full of ancient and modern Lacedemon. We crossed Arcadia and Messenia to Port Cyparissus, now Arcadia, and thence to the ancient Messene and the modern town of Calamata, near it. You know how famous Arcadian pastorals always were. We found the country still as beautiful as possible throughout, and still, as usual, covered with sheep and shepherds, though not the opera kind of *pastorelli* which one admires at the Haymarket. The people, indeed, disgrace the country, being a parcel of poor, miserable savages employed by the Turks, who are here few, but absolute.

Near a small village called Andriepna, about two hours' ride in the mountains, anciently Cotylum, we saw the remains mentioned by Chandler from Mr. Bocher's tour, the temple of Apollo at Bassae, near Phigalia. Its thirty-six columns and the whole ruin is still in the state he saw it. It is in a little basin formed by the higher summits of one of the highest mountains of the Peloponnesus, and from which the eye wanders over most of its southern provinces. How the temple got to so inconvenient a place is curious to consider. It certainly was strictly worshipping in the high places, but if I had been the priest I should not often have expected a full congregation.

The ruin has a fine effect, and its dimensions and plan are easily taken from what remains. We took with a cord the principal ones, which I have got in my journal. The pillars are Doric, and the architect, who, you will see in Chandler, was also the architect of the temple of Theseus, has followed the same bold and fine proportions. They are slenderer than the temples of Paestum and the old columns we saw at Corinth, but far stronger than our modern Doric, being in height only about five and a half diameters. The slender proportions now used have but a mean effect compared with the chaste and manly simplicity of the ancient architecture, and least of all agree with the strength and massy plainness of the Doric, which has suffered more from the corruption than any of the lighter orders.

I assure you the columns at Corinth, which are only three and a half diameters in height, are far grander than those at Nemea, which are of a late date, and are slenderer than the Athenian proportions. But you will say this is not interesting to you, who have not seen them.

The south part of Arcadia, then, we found beautiful beyond any country we had seen, except Monte Santo. The foliage of spring, and the mixture of its light greens with the sober brown of the olive and the dark verdure of the evergreens, heightened its beauties. The quantity of shrubs resembles Monte Santo, and they were now all in flower, and the ground covered with grass and every sort of blossom. The scenery is a suite of little retired valleys, with clear streams or rocky rivers down them, the sides ornamented with wood, which only opened to discover glades covered with flowering shrubs and verdure. Near these the scenes were perfect; their defect was that, seen from above, the higher hills, which below were hid, appeared bare and not picturesque. The views, therefore, are confined, but so sweet, still, and agreeable that I often wished you and Asphodel were by my side, and recollected with pleasure how often we had together enjoyed scenes of the same sort.

Were I to draw any parallel between Arcadia and Monte Santo, I should say that they were both designed by nature for what they have served, the first as a secluded rural country of shepherd lads and lasses, the other for the retirement of monastic contemplation. A monk, you will tell me, however, never was designed by nature, in which, as I perfectly agree with you, we must suppose it designed for your system of Irish solitude in russet gowns and pink ribbons; but as it now is, it has been strangely perverted from its intention. Perhaps my different ideas of the two places arise a good deal from having seen the one in spring, the other in autumn; they were quite the *allegro* and *penseroso* in the way of landscape.

At Arcadia we found some very hearty, good Turks. They were Lalliots, who were originally Greek renegades, and have little of the dignity and form of the Asiatic Turks, though their independence cures them of the fawning Greek character. Along all this part of Messenia we rode through an uneven, fine country, covered with forests of oak, till we approached the ancient Messene. We found remaining in it little but the walls and one of the gates, which is a large rotunda of eighteen yards across, forming a kind of bar. The stones over the doorway are extremely large, and some of the towers remain extremely well built. Burgh will tell you that they were the strongest walls Pausanias saw in Greece.

The plain of the river Pamisus, which extends from hence to Taygetus, is as fertile and as well cultivated as any part of England, near Calamata and Nisi. Its products are figs, oil, and silk chiefly; they have very large plantations of mulberry for the worms that pro-

duce the latter.   At Calamata we found a rich, pretty
town inhabited by Greeks, who have improved in our
opinion very much, as independence to a certain
degree had made men of them.   Our letters there were
in so strong a strain of recommendation that the chiefs
of the town disputed the honour of lodging us.   We
stayed very comfortably, and took measures to proceed.   We were the only English who had been here
in the memory of the oldest residents, and as it cannot
rain but it pours, just as we were setting off we were
joined by two others, whom we had known intimately
at Constantinople.

This naturally detained us another day, which was
passed in recounting our adventures and comparing
notes very pleasantly.   They had passed over partly
the same country, and it was with pleasure I found we
had left nothing unseen.   We were now in the con-
fines of Maina, of which I will give you some account
before I continue my journey.   Though the Turks
made a prey of Greece and the Grecian Islands in
general, yet it is not commonly known that one little
district has always resisted all their efforts.   What is
still more interesting is that this district is the ancient
Laconia, and that the men who have defended their
freedom are the descendants of the heroes of Greece,
for there is no place where families are less mixed or
have gone on for generations more than here.

Their soil, which includes the two promontories
of Malea and Taenarum (Matapan), is a barren rock;
but this circumstance makes their country defensible,
and, notwithstanding the fertility of the adjacent plains
of Messenia, they have had the sense to perceive the
superiority, like the country mouse, of "a hollow tree,
a crust of bread, and liberty."   They have never had
a Turk amongst them but as an enemy or a prisoner,
and as they never admit any Turks, and supply the
barrenness of their country sometimes by a freebooting
war all round them, their name is a terror to the whole
country, and the Turks, who consider them as rebels,

endeavour to hide their fear of them by their detestation, especially as they have not quitted the Greek religion. As they are under little government, and part of them ignorant and poor, those who inhabit the promontory of Taenarum sometimes commit such plunder out of their own territories that at Calamata they are dreaded beyond measure. The primates who were to answer for our safety entreated us not to go; as we found that we could go a little way safely we were determined not to stop till we could go no farther, and now we find we can go the whole tour we wanted to do, report as usual telling stories, or at least exaggerations. Our friends at Calamata are in terrors about us, and we are living with the people here with all the heartiness and good-fellowship possible.

To see patriarchal and primitive manners, a traveller should visit Maina. Their order of government is this. The land is still parcelled out in districts on Lycurgus's own plan; on every one of these lives a family, supported by the villagers and people of that district, who are as free as their masters, with their guns on their shoulders; and thus the head family commands about four miles round about, and is indulgent to the others, who would otherwise either destroy or desert it. These rulers often make war on one another, and the plunders then committed bring them into the bad repute their neighbours give them. They acknowledge one man as Bey, who is united by family to many of them, and if attacked by the Turks take their guns, retire to the mountains, and, with a force of six thousand or seven thousand men, carry on a war that is the terror of the Ottoman Empire. They sometimes make peace with the Turks, and pay tribute, if their country does not produce corn enough without importation, but if they can live they never submit to this humiliation. To give you some idea of their confidence in their own strength, and of the complete weakness of their enemies: a party of three hundred wanted to pass into Roumelia across the Morea to join

some Pasha then at war. All the Agas opposed their
passage, in consequence of which they had their
villages plundered and their troops beat. They sent
to the Pasha of Tripolizza to give them free passage.
He opposed them, and with this small force they
marched to Tripolizza and besieged him for seven
days in his very capital ; then cut their way forward,
and joined the Aga in Roumelia, where they wanted to
go at first. This you will say, I think, was no way
unworthy their ancestors, and it will convince us what
their laws must have been, which gave a spirit to the
country it has not yet lost, while all the rest of Greece is
sunk and degraded.   I will go even so far as to say that
the very first step in the country is enough to convince
you of the freedom of it; the rocks and sides of the
Taygetus, which is by nature as barren as ever mountain was, are cut into terraces to support the little
earth there is, and covered with corn springing even
from the very stones. The agriculture is clean, well
kept, and resembling any country more than Turkey ;
they have so completely made the most of nature that
scarce a foot of ground is lost, and it reminded us of
Switzerland ; and everything shows that the corn and
wine spring for themselves, and not for an absent
master.

Having thus in some measure, I hope, interested
you in the country, I will tell you how we have come
into it and how we travel across it. We entered it
yesterday, and soon came to one of the towers of its
chiefs, to whom we had letters. We found a spirited,
hearty fellow, who received us with open arms, welcomed us to the country, and entered into a very
interesting and animated conversation on the present
state of it. We naturally inquired about the safety of
it ; he said the wars that had made it dangerous were
now finished, and that the country had suffered much
misrepresentation from them. He said certainly there
were bad men in all countries, and that, added to the
enormities of these, many corsairs from Cephallenia

and Corfu had infested the coast, which were all
included in the bad reputation thrown by the Turks
on the Mainotes. He talked to us of antiquity, and
walked, with all his suite, to some ruins about a
mile off.

He then took leave of us, and one of his men,
armed, walked before us to the fair lady's castle,
where we now are—another battlemented tower, with
portholes on all sides in case of defence, surrounded
by a small village on the shore. At our approach, an
armed man came out to know our business, and
walked with our other guard before us to the house.
We were received by her uncle, the late governor of
the country, to whom, as well as to her, we had strong
letters. The lady is about twenty-eight; her husband,
who governed here, is dead, and she is mistress of the
territory. You will remember the freedom of the
ancient Spartan women, and the fine answer of the
wife of Leonidas when told " they were the only
women who governed the men," and she replied, " Because we are the only women who produce MEN." While
the sex is degraded at three hours' distance, they are
here free, simple, and happy. By what I am told they
are very virtuous, and it is the only instance in the
Levant. For all this they are as beautiful as angels;
it was a new thing to us to have audience of a fine
woman, attended by a train of damsels, most of them
pretty, and her sister, who was about eighteen, and as
beautiful as you can conceive.

CARDAMYLA, 12*th*.

I left off here to talk with our friends, and resume
my letter here, if possible still more pleased with the
Mainotes. The lady's castle was really enchantment;
her uncle, a hearty, fine old man, dined and supped
with us, and we were waited on by beautiful girls, in
the true mode of patriarchal times. He lived in one
tower with four daughters and his wife. Two of his

daughters were children, and visited us—they were beautiful beyond measure; and of his older daughters one was, I think, the handsomest woman I ever saw. To give you some idea of their style of dress: On their heads is a plain small circle, either of shawl worked with gold or, sometimes, a red or green velvet cap embroidered round with gold, forming a coronet. Over this floats a long veil of white embroidered muslin. One end hangs over their right shoulder behind, and the other, hanging loose across their breast, is thrown also over the right shoulder. They wear a tight, high camisole of red silk and gold, buttoned with coloured stones across the breast. A short waistcoat, which is cut quite low, and clasps tight round their waist, is made of muslin and gold, with small globe buttons. A red sash and long flowing robes of white muslin and gold are below. Over these they wear a red, green, or light-blue silk gown, cut straight, and entirely open before, embroidered in the richest manner, the long sleeves sometimes of different colours. On their neck are rows of gold chains in the English mode exactly. They do not wear trousers so low as the women in the other parts of Turkey. This is chiefly the description of the lady of the house; you will suppose the colours are varied for different tastes and different ranks. The contour of the dress is much the same, and as the women are naturally lovely, with complexions you would suppose born in the coldest of climates, you may imagine the enchantment of the place, and will conceive how we regretted leaving our lodging.

My draughtsman had taken two figures for me, one of the old man of the house, the other of one of the women. As I showed it the old man he was so much pleased with the compliment that our painter's fame spread over the house; he drew the little girl, his daughter, and the mistress of the house gave us permission to take her picture. The old man, who thought it improper, hindered his going, when, like a true woman determined to be mistress in her own house, she sent for him to give her uncle the slip, shut herself up with her women and him, and planted four or five men at the door till her picture was finished, as she was determined to see how a picture was drawn; and she chose we should remember her after we were gone. The old man found out our trick; but the lady had quite got the better for this time, and he would not say anything further. He astonished us while we stayed by the superiority of his reading to any we had long been used to. The first book I found in the house, to my astonishment, was Belisarius translated into modern Greek; he had also Rollin's ancient history in the same language. He talked to us a vast deal about ancient Greece, of which he knew the whole history as well or better than us; he was particularly well acquainted with the different colonisation of the country, and his eyes sparkled with pleasure when he talked of the ancient Spartans.

Everything we see reminds us of Switzerland: the same cultivation in a most barren country, the same freedom of mind, the same simplicity of manners. Their compliments are only the warm expressions of friendship and interest, and they do not tease you with fulsome or fawning civility. "Sans façon" was the only French our old friend knew, and he had a perfect idea of the comfort of the maxim. Indeed, I have not often been more at my ease than we are in this country, and as want of ceremony is always an increase of gaiety, we talked and laughed all day. We have met with as warm a reception at Cardamyla, a small village of the same style that retains its ancient name. We came on mules by a road impassable for horses, and enjoyed not a little being stopped by our guides in some of the villages with an apology that the Mainotes had never seen a stranger, and they wished to show their friends so new a sight.

We have at last got out of the Maina, and I will
finish my long letter.   We went in it as far as Vitulo,
and then crossed to Marathonisi.   These you will
find in any good ancient map as Oetylos and Gythium ;
in modern ones they are little known.   Since that we
left the Maina, and are now near the situation of
Sparta.   We still talk with pleasure of the Mainotes ;
we passed through the heart of their country, and
saw them thoroughly.   I have given you most of the
good traits of their character ; their vices and virtues
are those of a half-civilised nation, and they are the
direct contrast of the other poor slaves who have
fallen under the Turks, and suffer from their corruption and over-refinement.   The one is a nation
never made the most of, the other a people worn out.

Before Cardamyle the country is governed more
strictly by the chiefs than it is beyond, and the
common people are better off, as the land is less
barren.   Afterwards we were struck with the sight
of a range of mountains, which I can compare to
nothing but Kendal Falls, which was scattered all
over with thin corn, springing from little terraces of
earth scraped together, often not larger than a table.
The people, in consequence of dearth, besides exer-
cising their industry in this way, plunder everything
that approaches them ; and without the protection
of their chief every village is a band of robbers to
those who pass them.   At the same time they have
such an idea of hospitality that the houses of rich and
poor are open to strangers in the worst places, and
the very men who would strip you to the skin as an
enemy, if unknown, will if you claim the rights of
hospitality give you every assistance, and stake their
lives and families to defend and protect you as a
friend.   We were the only strangers, literally, that
the oldest people had ever seen, excepting Turkish
fugitives and deserting soldiers in the Russian war.

You can hardly imagine with what ceremony and satisfaction we were received, every one, as we were under the protection of their friends, doing all in his power to assist us and pass us safely, many owning themselves that though they could pass us in safety they were astonished at our venturing, and complimenting the whole nation of English as being the first that has ventured among them.

In case of an attack upon their country they arm both men and women, and their whole force amounts to about fifteen thousand. You would never do for a Mainote lady. It would be a disgrace for them to stay behind when their husbands and sons are in danger. Every little district is united by all the ties of kindred, and they are all brothers, sisters, and cousins in these villages. Fighting side by side, and with their wives and children around them, can you conceive a more formidable corps than the smallest clan so animated? I must allow that the ladies, beautiful as they are, are rather *farouches* in their ideas of honour, as at one captain's where we had a ball they apologised for not having better music, as a favourite fiddler having made too free either with the person or reputation of a fair lady here aroused the vengeance of the *softer sex*, and she shot him through the head upon the spot. The gentlemen, too, would have rather alarmed you as partners, for each of them danced with a large brace of loaded pistols in his belt, and by way of entertaining the ladies a shot was fired out of the window about every ten minutes to enliven the dance. At Cardamyle we saw the ladies exercise at throwing stones, in which, though comparisons are odious, they succeed better than your attempts generally do. We were often put in mind of the female gymnasia of Lycurgus, and the Spartan ladies running and wrestling. With all this they are beautiful, and, as far as I hear, very virtuous, so their education spoils neither their persons nor their minds. Such is the state of the ladies.

Of the men what I have already said will convince
you that they have many interesting traits of character, and all the virtues of poverty and independence
Their vices are violence in their enmities as in their
friendships, *fierté*, turbulence, and revenge.   In our
whole passage I saw no traces of the thieving or
pilfering tricks and ways of cheating we had so often
noticed in every other class of Greeks.   Their spirits
are open and high ; their robbery open war, but never
under the mask of friendship, which with them is a
most sacred name.   We liked them more the more
we stayed, and if we had pleased should have spent
much time there, for we never entered a house without
being pressed to stay there, and never left it but with
the regret that we should not be able to return expressed by the whole house.   We were, as you will
suppose, highly gratified with our tour, and with the
people we saw ; the more so as nobody else had seen
them, and their manners and spirit are very different
from those of all the other nations here.   In point
of antiquities we were able to fix the geography and
ancient situations of most part of the coast towns.
We found but few remains, and, indeed, where corn is
wanted, you may be sure the men of the country will
blow up old stones, and plough over the ground.   For
the poor ancients, therefore, " deep harvests bury all
their pride has planned," and the situations of their
towns are only recognised by an old wall or two, and
the slight corruption of the names of places.   They
survive here in a nobler manner, since certainly these
people retain the spirits and character of Grecians
more than we had ever seen, and their customs and
language are transmitted with greater purity.

We made stops at two or three houses from being
pressed to stay for a day, so are rather later than we
wished in our tour.   I will not tire you by dragging
you step by step with us ; you shall some time read it
in my journal.   We came here from Gythium, now
Marathonisi, and, meeting our English friends again

here, we rode together to Sparta yesterday. We found literally no remains worth mentioning but the theatre, which is very large, and of which almost all the stones are removed. We stayed to-day in hopes of bringing off two pieces of sculpture we found at Amyclae which are very curious, but we fear we shall not be able. They are two square marbles with a Lacedemonian lady's toilet carved upon them—the slippers, combs, mirrors, essence bottles, *étuis*, etc.—which are in very good preservation, and would be a very great acquisition if we could get them to England. We therefore shall do all in our power, though, I fear, we have no great hopes.

So much for ourselves and our motions. I was surprised yesterday by a large packet of letters from England, which had travelled up and down the Peloponnesus after us; I leave you to judge whether agreeably or not. It contained so much good private news that it was read, I assure you, more than once, and with more pleasure than you can imagine; being with you so well and happy, and promising so fair to make you all so, gives me a satisfaction I can hardly express. I am sure from your accounts that Henry's profession is the one he ought to have chosen, as it was chosen for him by nature, and, as a fighting officer who does not talk of his victories is rather a respectable character at present, I have no doubt of his making a good figure both in Flanders and by an English fireside, where, notwithstanding my talents for rambling, I should not dislike to be seated with you and the noble captain. We would talk over our travels in Holland and Greece, and should expect you to pay great attention. Tell him in a letter my packet contained I hear that a favourite Opposition toast for some months has been "The brave *followers* of the Duke of York." The pun is not bad, though somewhat sansculotte.

I have only one complaint to make of your letter; you seldom send Rover's compliments, and I know the

poor dog does, only he is not clever enough to write.
I have always favourites, you know. My poor little
Hungarian tired of his tour, and ran away at Smyrna.
I replaced him two days ago with a pet of the true
Spartan breed. He is a whelp, but means to be about
the size of Trusty. I train him to follow our horses
and guard our baggage. In Italy I mean to make him
follow and take care of our carriage, as I think a dog
from Sparta will have a fine effect in England, and
keep up what Stockdale calls the " hum " of our tour.
For the rest of our " hums," I have added a tolerable
bust found at Gythium to my collection, and my
medals flourish ; so Sir Robert and John Yorke will
frequent Rokeby on my return. As for John, he is
such an amateur of female beauty, I think when he
hears our stories he will travel to Maina, for neither
Lady Coventry nor the Venus de Medicis are much
superior to some there. You were in great danger of
losing us, for we were very often asked to marry and
settle, and think we should have made excellent captains of a Mainote band. I have bespoke a very handsome Mainote lady's dress, which I hope will meet us
at Cerigo (Cythera), and which, as I shall not always
wear, I will lend you when I do not want it, as you
will look very well in a muslin chemise and a blue
silk pair of trousers. We will attend Ranelagh as
Mainotes when my Wakefield friends give the second
exhibition of Annette and Lubin. I leave off my letter
for a visit from a Turk, who has sent word that he
wished to be allowed to *see* us ; you see we are quite
lions here. . . .

Our Turk is gone. He was an attendant on the
Aga on whom we had called this morning, and his
message was not, as I have written, so much to *see* us
as that we might *see* him, for it is the beginning of the
Bairam, or Turkish carnival, and he had on his gala
clothes, which were covered with breastplates and
harnessing of gold and silver, so that he really *was* a
sight.

Safely arrived at the Sign of the Bear. We are in a scrape here, which I know you will be wicked enough to laugh at ; it is quite *dans notre genre*. We have contrived in Maina and our route to spend all our money in buying medals, etc., and cannot get a farthing for our drafts on Smyrna or Constantinople. We have, indeed, found nobody who had any trade there, and of consequence nobody who would take our word for a farthing, so we are obliged to borrow a few shillings of the Consul and hope to find some at Argos—about five miles off. If nobody gives us any there, we must stay here, for we are very comfortable in the Consul's house. We little expected to find money so scarce, or we could have had it at Tripolizza. At present, like good Irishmen, now that we have got out of the land of robbers, we have nothing for anybody to steal ; while we were there we had money enough. Adieu. My love to all at home, and believe me

Your sincerely affectionate brother,
J. B. S. MORRITT.

CHAPTER IX

Aegean Islands : Crete

Some readers may be puzzled by Morritt's remarks about the paucity of remains, "nothing to see," etc., at Argos and Sparta. This was true until a very few years from the present time. Within the last two decades the labours of the various "schools" of Athens, English, American, French, and German, have uncovered much that was entirely concealed for nearly a century after Morritt's visit.

Similarly in Crete he finds no evidence of its former greatness. At Gortyna he writes, "There is little here"; and of the palace of the Minoan kings there was nothing visible of the vast remains uncovered in 1900 and the subsequent years by Sir Arthur Evans and his followers, which have thrown entirely new light on the history of "Aegean" peoples and civilisation, even while the inscriptions are still unknown language, Yet Morritt (see p. 240) was much nearer the truth, through his study of ancient accounts, than most who have discussed the question until a century after his time, when he rejected the current belief that the famous labyrinth was merely the quarry at Gortyna, on the ground that the labyrinth belonged to Gnossus and not to Gortyna, and supposed it to have been "a subterranean palace" there. The recent spade-work in Crete has fairly established the truth that the labyrinth *was* the great palace of the Minoan kings at Gnossus, whose multiplicity of rooms and passages has been uncovered; and there is much plausibility in the view that the name itself comes from the *labrys* or double-headed axe, which was sculptured as a sacred emblem in the palace. This implies that Morritt was

mistaken in his opinion that the Cretan labyrinth
was *derived* from the Egyptian. The great Egyptian
temple of the twelfth dynasty at Hamara was probably
rather earlier in date than the Minoan "labyrinth,"
which is not at present placed earlier than 2000 B.C.;
but it would seem that the *name* was transferred by
Greek writers from the Cretan palace to the many-
chambered Egyptian temple.

NAXOS,
June 4-5, 1795.

DEAR MOTHER,

We went to Argos from Napoli. In the plain
are the ruins of Tiryns, which you mentioned to me
in a letter, and of which, to give you an idea, I need
only translate Pausanias, who seems to have found
them in the very state they now are, and probably will
remain for ages to come. They are the rudest specimen of architecture in Greece, and form a breastwork
and parapet to a little hill which contained the houses
of Tiryns. The stones are not cut; they are a collection of rough fragments of rocks heaped one on the
other, the hollows filled with smaller stones to give
solidity to the fabric. When the Archbishop mentioned to you that many were thirty feet long, I
suspect he has found somewhere the measure given
in Greek, and has reduced it to English measures from
the most received opinions of the relative measures;
of which reduction I have more than once doubted the
accuracy, as, in many instances, it makes ancient stories
scarcely possible. Pausanias is more exact. He says
the smallest of these stones (not counting those in the
crevices) could not be drawn by a yoke of two mules,
which I believe true; the largest I saw were ten or
eleven feet in length by five or six in breadth and
thickness. We had seen other buildings of which the
stones were almost as large, but the striking thing in
these is the extreme rudeness of the masonry, which
carries with it the marks of the very remote and
early times of Greece, and one can't help seeing with

pleasure and wonder a wall which the Greeks themselves ascribed to the Cyclopes.

At Argos we found few remains: the walls of the
citadel, built up with more modern ones; forms of
buildings in the rocks; that of the theatre, notwithstanding what Chandler says; and fragments of architecture, with some broken statues, in the churches.
Of the famous temple of Juno, common to it and
Mycenae, we could hear no tidings; it seems to have
entirely disappeared, and a small church near the
situation is adorned with the only fragments of it that
are left, probably. We got at Argos, however, some
money for our draft on Constantinople, which was the
most agreeable thing we found at the place. The
next four days were employed in a fool's-pace journey
through the Argolis. We endeavoured to persuade
our guides (one of whom weighed about twenty stone)
to go faster, and, indeed, horsewhipped them a little;
by which means we very near lost our horses entirely,
and were glad at last to go at any rate. We slept in
villages as miserable as possible.

The objects that made some amends for the *désagré-
ments* of our journey were the remains of the temple
and buildings sacred to Aesculapius, near Epidaurus.
Chandler gives a detailed account of them. The
theatre, in particular, remains the most perfect of any
we had seen; almost all the marble seats are in their
places—we counted above fifty rows; the passages
between them, and the communication through the
body of the theatre, are still seen. We had often been
struck before with the shape of these seats—they are
very broad and low, and they rise like steps one from
another. It makes us think that the ancients sat then
as their descendants often do now, with their legs
under them *à la Turque*; if they did not, they must
kick one another's *dernières* during the whole representation, which I do not find mentioned in any book
of the times. Five miles from this is the city of
Epidaurus, now a village of about five mud houses.

Nothing but a little old rubbish, overgrown with weeds, remains. The situation is fine, and partly on a small promontory jutting into the sea, and forming a convenient port for the town. Aegina lies before it, and the sea-view is beautiful. We now continued along the Argolis, leaving Troezene on our left, and came in a day and a half to Hermione. The country is uneven, wild, and uncultivated, though naturally very fertile; I believe, however, that throughout it, and particularly near Troezene, the air is unwholesome in the great heats, and the water bad.

You know the whole coast has been changed by earthquakes and volcanoes, and several small islands have been thrown up by them; we saw near Didymos (a little village in the inland part of Troezenia) a curious effect of them. The fire having consumed the earth below, the undermined surface has in two places fallen in, and forms two regular circular basins in the middle of the plain, the least near forty yards in depth and eighty or ninety diameter. The sides are an upright wall of brown rock, and so regular we could hardly believe them natural. In the bottom is a little chapel and some vineyards. The largest is on the side of a hill, by consequence not so regular. The people of the village find much saltpetre in it, of which they make a little commerce. Near Hermione we had the pleasure of riding along a stream between two high winding screens of rock covered with foliage, particularly pine and firs. The scenery, of course, was gloomy and picturesque, and when we had got through this defile, which is about four miles long, we crossed a fine plain, much cultivated and wooded, to Hermione (now Castri), which is in a beautiful situation, with one of the best ports in Greece. The isle of Hydra is opposite, and screens the road between them from wind and weather.

At Hermione we found the broken-up seats of a small theatre on the shore. They are different from any we had seen, as they are a stucco of small stones and mortar, and the whole theatre has been almost in one piece. We found the foundations of some of the principal temples, and, near that, we suppose, of Ceres, a hole in the ground which has made a great figure in story. It conducted to hell, which was in the neighbourhood, and was the road by which Hercules dragged Cerberus to earth, and by which Pluto dragged Proserpine to hell. I found a ridiculous story in one of our books in speaking of this place. The people of Hermione were so persuaded of their nearness to the infernal regions, and of the neighbourly friendship of their inhabitants, that they did not in their burials put Charon's pay in the mouth of their dead, as the old boatman carried his next-door neighbours for nothing. The boatmen in that neighbourhood do not go for nothing now, as we found at Hydra, where all the boats have lately gained so much in their corn trade to France and Genoa that they won't go on any other business.

Hydra is a considerable town, built on an island, the pasturage of which would hardly feed a horse. The whole is a barren rock, and the port was some years ago a nest of pirates. Commerce and application have made it a respectable town; the port is full of boats, and even ships; they are the best sailors in the Archipelago, and the town is neat; though built on the side of so steep a hill, the houses rise over each other in steps. They have nothing to eat but what they import; a little mutton was the only thing we got there, and every sort of garden stuff is totally unknown except a vessel is driven by accident to Athens or Corinth and thinks it worth while to bring a few cabbages or turnips. The people, enriched by hard application to commerce, have no idea but money, and we regretted our stay there, which was prolonged by a foolish holiday, during which they would not stir.

In sailing from it to Cape Sunium we were driven by weather to Poros. We rested a little while in a

cave and then ran to Zea, with a very rough sea, or,
in plain English, a storm, and arrived late at night.
The next morning we went to the town, about three
miles from the port. Here began our tour of the
Cyclades. We are woeful sailors, for as sure as ever
we are in our boat one of three events takes place,
viz. a calm, a storm, or a contrary wind. The Greek
islands, which are generally the beaten track in a tour
through the Levant, are just the part of it that offer
the fewest objects of antiquity or curiosity. The
reason is very obvious : they are much more inhabited
and much frequented by merchants; the inhabitants
pull to pieces old buildings and build new ones, and
the merchants carry off statues and marbles when
worth the trouble ; but in return the modern state of
the Isles is much more agreeable, and a man finds
much more amusement and better fare than in the rest
of Turkey.

The Cyclades and all the islands in that part are
entirely in the hands of Greeks, and the Turks make
them pay an annual tribute, and give them very little
other trouble. At Zea, Tenos, and Myconè we saw
very few remains of antiquity worth notice ; they are
barren and rocky, but, from the peace and freedom
they live in, are much cultivated, and Tenos particularly is covered with villages and gardens. Their
great trade is silk, and all the Tenians, from the
highest to the lowest, are knitters of silk stockings,
gloves, etc., which is for such an island no inconsiderable branch of commerce. As we were detained by
weather at most of these places, we kept ourselves in
good humour by giving balls to the *belles Grecques*
and teaching English country dances and waltzes *à la
mode de Vienne*.

You hear often in England of the beauty of the
Greek women; I assure you the account does not
exaggerate it, and at Tenos, but above all at Myconè,
no account can. A fiddle is a general *point de rallie-
ment* for the whole town, especially as at the Consul's

houses we were usually a large party of young people
and had our partners in the house, as most of them
have families.   You will conceive, therefore, that when
we had bad weather out of doors we had generally
very good within, and as they are lovers of dancing,
at Tenos particularly, when we had not a fiddle we
sang, and danced from morning to night so.   We make
great progress in modern Greek, and begin to talk
pretty intelligibly, so that we at least gained something by our misfortunes.

I picked up two small statues at Tenos, which will
figure in my collection.   Delos is perfectly desert, and
covered with old broken marbles ; the neighbouring
islands carry off marbles for ever, and its columns and
stones are the ornament of a thousand churches about
its neighbourhood.   While we were walking over it
we were not a little surprised by meeting the young
Englishman from Smyrna (Hayes), to tell us that a
French corsair was in search of us.   He had received
the news at Myconè, and kindly followed us in a boat
to inform us that we might be on our guard.   It proved
a false report, though there was a small boat at Tenos
which had occasioned the story.   As it was only a
boat of four or five men, we gave ourselves very little
trouble about it, and afterwards heard it was gone on
for Smyrna.   It was manned by an officer and three
sailors of the frigate Captain Paget took last year at
Myconè, which, being taken in a neutral port and
looked upon as no prize, enraged the French beyond
measure.   We were shown the scene of action, and it
was certainly a proof of French courage by sea that
they durst not, with equal force, near twice the number
of men, and a new frigate, sally out and attack the
Romney, which is an old, crazy vessel.

Besides this, on Paget's first broadside, instead of
standing to their guns half the crew leapt overboard.
We have heard a story still more honourable for the
English since, which has done us much good.   The
three English frigates had blocked the *Sensible*, of

thirty-two guns, at Chismé, and challenged her to come out and fight any of them singly. The Frenchman chose for his antagonist the *Dart*, a sloop of twenty-two guns, and insisted on writings being drawn, that if the others took any part in the engagement, the ship was not a fair prize. These writings were signed and agreed to by the English officers and the Turkish governors of the two ports. The next day the shore was filled by Turks to view the engagement. The *Dart* sallied forth and fired a signal. As the other did not come out she sailed into the bay at Chismé and made another signal, and the French, not daring to attack her, though they had been reinforced by the crews of their other sloops at Smyrna, stayed in port, while the Turks on the castles and the English sailors on the yardarms hooted them for their cowardice. I do not believe there is a ship's crew in England but would have thrown their captain overboard, if he had disgraced them in such a manner. Such is the vaunted courage of the mass of the sansculottes, when at all equally matched in skill or numbers.

The Christians at Naxos are under two slaveries —that of the Turks, owing to their weakness and cowardice; and that of their priests, from their ignorance and bigotry. If the first were taken away the other would have the power in its hands, and by the use which has generally been made of it elsewhere, I think one may conceive the country would not be much better for it. You see what a vision it is to think of seeing the ages of liberty revived here: driving out the Turks would be only reviving the Empire of the East, the weakest and worst of all governments. Upon my word, but for the Turks I do not believe the country would be fit to be visited. The Greeks would not be able to hinder corsairs and robbery, would cheat with more impunity, and have no masters more honest than themselves to appeal to. The only remains of ancient times in Naxos is the doorway of the temple of Bacchus, on a small island off the port.   It is composed of three stones, one on each side, and one across is about eighteen feet high and of the most beautiful marble.   The work is plain, and the size gives it grandeur and simplicity.   The temple is ruined.   When Orloff was here he tried to carry it off to Petersburg, but, the stones being too large, wreaked his vengeance by firing balls at it. This is a good deal like Xerxes whipping the sea, and the stones of Mount Athos ; and gives a fine specimen of Russian taste.   At Paros we saw specimens of another sort, a castle built entirely of old marbles, columns laid crosswise, inscriptions topsy-turvy, friezes sideways, and bas-reliefs with the flat side outwards.   Most of the valuable marble has been carried off from this place.

At Antiparos we saw the famous grotto.   It is an immense natural cave, very deep underground, and most beautifully hung with spars and stalactites. The light, as we moved about with our flambeaux, had a thousand pleasing effects.   It is a much larger space than any part of the cave at Castleton, and the spars infinitely finer ; I find, however, one hole in the ground so like another that I have given up grottos for the future, as none can be finer than this, and they are all very difficult to enter, and very dirty to stay in. My future answer will be that I have seen the grotto at Antiparos, as superior to all other grottos as Westminster Bridge is to ours on the Tees.

We had a very rough sail to Amorgos, and slept on the shore of a small creek in Paros the first night. At Amorgos we saw only a poor town, and poorer country, convents, and miracles, about which you will excuse my silence, I think.   We stayed one day, and then, after sleeping again on the sand, set off to Cos. We arrived that night at Astypalaea.   How shall I describe it ?   You have been in Scotland ; but you have not seen Astypalaea.   As the old woman in "Candide" tells Cunégonde, "Vous avez vu beaucoup, mais, Mademoiselle, avez-vous jamais eu la peste ?"

All the inhabitants live in one single town situated on a high rock, and surrounded with a high wall. The largest streets are not above eight feet broad. The staircases, which in Greece are always on the outside of the houses, take up three feet on each side; the middle is taken up by a gutter without water, which seems the general receiver of all the filth in the neighbourhood. In this, however, we were un-deceived, as we found in the first house we entered a chamber without a door adjoining, and open to the parlour, contained that of one family at least. Beds were brought for us, and we sat with patience during their making, till we had counted fifty bugs, but when we advanced upon the other half-hundred our courage failed us, we hurried down to the shore, and slept again very happily on the sand. Early the next day we set off and arrived safe and well at Cos. What a change! Cos is certainly by much the finest island we have seen. The view of it from the sea is as charm-ing as the view of any town I have seen. It is Turkish, and the whole is varied, and enriched with orchards, spires of cypress, palm trees, and the tall pillar of the mosques that rise up from a bed of foliage, the whole town being full of gardens. The plain all round is covered with a forest of oranges, lemons, pomegranates, almonds, and figs. The large trees are planes, and nothing can be more beautiful.

The Greek towns are by no means so beautiful: they are generally a flaring heap of white houses; and they are too idle to have the luxuries of the climate. A Turkish town is, on the contrary, full of fountains, and of shade where a tree will grow; they are very susceptible of these luxuries, and spare no pains to have them. I have seen them sit under a tree in the streets for near a day together, and enjoy the open air sheltered from the sun.

HALICARNASSUS (Now BOUDROUN),
June 16.

We got here yesterday with a passage of four or five hours; the distance is about fifteen miles, but we had no wind. The present town here is a poor Turkish village, much scattered, but has, notwithstanding its poverty, a pretty appearance from the entrance of the port, as it is full of trees and gardens. We are eating apricots and figs by thousands, and you will imagine fruit is in plenty here. At Naxia, lemons are in such plenty they are sold for about ninepence the thousand; in one garden belonging to a convent, the annual product is 150,000 oranges, 25,000 lemons, and 10,000 citrons.

We have found fewer remains here than we expected: six Doric pillars stand near, half buried in the ground which has accumulated, and support their entablature. It seems they have belonged to some portico, the ruins being longer than any temple, and not in that shape. Some broken ones mark the continuation of the line. We saw the theatre, in which many rows of seats remain; the ancient wall is traceable behind the town, enclosing with the sea a space of near six miles circumference at least.

A report is come here from Constantinople that we have peace with France. I suppose it is owing to its being concluded with Spain and Prussia, and the Turks know no difference. We, however, parade these seas, the English flag flying at our mast-head, in perfect security, as the French have no vessels out. The constant north winds that reign in the Archipelago during this season have made our voyage very good, since we could take advantage of them; and we hope to get to Candia very well. Our short tour on horseback threatens the most fatigue. You have not a notion of the heat we now are exposed to, which increases every day. We must conform to the plan of the country, and sleep during all the middle of the day, travelling only very early and very late.

We have been seeking in vain for the Mausoleum here; it has entirely vanished, or exists only in some inconsiderable and irrecognisable ruins.[1]

June 17.

My prophecy was right—we are at Boudroun another day; at this rate when we shall arrive at the end of our pilgrimage I do not know; we have been so sulky, as very near to order our boat and sail to Cnidus and Rhodes in a pet, leaving Mylassa and Stratonicea for other people; we have, however, thought better of it, and shall, I suppose, get off to-morrow. Indeed, if there had been a favourable north wind it might have changed our expedition; but one good reason for not taking our boat is there being a dead calm just at present.

The day is again hotter than you can imagine; and if I walk five yards I melt, like Sir John Falstaff in the buck-basket.

My long letter is full, so I must take this little scrap of room to bid you adieu, and say how sincerely and affectionately I am yours,

J. B. S. MORRITT.

Sent from Rhodes by Leghorn July 1.

DEAR ANNE,

I begin my letter from Rhodes, where it will very possibly be almost finished, as we seem rather to be fixtures here, and in no very agreeable manner, from our party's falling ill. Stockdale and I are, thank God, now well. On our first arrival here, our voyage in Asia had been so extremely fatiguing, and our living so bad, that even I was at last knocked up,

[1] It was not till 1857 that Sir Charles Newton discovered *in situ* the remains of the Mausoleum, of which the more important are now in the British Museum; and from these and the descriptions in ancient writers established with tolerable certainty the form and character of the building.

and for four or five days was laid up with a slow fever, which has now left me.   The day after I fell ill, my poor draughtsman and my servant both followed my example, so we were a pleasant travelling party. They are both now better, but as they were worse than me they mend slower.   In this climate, and at this time of the year, a fever is not an illness that trifles.

Our tour in Asia (though, as I tell you, it made us all ill) repaid us for our fatigues in some measure by the monuments we saw and found; and few parts of our tour have been more interesting.   I finished my mother's letter from Halicarnassus; it is a two days' ride to Melasso—that is, when one can only ride mornings and evenings, and go on the beasts of the country, which are never suffered to go out of a slow foot's pace.   The country is in parts rather pretty, in general hilly and uninteresting.   We were in a caravan composed of Jews, Turks, and Greeks; so the different ceremonies in the party were sometimes ridiculous enough.   At Melasso we stayed a whole day besides the evening of that we arrived on, and were very busy the whole time.   It was anciently Mylasa, one of the principal cities of Caria, and belonged, amongst others, to the famous Artemisia; and on the wall of a large square marble building here, which is now built up into Turkish houses, we found a dedication inscribed by Mausolus to his father Hecatomnus.   We made here a famous harvest of inscriptions, and this was not all.   About a quarter of a mile from the town we saw one of the prettiest little bijoux of a temple that you can imagine.   It is most like a square summer-house; the lower part is a plain marble cube with a door into it, and a bold, plain cornice.   On this, as on a pedestal, is an airy Corinthian colonnade of four columns on each front, that support a marble ceiling carved on the inside with a richness and delicacy I cannot give you an idea of. The compartments of it are in lozenges, the largest in the centre, each adorned with ovola and a rich scroll, and all this remains almost as entire as when first put up, so that it looks like a pretty pavilion at the end of a modern garden more than an ancient ruin.

The whole country is very mountainous, and the chains of Latmus, which continue as far as here, want neither wood nor boldness of outline. At the end of our ride we found a temple, which was indeed the object of it. It is situated on one side of a fine plain covered with groves of olives, and a thousand other trees and shrubs; bounded on the south by woody hills, and on the north by a bolder chain, with very high rocky summits in the distance, all softened and tinged by a setting sun whose effects here even painting can scarce make you conceive. The ruin is shut in by a woody little dell, and stands under steep banks of foliage. Fifteen columns of it are standing, and a part of the doorway of the cell, of most exquisite workmanship. The rest of the building lies in a picturesque heap within them, overgrown with shrubs and small trees, out of which the columns seem to rise.

It is in its present state as beautiful an object, as a picture, as it has once been magnificent in the pride of its architecture and the brilliant symmetry of its proportions. These columns are of the Corinthian order, and nothing can exceed their neatness and lightness ; they are about twenty-seven feet high with their architraves, which remain on them. The cornice and frieze, which remain on some, are about three feet more. The whole is of the same white marble we had admired before at Melasso, discoloured a little by the air and weather. But what made the ruin more interesting is that the columns are inscribed with the name and dedication of the people who raised them ; and by this means we date them, as we think, to the time of Philip of Macedon, as some have been erected by the mad Doctor Menecrates, that called himself " Jupiter," etc., and who was famous at the Court of Philip for his follies, and the lessons he received.

The country beyond Melasso is a continuation of higher and higher chains of mountain with large, rich plains; the hills are covered with pines, and the road is pleasant; nothing can be richer and more pleasant than some parts of the plains, for here oranges, myrtle, and lemons overrun the country, and round some of the villages it has the air of a perfect suite of gardens. Nothing, however, can equal the neglect of cultivation, and the consequent misery, depopulation, and poverty of the whole of it. Do you want a dinner, buy a sheep, or, what is better eating here, a goose. You must send after it, kill it, do everything yourselves; not a soul will stir for money, as money cannot be eaten, and does them scarce any good. We had no bread, none is to be bought; the people make a bare provision, and that very bad, if they are fortunate enough even to have flour to make it of. We must buy flour, and get it made into cakes by a baker, if there is one; if not, by our own servants. In Moglah, a considerable town towards the end of the Gulf of Cnidus, we could not get bread for our breakfast, till a good-tempered Turk bullied the baker out of a loaf or two, which would in better times have scarce served me alone; and the inhabitants were on an allowance of so much a day, as if the town had been besieged. Would anybody believe this possible in a country which, if cultivated, is capable of supplying half Asia, and where once nothing was seen but large, flourishing towns, ports full of commerce, and every necessity and luxury of life?

Such are the real Turks, for this is entirely a Turkish country—lazy, ignorant, poor, and labouring under every evil their horrible government can create. Beyond necessaries nothing is ever done; yet the Turks here, with all their prejudices and poverty, are a quiet, brutish people, and the country is perfectly safe and uninfested by robbers, which abound in every part of the European dominions. We found them, however, more bearish and uncivilised than the northern parts of Asia, where we had admired and liked them before, and we were often suspected of seeking for treasures, and still oftener of being Russian spies, by the more ignorant part of them, that is, nine out of ten.

Approaching the end of the gulf, we saw higher and higher mountains eastward, many capped with perpetual snow. These are in Lycia, the beginning of the chain of Taurus. We crossed a very high mountain the evening we arrived from Moglah to our boat, which met us at the end of the gulf. For three days, with a contrary wind, we beat down to Cnidus. We got some little bread at a village one day, which we had to send to at two hours' distance; this and a little ham was all we had, and every day made our allowance less. We more than once wanted water, and when we arrived at Rhodes had slept above a week in the open air. At Cnidus there is now not a house. Many columns and temples, but all destroyed. The walls, the two ports, the ruined theatre, are all that remain. The next day we ran to Rhodes, and arrived so late that we only found for lodging a shed at the door of a coffee-house in the middle of the quay. The last day I caught a *coup de soleil* in the boat, which had given me the headache, and this bad night finished me off and gave me the illness I am just getting better of. At Rhodes we have yet seen nothing but the view from our chamber windows; the town is large, and, though commanded by the Turks, and entirely inhabited by them and a few Jews, yet is more comfortable and better in appearance than most of their towns. We have only been out once to call on the Pasha, a piece of civility which procured me a good headache and fever for the evening; we were, however, civilly received.

Parts of the hills and the shore are picturesque; the island in general is certainly finer, and more favoured by nature, than any we have seen, but is much more neglected than those that are entirely in the hands of the Greeks, and yields far in this respect to Chios, Tenos, and Naxia, though naturally superior to any of them. Lindos is a Maltese-built town, and the houses are neat and comfortable. We were much disappointed in the antiquities we expected to find there. The only thing we saw, besides a few inscriptions, was a cave in the rock, before which a row of Doric columns had been hewn out of the natural stone, in which above remained the entablature, with the triglyphs, and some indistinct figures which had ornamented the cornice. All this is worked in the stone, and is not delicately carved. The pillars are broken or removed. On the top of the cornice a row of large marble altars has stood, one of which is up at present; a few of the others lie overturned before the building. They are ornamented with festoons, and are by better hands than the rest of the building. A Turkish castle occupies the situation of the ancient Acropolis, and contains nothing remarkable. There are two small ports, which were good for ancient vessels, but make no figure now.

CANDIA.

I finished my first sheet at Rhodes; I begin again from Candia, which we have had no small trouble to arrive at, though, now we are here, I can't, as usual, say "More fools we," for we have certainly changed for the better. We stayed at Rhodes some days after our return from Lindos, in the same dull manner; my servant chose very near to kill himself by having ideas of his own, as all Frenchmen have, when they are ill; and the great ass was so determined *de se rafraîchir* that, though he had taken James's powder the day before, and we had twenty times told him the effects of it, yet the first thing he did was to get his head washed, and eat all the fruit and trash he could find. I leave you to judge what a state it brought him to; he was as near dying as possible. We are now, however, in better condition.

At Rhodes, as I told you, we wished to find some vessel bound towards Zante; we were not lucky enough, and were at last obliged to take Crete in our way. We hired a pretty large boat, and set sail as soon as our people's health would permit. No poor creatures were ever more unfortunate by sea. After being out two days, a storm drove us to the little island of Chalchi; there we stayed, the storm continuing three days, scattered along the shore, and sleeping among the rocks. The people of a village about two miles off brought us our eatables, but the village was so miserable we preferred sleeping on the shore. Our shelter was a large cave, and we lived very primitively, in the true taste of the Golden Age, which, however, is very far from being mine, notwithstanding the practice I have had.

We got off at last, and aimed to anchor in the evening at Stagia, another little islet about half-way to Crete. The wind was so strong from the west as to drive us to leeward of it, and oblige us to stop at a small desert isle off Caxo. Here we spent two more days, and though only about twenty-five miles from Setia, the port we aimed at in Crete, we were three whole days more in beating up to it, so that for a passage which may easily be made in two days with a tolerable wind, we employed ten, and found in our road only desert shores and uninhabited islands. Carpatho and Caxo, along which we passed, are like most of the islands in these seas, bare and not remarkable, extremely rugged and stony.

We should, I believe, have got sooner to Crete if we had gone all night, instead of running down to Caxo, as our captain wished to do; but Stockdale interposed, being what Will Horn calls "ratherly shy o' t' watter." However, we arrived safe. The moment we could get ashore, S. and I left the boat to make the best of our way, and landed about twenty miles below the harbour, on a promontory to which the wind drove us. We began our tour of Crete then by a walk of about ten miles, with a sun fit to broil us. Our Greek servant followed, beseeching pity; and, indeed, a pair of English legs show the natives of a hot climate no little play when they come in competition.

We stopped at the first habitation we found, where we arrived late. It was a Greek monastery, and pretty comfortable, but the whole country on this long promontory is exactly like our moors—hilly, stony, and covered with heath and wild thyme. They had a pretty little garden, where we passed the next day, our boat not being able to make the harbour. The next day we got mules and rode about ten miles more to Setia, where our boat and people were at last arrived.

In the time of the Venetians this was a considerable place; there are now only a few warehouses on the quay, the whole town having been destroyed by an earthquake. We stopped at a village about two miles from the port, which is at the bottom of a bay formed by the promontory of Spina Longa on the west, and on the east by the point where S. and I landed. The country here is really pretty: an uneven and narrow valley is shut in on every side but where it opens to the sea by bold hills, whose outlook is fine, and which only want a little more wood. The valley itself has enough, and the vines with which it is planted, being now in their full beauty, more than supply the place of pastures and meadows, which are not beauties of a warm climate. We sent the invalid part of our suite to Candia by the boat, and took mules to Girapetra. The road leads up this valley, which we therefore saw in its whole extent. Several pretty villages are seen on the brows of low hills or mixed amongst the trees, which are chiefly planes. There are besides many olives and oranges, which often make a pretty mixture among the greens, and a good many streams of no small beauty or comfort here.

We set out from Setia about five o'clock, and as we had a full moon travelled all night, except for about an hour and a half, and got to Girapetra about eight the next morning. I think I hear a certain saucy person observe:

"So you travel all night by way of seeing a country!"

I, in answer, shall observe that a full moon is no bad light to see a pretty country by, and that it is better to go even in the dark than by the sun, of which really you have not an idea. There is a low chain of hills, and on each side a high range of mountains, between Setia and Girapetra. This last is the usual name in maps of a small town on the southeast part of the island. The Greeks have preserved one of its ancient names, and call it Hiera Petra, though formerly its most usual name was Hierapytna.

I have often told you how European nations and map-makers have confounded and disfigured the geography of this country by writing down the names they learnt without understanding the language, and then they think the ancient name is changed. In fact, the ancient names are in general preserved, and it is usually only the fault of not understanding the pronunciation of the country, which in many instances has at least as fair a chance of being right as ours.

The town stands on a large, shallow bay of the southern shore, and the country round it is remarkably fine. A very rich plain extends behind it, and reaches along the shore of the bay. Groves, or rather forests, of olives are scattered all over it. The mountains, which are more adorned than towards Setia, are on the west and north, a very high chain, with many crags and hollows, besides trees that break the lights and shades very finely, and prevent that "pleasing uniformity of tint" which you and I admire on the high moors. The plain produces corn, vines, and gardens; scarce a tree in it but supports a vine, which I think is one of the most beautiful objects possible.

The ancient town was nearly on the situation Girapetra now stands in. We found one of its temples, that is, a foundation with some finely wrought ornaments scattered near it, in a field. A large basin, now dry, was the ancient port. At present they have none, except in summer, when the north and west winds blow, for with a south wind the bay is perfectly exposed. We saw the aqueduct and cisterns that once supplied the town, and are now in ruins. Some large columns thrown down, the foundations of a thick wall round the port, broken pillars and bits of marble up and down the town, *voilà tout.*

We lodged at a Turk's, the commandant of the town, and as all houses are open in this country, had men and women in the chamber, on the stairs, and in the yard merely to stare at the animals. This having since happened in every village we have been in, we begin to be more accustomed to the mode of the country; but though we had been a good deal used to this before, I never saw curiosity so highly raised or so disagreeable as among the natives here, for we could neither eat nor walk in peace, but were everywhere followed by two or three hundred people.

At Girapetra we were at last obliged to shut the court gates, and when they were to be opened, a man held his arm across the door to prevent people coming in, as the street was full. I wish you could have seen us there. A pack of cards was discovered in our suite, and we had a most amusing game of Trente-et-Un with the son of the Aga and a large party of Turks and Greeks for *paras* (about our *halfpence*). There was not one of the party could count but by the fingers, and so the thirty-ones were not always so accurate as to have been allowed at Brookes's, and were very often revised, to their no small annoyance. The young Aga, who was rather a *bon vivant*, and not much of a

Mussulman, used to skip up from the party when his papa came in, as games of chance are a scandal to the faithful, and a very sharp look-out was kept that we might not be surprised by any of the graver part of the village.

Au reste, the Turks of Candia are almost entirely metamorphosed. They live and eat with Christians without any scruple, almost all drink as much wine as they can get, and their women, instead of being in prison or muffled up, walk about with the same dress and freedom as the Greeks.

In Candia (the town) they are more like the rest of Turkey, but in the villages Mahomet is very much on the decline, and the Agas we saw even made an open joke of the prohibition of wine, and were not more scrupulous in talking about their women, a subject on which a real Turk is as silent as a Chartreux. In revenge, however, we found much cheating and black-guard behaviour amongst our attendants from place to place, and more interestedness than we had generally met with amongst them. We meant to take the ruins of Gortyna in our way to Candia, and were hindered partly because we had not been presented to the Pasha, who is at the town, and partly by our janissaries and guides, who cheated us. I will not give you an account of our squabbles; but they finished by our going directly to Candia. From Girapetra, after crossing the plain westward, we were engaged in the passes of the fine mountains I have talked of. Their gloomy clothing of firs, the olives, equally gloomy, in the plains and dells, formed amongst these scenes not an unpleasing contrast with the rich plain we left. The day after we crossed a high mountain, with many springs and cascades, verdure and foliage in the dells, and an amazing quantity of the finest myrtles I ever saw.

Candia is at a day's journey from these mountains, across an open, fine country, though not cultivated as it might be. It is better, however, than most of

Turkey, and far the first and finest of the Islands, which have no pretensions to compare with it, either for picturesque beauty or fertility. Naxia and Cos have the most of the first, and Rhodes and Paros of the latter, but Crete is far superior to them all. We passed the ruins, or rather the situation of Cnossus, near Candia, and saw a few chambers cut out in the rock, with niches for urns and sarcophagi where the Cnossians were buried. An old bit or two of wall is what remains of Cnossus; the tomb of Jupiter and other monuments we inquired for in vain.

I am and shall be very well content with the frosts and coal fires of a Rokeby Christmas, when I think how little the summers of warmer climates are to be envied, and look round me at the indolent, enervated people that inhabit here. In the Turkish language, a French author observes, there is no term for *promenade*, or a walk; and, indeed, they have not an idea of even stirring from a sofa unless for business. There they sit, sipping coffee every two hours, and smoking all day, so that even Stockdale, who does not fidget, and much more I, who do, are objects of general remark in a house, for they have no notion that we should so often stand when we can sit, or that we should ever walk backwards and forwards in a room, but for the sake of fetching something. The heat and manner of living in their towns is such a hindrance to going out that when we are detained there some days we die for want of exercise.

I have got an old book in my travelling library that gives an account of the Turks in the time of Soliman II., when they extended their conquests to the gates of Vienna; it was written by Busbecq, a German employed as Ambassador by the Emperor. Nothing can form so striking a contrast as what he found them to what they are now, and I have been a great deal amused with tracing the difference. Their great Sultan was then at the head of an army of two hundred thousand exercised cavalry and a veteran

infantry that had conquered the whole of Hungary,
Wallachia, Moldavia—in short, from the walls of Constantinople to those of Vienna. What would he have
said if he could now see the soldiers, a parcel of lawless, armed vagabonds, without discipline, without
honour, and without courage, formidable only to their
miserable fellow-slaves, and successively beaten by
the Mainotes, the Albanese, and the Russians? The
Pashas and Agas, who were the best commanders then
in Europe, are now a party of effeminate men without
principle, that go with the Vizier merely for plunder,
and are more occupied in the intrigues of the
Seraglio, and in ruining each other to enrich themselves, than in defending, improving, or aggrandising
the country.

Everything is some hundred years behind the rest of
Europe, and war more than any. Their blindness and
infatuation, " de la chute des Rois funeste avant-
coureur," is beyond what can be imagined. They all
talk and ask about the Russians and their designs with
a tone that betrays their fear and their weakness.
They see them at their gates, within a few days' sail
of Constantinople, with an increasing fleet that has
always beaten them and without anything to oppose her
but two small fortresses on the Bosphorus, which they
do not know how to defend or to make use of. For
all this they are at peace with her now, and, instead of
employing the interval to strengthen their coasts and
restore their army and navy, they are thinking of anything else, irritating us and every other nation by an
open and shameless breach of neutrality in favour of
the French, who are the heroes from whom they
expect assistance. They expect a French fleet in the
Black Sea, and forget that it is blocked at Toulon,
while the Russians have the best pretext in their conduct for beginning to swallow them as soon as ever
they have digested Poland.

I write now in our cabin in my way to Zante. The
wind is not favourable, but we advance. We set off

last night, and slept comfortably, as our cabin is fitted with beds; and we are now (about noon) near the island of Santorin. Beyond this, we expect a north-east wind which will enable us to make Cerigo and run along the coast of the Morea. Candia is almost out of sight, and we are looking for the rocks and small islets about Santorin that have at different times, and even within memory, been thrown up by volcanoes. So finishes our tour in the Archipelago, which has quite given me enough of sailing for pleasure. Adieu, my dear Anne; you know how affectionately I am always yours,

J. B. S. MORRITT.

SHIP OFF MILO,
August 27, 1795.

DEAR FRANCES,

As I have more than once written to you since I left you for *your* amusement (in which the intention, you will own, was good, whatever the success was), it is but fair that when I have nothing else to do I should for once write to you for my own. Indeed, we are now in prison, cruising between the isles of Milo and Argentiera, and if I had not the resource of holding a little prose with you I should only have the choice of twirling my thumbs upon deck or going to sleep in the cabin, both which you know very well are not at all in my way. The few books that are in our party I can almost say by heart, so I will venture to hold a little talk with you, at the risk of having very little to say, especially as I know from old experience that in the minster yard that little will be not without interest, though it should tell you only how we eat and sleep, and what squabbles we have with our old enemy Aeolus, who is not yet tired of persecuting us. The interference of this gentleman has often made a figure in sublimer writings, and thwarted sublimer heroes than us; and as we have no interest with any of his superiors, we are left a prey to his ill humours—and how long he intends us to be in our road to Zante I can't guess, as we seem to be in danger of taking another turn in the Archipelago. We have, however, got off from Candia, which had cost us so much time and trouble, and are not in an uncomfortable vessel, since I can write to you in it, which was not to be done in the open boats and skiffs we have hitherto sailed about in. A gentle sail in the Archipelago : at the distance of England, what an elegant sound that has ! I remember when I thought it abounded in quiet breezes, pretty islands, Italian skies, and, in short, everything that could make a voyage what we call " sailing for pleasure." I have bought experience since, and become wise. This, therefore, is a more exact account.

The Archipelago and Mediterranean are subject all the year, except just at the Equinoxes, to regular trade winds ; during the summer these are from the north points in the Archipelago, and from the west in the Mediterranean ; in winter the contrary. These gales are constant and last for months ; indeed, without them the islands would be scarcely habitable but by blacks, or Arabs at least, as they would be many degrees hotter than they now are. Whichever way, then, you plan a tour in the Archipelago, unless you make half the round before the Equinox, and half after, you cannot avoid contrary winds, and these are frequently such squalls in the summer as to confine even large vessels for weeks. This is the reason why our tour is not already finished safely, and our party settled in Italy, for which we are scarcely less anxious than if we were on our immediate road home. We have exhausted Turks and Greeks ; I know the nations by heart, and do not wish to see any more of either. A few remains of ancient Greece, the only objects interesting in these climates, will delay us some days on the coasts of the Morea and Epirus—afterwards, adieu to Mahomet.

I have given you accounts of most of the large

islands; the others are all barren, brown, stony cliffs, inhabited by poor Greeks, who change their fear of the Turks for their fear of corsairs, and, when the seas are much infested by them, are alternately pillaged by the Maltese as under Turkish government, and by the Turks as harbouring Christian pirates. Milo, which we are now within a hundred yards of, seems in general without cultivation or trees, the soil chalky, and the ground like a bad part of our wolds burnt up with the sun. Round the town there is something like tillage and a good large port; the mountains are only pasture for goats and sheep. Argentiera is smaller, and if anything worse in the same way. Santorin is cultivated on one side with vineyards, and the soil is volcanic, but they have not a tree, I believe, in the island. This is in general a description of most of the islands of this sea, and the rocks that surround them. In Milo and Argentiera the cliffs are white and chalky, with a sort of earth from which they make some profit. They load ships with it for different parts of the Levant. It is fat, and they use it at Constantinople and the great towns for soap in the baths and washhouses. It was more famous anciently, and entered into their physic; it is mentioned as the *Cimolian* earth; Argentiera is *Cimolus*. It had been called Argentiera from its silver mines, of which there are traces. Nobody dare work them, however, as the Turks would make them pay more than they gained— their usual practice wherever there is an appearance of industry or riches.

You now, I think, begin with me to be tired of the Cyclades and Sporades; you may find a long account of them in "Tournefort," which has so heartily tired me in reading that it has taught me to have mercy upon you. I remember, however, that in my sister's letter, which I yesterday finished, I said nothing of the town of Candia, Gortyna, or the Labyrinth. These great names will raise your expectation as they did mine, so I must set you right, as experience has set me. Candia is a large and well-situated town, which, thanks to its Venetian possessors, is still better built and handsomer than the others of Turkey, and has some streets wide and convenient, which is no small praise after seeing the holes and corners they generally live in at Smyrna, Salonica, and Constantinople. It is strongly fortified with Venetian fortifications, which are now, as usual, neglected, but not much injured, and would still, I should think, stand a strong siege if defended by anybody but Turks. We lived in a great rambling house of the Venetian Consuls, and were comfortable enough; we were often visited by some of the principal Beys, who appeared to us humanised and civil, one or two even clever in comparison of what we have been used to; we therefore made no small acquaintance for the time we stayed. The Viceroy of the island is an old man, who has been Grand Vizier; an office not now always fatal to its possessors, as it was in the flourishing times of the Empire, when Turks were savage and rebellious by nature; now their character is somewhat altered, and the only possession fatal to them is that of great riches, which the Sultan appropriates by cutting off their heads and transferring the *dirty* gold and silver to the treasury. In every rank here a low interest has succeeded to their old more fierce and untractable barbarity, and as, in the times of their strength, nothing was to be done with them but by force, so now everything may be made of them by money; and the corruption is general. Nothing so precarious as offices and governments here, and in the year's residence we have had in Turkey, more than one of our rich acquaintance have *surrendered* (a term equivalent to *resigning* at St. James's) their necks to the bowstring.

The Pasha of Candia at first refused to let us see the island, Candia not being mentioned in our travelling orders with sufficient precision; however, by a petition, enforced with a sop to every Cerberus-like agent that surrounds him, he thought better of it, and we went our tour. This governor has the command of every office in the island, and, as Pasha of three tails, has the power of executing summary justice, or, in plain terms, of taking off the head of any person in the island, responsible only to the Seraglio, who may probably retaliate in the same summary way upon him, if any secret and powerful enemy takes the pains to supplant him there. *His* power is in some measure checked by the privileges and power of the janissaries, who in every fortress, as in Salonica, Larissa, Negroponte, and here, enjoy rights they well know how far to exercise. They are a fierce, lawless, armed rabble, responsible only to the commandant of their own regiment, who is one of their own corps, and often of low rank, raised by cabal, or by military merit, that is here superior strength, or brutal courage. He alone punishes them, and will not unfrequently screen them from the civil jurisdiction, and even from the Pasha himself, if he has interest at Constantinople. By this means all the towns, where they are established, are the centres of military sedition, disorder, and even rebellion. None but the great Turks and the soldiers are safe from insult, and Christians are exposed to every injury and even assassination on the slightest quarrel with them.

I do not recollect I ever talked to you before of this extraordinary government; but this short sketch will give you a general idea of that which prevails in the great towns here. For illustrative examples I could tell you that a little while before we arrived a Greek bishop at Candia had refused some money which a janissary thought he had a right to demand of him. The day after a large party of them rushed into his chamber, and he was murdered by repeated stabs and pistol-balls. In vain the public justice pursued the offenders, the janissary Aga only strangled one of them, and him not the ringleader. In short, above forty assassinations had happened in a few months, and the country was every day still exposed to robbery and iniquity of all sorts—so much for Candia.

Gortyna is at a village about twenty-five miles distant, at the foot of Ida, separated from the plain of Candia, and of Cnossus, by a chain of hills chiefly barren, stony, and uninteresting, though some of the dells on the western side are more deserving of notice, and have pretty and picturesque aspects. Gortyna is in the largest and finest plain of the island, opening at one end to the southern sea; it is rather fertile than picturesque, but now is thinly inhabited and ill cultivated. There is little to see here: old, prostrate columns, ornamented fragments, well-known inscriptions, and a stripped theatre as usual. The little river Lethe, which crosses it, still, as of old, overgrown with plane trees, and the shade famous for the amours of Jupiter and Europa, we looked at with more interest, as it applied more to our fancy than our eyes, and I have often experienced how much a pretty story, consecrated by anciently received opinion, gives consequence to scenes in themselves indifferent. Who did not look with pleasure at Shakespeare's mulberry, but the parson who cut it down? So the story of this little brook, with its reputation for oblivion, made us not pass it by, though it is a good deal less remarkable than the Greta. We don't want to forget or be forgotten, so I think did not take any draughts of it.

A mile beyond is what is called the Labyrinth. It is in a mountain, a large subterraneous range of passages, unequal in breadth and height, many crossing into one another, most ending at large, irregular chambers hewn out in the rock, and sometimes meeting or branching off from opener parts of the cave, which it is true make the road difficult to find, though not so difficult as has been represented. You ask me what I think of this; to say the truth, neither more nor less than a large stone quarry, of which some of the passages, where low, are rather choked up. It is everywhere full of the cuttings of stone, and in these open chambers, which I conceive only to be the working out on all sides of the better veins, the marks of the chisel are everywhere seen, and the sides, not being even but cut in irregular steps, seem often to show the very places where blocks have been taken out. I believe, therefore, this was the place Gortyna was dug from. This is contrary to Tournefort and the received opinion; however, I cannot think it the ancient Labyrinth, which, built on the model of the one in Egypt, was designed as a subterraneous palace—a habitation at least. One reason is unanswerable: the Labyrinth belonged to *Cnossus*. There was the Court of Minos, and they represented it on the current coin. Gortyna never did, and this is a mile from Gortyna, in the plain of Gortyna, and separated by a range of hills from that of Cnossus, which is twenty miles distant. Much is said on both sides; I own I only saw a deep-worked, intricate stone quarry, on a larger scale than the marble quarries we had seen, but much resembling them; and as one reason against this idea is drawn from difficulty of its access, and the lowness of some of the passages, I wish only to set those who object to this at the end of the high quarries of Paros or Pentelicus, which nobody doubts, and they must own they were answered.[1]

[1] See p. 210.

CHAPTER X

OLYMPIA AND THE IONIAN ISLANDS

MORRITT is no less keen to discover in Thiaki the places described in the Odyssey; the topography, he says, "I think we have reason to suppose nearly as exact as we had already found the Iliad." But it should be noted that here also the identification is being disputed; among other reasons, because Thiaki (the Ithaca of historical times) seems too far from the mainland to suit the narrative of the Odyssey. Dörpfeld is held by many to have proved that the island of Leucas was really the Odyssean Ithaca.

Morritt always retained his conviction of a single authorship for the Homeric poems (see p. 255), in which belief he has had many adherents of the present generation—notably Andrew Lang. In Scott's diary, under April 22, 1828, there is the following entry : " Lockhart and I dined with Sotheby, when we met a large party, the orator of which was that extraordinary man, Coleridge. After eating a hearty dinner, during which he spoke not a word, he began a most learned harangue on the Samothracian Mysteries, which he regarded as affording the germ of all tales about fairies, past, present, and to come. He then diverged to Homer, whose Iliad he considered as a collection of poems by different authors, at different times, during a century. Morritt, a zealous worshipper of the old bard, was incensed at a system which would turn him into a polytheist, gave battle with keenness, and was joined by Sotheby. Mr. Coleridge behaved with the utmost complaisance and temper, but relaxed not from his exertions. 'Zounds, I was never so bethumped with words.'

Morritt's impatience must have cost him an extra sixpence-worth of snuff."

ZANTE,
August 29.

From Milo, with a fresh gale, we crossed to the Morea, glided past Cerigo and round Cape Matapan, and then coasted northward along the shores of Arcadia, near enough to observe its beauties; everywhere a woody, hilly country. I described it once before, and am soon returning to part of it again, near Olympia. We beat about with west winds, but arrived at last at Zante. I have thousands of letters—news from old England, news from you—and our satisfaction and pleasure are not to be expressed. The Consul here is really a gentleman, and we are doing very well. By an unlucky accident I missed a letter he sent me, and we have not managed, as he wished, to avoid a quarantine; we therefore can't go on shore without being put in a lazaretto for thirty days, the plague being much spread at Smyrna and other places.

Everything here rings with the cowardice of the sansculottes by sea, and we witness it in these seas, where, on board the Smyrna frigate, the French have stabbed their captain because he gave the signal for fighting; if this continues we are in no great danger. I am as affectionately as ever, and more so cannot be,

Yours sincerely,
J. B. S. MORRITT.

PYRGO,
August 27, 1795.

DEAR MOTHER,
We have just been dining with a Turkish Aga, and sitting cross-legged half the evening seeing a parcel of fellows making fools of themselves to amuse us and him; a sight which never fails of making me melancholy, but which a Greek or a Turk thinks the

height of merriment and jollity. Nothing is there, I am convinced, which is so difficult as to make merry; it does not consist in singing, dancing, or getting drunk, and is by no means synonymous with making a noise, and though very few people, except men of sense, can be really *merry* fellows, yet every ass one meets always pretends to it. Such have been my internal reflections this whole evening, and such they have frequently been in other places than Turkey. In Germany, France, etc., the English are renowned for the jollity of their parties; therefore, when you are complimented by a *partie à l'Anglaise*, as I have more than once been abroad, the first thing done is to be *bongré malgré* extremely noisy, which always ends in half the parties being stupidly drunk, and the other half being as stupidly sober. This latter, how-ever, is, thank Heaven, my present case, and as no recipe is better, after being *ennuyé*, than conversing with a friend, I begin with no small pleasure to be-stow some of my tediousness upon you. I am, indeed, in a little better humour from an acquisition I have just made, viz.: an ancient brazen helmet found in the Alpheus, by Olympia, with a Greek inscription upon it; it is a little worse for wear, and has cost me about tenpence, which I would not have given if I had not thought it had covered wiser heads than are now to be found in the country.

Our reception at Zante was ridiculous enough. As it belongs to the Venetians, a lazaretto is established, and, having missed letters from the Consul by not going to Canea in Crete, we were exposed to a quarantine and not allowed to come on shore further than the health office. Here we held parleys with the Consul and such other people as chose to wait upon us in our adversity. As we flatter ourselves we carry no small marks of health in our faces and per-sons, we could not help laughing to see a party of old, quizzy, shrivelled, green and yellow figures skewing round us as if we were chimney sweepers, and avoiding, with no small difficulty, the touching us even. The Zantiots—that is, those who are not Greeks—are Venetians *de la vieille Cour*, fine-sitting figures with striped coats, bags, silk hats, and swords; so that, as we sat in a narrow passage near the health office, we were a great nuisance, and swords could hardly pass.

We determined to make our tour in the Morea and return afterwards to Zante, as by landing without bustle we could escape being shut up, which now was not possible. We got a boat, then, and, as we were detained by winds, Signor Foresti smuggled Stockdale and me into his house about ten at night, leaving our party on board. We lay *perdus* one day there, so saw little of Zante. The inside of his house made us amends, for we found it quite *à l'Européenne*, and lived like Christian people for the first time. Nothing can be more attentive or obliging than the master of it, who is a great friend of Frederic North's, and procured his consulship through the Duke of Leeds.

As, in describing a country, one ought not to omit any of its peculiarities, I must tell you that we were a little struck with the gentle manners of Zante: in the two days that we stayed three different people were shot in the market-place in quarrels; the survivors make their escape very easily, or if, by bad luck, they are ever imprisoned, their liberty does not cost above seven or eight piastres (about twelve shillings), since the laws of Venice are as mild as possible on these trifles. We are assured that these events are still more frequent in the currant season, when the villagers assemble, and very few nights pass without one or two murders there, a man being esteemed nothing who has not killed one or two antagonists. The same softness of character prevails throughout the Venetian islands and their Sclavonian territories, where whole families, like the Capulets and Montagues, have no other employment but cutting throats from

generation to generation.   We had likewise the amusement of an earthquake the morning we left them, and
yesterday, on arriving here, had three more smart
shocks during the afternoon—but this happens eighteen
or twenty times every summer; for my part, I own
I was not perfectly at home while the house was
rattling round me, but our host and his party sat very
composedly and begged it might not spoil our appetites,
as we were then at dinner.

Pyrgo is a small, neat town almost opposite Zante,
at about two or three miles from the shore.   It stands
in a fertile, agreeable country, as all this side of
Peloponnesus is.   The mountains Cyllene, Maenalus,
and Lycaeus retire behind a rich plain and varied
chains of hills which bound it.   On a cape near
Pyrgo are some old ruins, of which it is not known
what the ancient name was ; it is supposed Cape Pheae.
The ruins are an old wall or two.   Olympia is about
three hours distant, and we are going there to-morrow.
We stayed to-day to dine with the Aga, who pressed
us very much, and it succeeded, as I have told you.
He was surrounded by Greeks and Zantiots, who
laughed, sang, danced, and wrestled as he bid them.
Good God! if a free ancient Greek could for one
moment be brought to such a scene, unless his fate
was very hard in the other world I am sure he would
beg to go back again.   An old Lacedemonian, on his
return from Athens, made a remark, which may be
very truly said on leaving Turkey, " that he came
from a country where nothing was thought dishonour-
able," and this is the character I shall give of the
Levant.

ZANTE,
September 6 *to* 19.

I left off my writing at Pyrgo, and have not taken
it up again for some days, and for a most disagreeable
reason, as in our tour I caught, some days after, a
most violent *coup de soleil*, which made it impossible

for me to use my eyes or my head in anything. It lasted but a short time, during which I was most seriously ill, and my head so inflamed that I was confined a day at Gastouni, and could scarce rise from my bed. I am now quite well again, and do not think of past evils; these things will happen in a climate like this.

Our tour was pursued the day after I wrote to you from Pyrgo. Olympia is at about nine miles' distance from it. The situation is upon the Alpheus, in a very flat part of the plain, shut in by hills all round, without any opening but at the river; nothing remains but a foundation, supposed that of the temple of Olympian Jupiter. We slept at Lalla, a village about nine miles from hence northward, and in a high situation, the mountains here rising all the way to Mount Cyllene. As high as Lalla the country is fine, that is, covered with wood; but beyond the hills are very bare, and Cyllene is a pointed high cone of brown stone. The Aga's where we slept is the head-quarters of a savage tribe of Turks, by turns thieves and thief-takers, according as the Pasha is in favour or not with them. This system of robbery is exactly like what used to be called private war in that regretted age of chivalry and *feudal liberty* Edmund Burke talks of so feelingly—that is, it resembles a good deal the wars which are so righteously carried on along the coast of Africa, raised by the slave-dealers, and consists in a happy mixture of kid-napping for ransom, and plundering villages and *protégés* of the adverse party. We, as strangers, are always friends of the strongest, and wished to acquire an escort from this great man, though, indeed, just now there is little to fear, and the people about these parts are at peace.

We saw nothing remarkable enough to mention here; the Aga treated us courtly enough, and, I believe, had received such handsome presents from a friend of ours (Mr. Hawkins) that he expected more from us, for the rapacity of these middling Turks is insatiable.   Their dress is that of the Albanese, of which, indeed, they are a branch, and inherit all the fierceness, rapacity, and avarice of their originals. We heard of ruins, and determined to push our journey eastward where they were, so set out the next day in that direction.   We descended through a woody country, and at length came to a steep descent terminating in the vale of the Erymanthus, now the Hana.

We crossed the valley, not above a mile broad, and climbed the opposite hills.   After winding amongst them for about half an hour we descended into the enchanting vale of the Ladon, famous for the story of Daphne, and more deservedly so for its picturesque beauties.   After passing a very deep ford, we found a poor village called Vanina, where we had the additional satisfaction of discovering the ruins and, in consequence, fixing the situation (by help of Pausanias) of the ancient Thelpusa or Telphussa.   It is along a gentle slope of the left bank, commanding the most picturesque view of the river and its accompaniments. We found the ruins of two temples mentioned by him, which, however, only consist of the moss-grown stumps of a part of the peristyle, the columns of which in one were fluted.   The remaining broken bits of building show the place to have been of a great extent, but we found no inscriptions, nor anything further worth mentioning.

We from Elis returned by Chiarenza, and escaped quarantine by landing at midnight and immediately taking refuge at the Consul's.   For Zante, I will describe it in my next; we have all round had fevers and agues, we and our servants, but are, thank God, refitted and fit for work again.   We are winding up our clues, and shall soon sail for Ithaca, Corfu, and Italy, for the bad air about Joannina frightens us, and Mr. Hawkins, whom we found here on our return, assures us there are no objects in that part worth our attention ; we shall therefore hurry to Brindisi and quarantine as fast as we can. Such are our life and adventures. Adieu. Believe me, my dear mother, most affectionately yours,

J. B. S. MORRITT.

BARLETTA,
October 17, 1795.

DEAR AUNT,

At last I write to you from Italy, our labours finished and ourselves closely locked up and strongly guarded in a lazaretto, where we are to perform quarantine in our way to Naples. This, you will suppose, is a charming situation for letter-writing, and indeed, as close prisoners, we have nothing else to do but talk to you at home about what we have seen, and wind up the scattered ends of our tour, which from Zante here contains some circumstances that I think will interest you, as at Ithaca, Corfu, etc., we have been pretty busy with Homer and the Odyssey, which I think we have reason to suppose nearly as exact as we had already found the Iliad.

We stayed at Zante, after our return from the Morea, near a month, refitting after fatigues and nursing our agues and fevers, from which five of the party out of six were affected, thanks to the vile air Chandler commemorates in the plains of Elis and Olympia. I wrote in my last to my mother our history as far as Zante, and I will now go on with it. There is scarce any island in all these seas that offers a prospect of fertility and industry equal to Zante. The town is on the eastern shore opposite the Morea, and the harbour, a large, shallow bay, is only fit for large ships, though a mole is run out for smaller vessels. On a low range of hills behind the town an old Venetian castle stands, which once was the town, and which, from a few traces of ancient buildings, seems to have been that of the ancient Zacynthus.

Behind these hills is a large plain containing the real riches of the island. Nothing can exceed it as a pro-

spect of luxuriance and abundance.   It is in this plain
they cultivate the small grape for currants, and it is
besides covered with wine and olives, eighteen or
twenty villages, and a thousand pretty villas of the
Zantiot gentry, with gardens full of oranges, lemons,
figs, pomegranates, etc.   At one end this valley ends
with a view of Cephallonia and the strait between it
and Zante, and at the other, catches a peep at the sea,
which runs up in a bay south of the town.   The back-
ground of this valley is a long range of pretty high
hills that bound all the western and southern shore
of the island.   They are at a little height stony and
barren, but the hills between the town and this plain
on which the castle stands are covered with houses
and gardens, each commanding the prettiest views you
can imagine.   This is all that is to be seen at Zante.
Society there is some steps above Turkey, and many
behind other countries.   You would not be able to
live there, for the ladies are more closely confined
than even in many places of Turkey, except those of
the lower order.   I supposed this owing to the remains
of Oriental manners, but was more surprised when I
heard the reason.

The island is so completely neglected that, besides
murders being committed almost every day in the
streets, if a lady had the misfortune to attract notice
she would very probably be run away with by force,
even from her own house, as bravoes may be hired
here to commit every sort of enormity, and all offences
are connived at by bribing the governor, who therefore encourages them, as they bring him money.   It
must be allowed he is reasonable, for murder does not
cost you above a guinea ; but you must not shoot
strangers like us, or at all annoy a native Venetian,
which are not thought game in these courts.   In short,
the only thing that hinders Zante from being as bad
as Turkey is that property is more stable and goes on
in an hereditary line, while the other is constantly
seized by Agas, Pashas, and, finally, by the Sultan,

which damps all industry and desire of acquiring
riches. For the rest of Zante I refer you to Chandler.
We found a hearty and comfortable reception from
the English Consul, and at last left him with a small
row-boat and six oars, in which my aunt Mary would
not have liked to go to Italy. These are the best for
expedition, as in a calm they row very fast, and from
the situation of the islands in our road we had always
places to put into at night or in case of bad weather.
We set off early, then, lay a few hours at night off
Cephallonia, and rode early next morning to Thiaki.
This has been thought Ithaca, and I was full of the
local descriptions scattered up and down the Odyssey,
which I hoped to find realised. I have not been disappointed, and I think you will be glad to hear the
result of our inquiries and observations.

Read over again the account of the port, and landing
of Ulysses by the Phaeacians when he first returned
to Ithaca, you will have the description of the harbour
that received us—a very deep, winding inlet terminating in a large basin, defended without by high, rugged
shores, and where boats might now ride without
anchors. It runs about two miles inland, and is so
remarkable I do not wonder it struck Homer's attention; the present small town stands on it. We, of
course, did not forget its leading distinction, the Cave
of the Nymphs. The people told us of several in
other parts of the island, which we did not visit, as
they did not agree at all with its situation; but it
exists—for a Venetian officer I knew afterwards at
Corfu assured me he had been with some travellers
to a very curious cave just above that port, which,
piercing the mountain, has two entrances, one north
the other south, though he had not gone in beyond the
first entrance. The port is on the north-west of the
island, where the ship from Phaeacia, or Corfu, would
of course arrive. Behind the town the hills of the
island rise to one point, in which we recognised Mount
Neritos, mentioned by Ulysses in his first account of

his country to Alcinous. At the foot of this is an old
ruined fortress, of which a few stones remain, on an
eminence over a valley that extends on the west end
of the island, and which contains almost all the cultivation of the country, the hills being only fit to feed
goats and Eumaeus's pigs.

This may have been the situation of some less
ancient date than Ithaca, but the capital was most
likely somewhere here; and another port nearer it
than the deep one was that of the town from which
Telemachus sailed with Minerva to Pylos, and such
a port exists there now. What shows, besides, his
great exactness is the mention Antinous makes, at the
end of the 4th book, of the strait between it and Same,
or Cephallonia, and the circumstance of the suitors
landing to lie in ambush for Telemachus at an islet
called Asteris, which agrees only with Thiaki, as no
other island forms a strait with Cephallonia (except
Zante), and at a small distance from Thiaki there is
a rocky islet which forms a port for a ship to lie in
between it and the shore of Ithaca; which, therefore,
has two mouths, exactly as Homer describes. The
accuracy he everywhere shows, in the most trifling
traits of description, is wonderful; and exalt him
as poet, geographer, and painter beyond any author
I know. I wish our friend Gray had been as exact
about his "woods that wave o'er Delphi's steep"; but
alas! excepting there being isles in the Aegean, the
other three lines are only poetry; for the steep of
Delphi is a barren rock that would scarce grow a fir;
the *cool* Ilissus is almost always dry, and never was
but a torrent; and the amber Maeander is more muddy
than the Nid in a flood, and never was other, for it
runs in a sand-bed.

However, as Homer has not used us so ill, let us go
on with him; for I have not done, and have been so
believing in him that I almost looked for Eumaeus's
pigsty. We sailed and rowed on; first to Santa
Maura, which the Greeks, however, still call Leucadia.

We reached Corfu the next day. You know this was
Corcyra, and in Homer's time Phaeacia. Nothing is
more rich and pretty than the scenery of the island as
you run between it and the shore. It is in general
broken in knolls and low hills, covered with olives,
vines, and gardens; and though not so well cultivated
as Zante, yet its happy climate and soil make it still
the paradise Ulysses found it. Read, therefore, once
more the description in the Odyssey, where he cele-
brates its fertility in the 7th book; it is as true an
account as I can give you, and more animated and
entertaining. There are now no antiquities in the
island; but when Homer has described a place, the
very stones are antiquities. We therefore traced, by
inquiry at least, Ulysses and Nausicaa to the town of
the Phaeacians. Ulysses landed on the west shore,
opposite to where we were. The shore now is all
along steep and rocky there, and a small river runs
into the sea—which is, I suppose, the one he swam to.

At about two miles' distance is now an old ruin
called Palaeo Castritza, "the old castle," situated, like
Ithaca and all the other most ancient towns, on the
top of a rugged eminence. When the town flourished
after, in more civilised times, as Athens, etc., the old
town served as citadel, and they extended the other
in the plain. This precaution in early times was
necessary, on account of corsairs and banditti; and
also they never are on the sea-shore, though generally
not far from a port. There is a small one in the plain
below this place, and at the mouth of it a small rock,
which resembles a ship so much that the Greeks now
call it "the Ship," both among peasants and sailors.
Can anything be more marked than this situation,
and the idea on which Homer built his fiction of
Alcinous's ship being petrified there by Neptune on
its return from carrying Ulysses? This place, I am
sorry to say, I did not see; but I can vouch for the
fact, as my inquiries were not only amongst people
who had seen, but people who had lived at the place,

which is about eighteen miles from Corfu. Don't call me stupid for not going! We only meant to stay one day at Corfu, and in that day I fell again ill of the ague. This detained us a day more; and hearing of these classical objects, I meant, if all was well, to go the third to them. Our boatman, however, represented strongly that we had now calm weather to cross the gulf of Venice; and that, slipping an opportunity at this time of the year, the weather evidently breaking, we should be detained probably many days.

So we left Corfu, were confined three days by storms at Fano, this small islet, and then rowed in a calm to Otranto, about seventy miles' open sea. We entered into quarantine there, and came on to Barletta, along the coast of Naples, to a tolerable lazaretto; but suffered again our usual labours—sleeping on the deck of a small boat—which we could not avoid in many places, as we were not to approach a house till we were out of quarantine. Here we are, however, safe and well, with good living, in a Christian town. A traveller makes or finds friends all over. We carried a letter, given us by a merchant, to the Neapolitan Consul at Corfu, and he, after the greatest kindness, gave us letters here to a man who sends us, in consequence, all sorts of good things every day. We have no more fatigue to undergo, and are in high preservation.

I am, most affectionately and sincerely yours,
                                      J. B. S. MORRITT.

BARLETTA,
October 27, 1795.

DEAR ANNE,
      Perhaps you will wish me after dinner many happy returns of this day. I am much obliged to you, but I don't myself, for *this* day is not only spent in close confinement, but has brought me the pleasing news from Naples that our applications are in vain,

and we are to be kept in captivity for our quarantine nine days longer.

You are not exactly informed of our last motions before we got to Italy, so I will tell you them. When we arrived at Corfu affairs began to wear a different aspect; we found with pleasure a large European town (for I hardly call Greece Europe), and saw genteel people for the first time. The town is divided into the members of the Venetian government, whose chief holds a little Court here, and the Greek nobility, of which there are many large families, natives of the island. Stockdale was rather ill, and confined to his room at the inn, but I met with a very agreeable reception, as we brought letters to a Conte Honstein, member of the first, and to the Consul of Naples, who introduced me to the second society. Honstein I found an agreeable, polite man, and he went with me, in the evening after our arrival, round part of the fortress, which is very strong, and of which he explained to me the nature, and afterwards to the ancient situation of Corcyra. It is a little south of the present town, and commands a view the most charming and most picturesque. The old port runs very deep inland on the south, and with the harbour of Corfu on the north a deep, gulfy bay forms this point into a peninsula. The whole, as well as the slopes of the hills beyond the two ports, is covered with old olive-grounds and gardens ; these, intermixed with villages and the walls of Corfu, you will suppose have a beautiful effect. We walked about till late with much pleasure, as I soon found my companion had eyes, and a conversation as interesting as it was void of pretension. At night the Consul of Naples, who was equally eager to oblige us, carried me to a conversazione at the house of Conte Bulgari, a Greek of the first distinction there. I there found many pleasant women, and heard guitars and harpsichords that made a noise rather more harmonious than Turkish howling, which is literally "no' but making

a din, for nobody ever thought them guilty of singing."

At this rate I passed two days very happily, hunting
medals and antiquities all morning, and flirting with
the moderns in the evening. A man always gets information by going abroad. I called one morning
on an old, snuffy antiquary here, who has a fine collection of medals of Epirus, Corcyra, and these coasts.
I inquired about the country so celebrated in the
Odyssey, and learnt with some surprise that he and
several other great men here had found out that it
was *not* written, as folks foolishly say, by Homer, for
two such *unequal* works as the Iliad and it *could not*
be of the same hand.[1] He, however, could not tell
me exactly who did write it, which gave me much
concern. Pray, do you know anybody that had a
hand in it? Now I almost broke his foolish pate,
for (but don't tell) the Odyssey is a very great favourite
with me, and though there are finer passages in the
Iliad, yet Telemachus and Penelope often balance in
my mind the fire and sword of the heroes before
Troy, who, though greater people, are seldom so
pleasant, like all other great people. And that this
man of taste should show me for two hours some
of the prettiest engraved stones I ever saw! I had
a very stealing itch at my fingers' ends, for he plagued
me with remarks that showed his eyes knew as little
of beauty as his understanding. N.B.—They were not
of his collecting, and had just power enough on him
to make him an ass.

We at last left Corfu, and saw, a little beyond, some
modern ruins with old stones at Cassiope, now
Cassopù. We stayed two days for fine weather at
a small island, Fano, north of Corfu, opposite

[1] It should be noted that this year (1795) was the very year in which Wolf's
famous "Prolegomena" appeared, maintaining the theory of separate authorship for the Iliad and Odyssey. It is just possible that the "antiquary" may
have seen his work; but it is also possible that he may have formed his
opinion either independently or from the Neapolitan Vico, who made the
same suggestion, without argument, in 1730.

Otranto, where we witnessed a melancholy scene. Some Albanese who were there with a boat, and with whom we made a great acquaintance, sailed off that evening, with a young Greek and his mother, to a small island near in their way home, where one of them, who was jealous of the young man's acquaintance with his wife, burst into the room where he slept, and had the barbarity to sabre him before his mother, who received a blow that almost cut off her wrist in attempting to save her son. They came back to the island where we were, and the ruffians went home; the young man, however, died the next day. This will give you some idea of the civilisation of Albania. These men were Christians, and at constant rebellion with the Albanese Turks, who are renegados within one or two centuries; but both parties are more savage than you can conceive. They make excellent soldiers, and the King of Naples has about four thousand in regular pay. They are called Regiment of Macedonia, and a large body of them was cut to pieces at the evacuation of Toulon, where the English were employed in saving their own men. I am told these men fought the French till not one remained, and would never hear of surrendering their arms. If the man had cause for jealousy the punishment was what might be expected, for such an injury there is never forgotten or forgiven; but the situation of the mother was shocking beyond description.

We at last had a calm day, and with our oars reached Otranto on the point of Italy, about seventy miles, and you would have stared at our boat, for it was not much larger than those on the Ouse. It carried us in safety, however, above four hundred miles, and on reaching Otranto, October 8, we began our quarantine, and were never admitted beyond the beach of any port till we arrived here October 13, where we heard the best lazaretto was, and which had the convenience of being nearest to Naples. We looked very hard at the castle of Otranto, in hopes

of seeing the plumed helmet, or the giant's leg and
foot, but were disappointed. The whole coast is
extremely flat, but the country is full of large towns,
and fine, though eaten up by myriads of convents,
whose houses do not seem calculated for the vows
of poverty. We had a good scene at Brindisi. The
governors of the health office admitted us into the
little room of the office, with proper guards, to eat
and pass the night. Soon after the door opened, and
a party of Calabrese ladies, escorted by some good
figures, made their entrée to visit us. They had heard
we were Venetians, but when we told them we were
English the scene was much better, and *sono Inglesi*
was whispered about with great amazement.

At last the spokesman observed fairly that in the
corner where we were the ladies could not see us,
and begged we would turn out into the light. You
may suppose how we laughed ; and consented on
condition the ladies would make the same display ;
they had never in their lives been out of the heart
of Calabria, and were now in two minds ; for on one
side was the fear of catching the plague, and on the
other female curiosity to see Englishmen. To do
them justice, they were better worth looking at than
us, for they were very pretty.

As we were in our travelling dress, and English
modes are all in all here, I have great hopes that all
Brindisi is by this time in jackets and trousers, with
white or straw hats, by way of being *à l'Anglaise*.
We supposed at last, from the length of their visit,
that they intended to observe, like Mademoiselle
Kerhabon and Mademoiselle St. Ives, "Comment dor-
moit un Anglais"; but they restrained their curiosity
in this point, and left us highly amused with their
simplicity, and the originality of our adventure.

We got here at last safe, after a most unpleasant
journey, being almost always confined to our little
boat with six sailors ; so you may suppose how comfortably we slept upon deck. We are perfectly re-

established here by the lazy hours we lead; and since our arrival our life is a perfect blank, very different from the entertaining change of scenery that we have had, which has spoiled us for sitting still.

Affectionately yours,

J. B. S. MORRITT.

CHAPTER XI

NAPLES

NAPLES,
November 18, 1795.

MY DEAR MOTHER,

.   .   .   .   .

Now, my dear mother, to talk of myself. We have been about a week in Naples, and the scene is totally changed once more—after my letters from the lazaretto, I need scarce add for the better. Suppose us, then, even superbly lodged in one of the best hotels of Naples, with a full view of the bay and Vesuvius from our chamber windows, with a boudoir that you would really envy us, commanding all the views, and fitted to your liking. Suppose also a return of English porter and English cookery to our dinners, and you will conceive us to be pretty comfortable.

In the mornings we drive about to see pictures and statues, in the evenings to the opera; for as the Ambassador is at Caserta, where the Court now is, and as we brought no letters besides to anybody here, we have not yet got an entrée to the fashionable circles, which, however, gives us only more time to see what is to be seen at first. Naples has lately had a great acquisition in this respect, as the King has bought the marbles of the Farnese Gallery, and brought them here from Rome. They have been a lounge for us two or three times already, and will afford us many more before we have done. The famous Hercules is a noble animal, and surprised me, though I had seen so many casts and pictures of him.

259

I do not think it possible, even in idea, to imagine a human figure more expressive of excessive strength; and the justness of the proportions is at the same time very striking; the whole figure is about 10½ feet high, and, except the prop he leans upon, no part seems to have been restored by modern hands. His countenance has a fine expression in it of a man resting after success; and conveys well, I thought, both the pensive air of fatigue, and the tranquil satisfaction of having obtained the Hesperian apples which he holds in his hand. We saw several others, but all thrown together in a lumber-room, which scarce gave any of them fair play; we, however, distinguished some beautiful figures and groups amongst them, though in the dark, and almost covered with the dust and dirt they had been packed in. A description of them is too like a catalogue, however, and will give you little or no idea of their beauties unless I can get drawings or casts of them, as perhaps I can of some.

This, with a few churches, is as yet all we have seen of Naples, for since we are here it has rained incessantly; and we have not been able to make one sally to the environs, where everything is that is worth seeing here—Herculaneum, Pompeii, the Royal Museums, etc., with which we shall begin the first fine weather. *En attendant*, we dowager about in our carriage, and visit church after church, where we always find most splendid knick-knackery, and sometimes good painting. The provoking part of the story is that these poor pictures, often by some of the first masters, are often crammed into some corner chapel or a dark sacristy, where it is all one can do to see them, while tawdry saints and ugly, miraculous Virgins are staring you in the face on all sides of the churches; and it requires great hunting to find these pictures out, for the priests in general know no more about them than we do. So we exercise our connoisseurship, and shall soon set up as great masters.

I saw two days ago a beautiful specimen of modern

sculpture in three figures, carved for the interior ornaments of a new chapel.   One was a figure of Modesty,
veiled from head to foot; another allegorical of an
angel freeing a man from a net which covers him; and
the third a dead Christ covered with the winding-
sheet.   The effect of the features and limbs in the
first and last appearing through a thin drapery was
such as I should not have imagined marble capable
of expressing; and you may imagine what a work the
other is in marble when I assure you it is almost
necessary to touch the net to be sure that stone can
represent it so accurately.   All the drapery and
accompaniments of these figures are equal if not
superior to antique works; still, is it not strange
that all the limbs, the head, and flesh that appear in
them without drapery are little above the common
style, and cannot approach the ancient sculpture,
which really seems almost a lost art?   For all this,
where his veils cover the figures, you think you see
them hollow from the different bends of the limbs;
the features are just distinguished through; and by
an art almost inconceivable, the strongest traits of
death are expressed in those of the Christ, though
only seen through the drapery.   To have an idea of
this, however, by description is but very imperfect,
and works so admirable are easier felt than described.
This is still more the case when I have to talk to you
of many other statues or pictures, where the beauty
consists in the expressions of passion in the countenance and figure, which of course are still less
describable than the effect of a well-executed drapery.

I must tell you one advertisement which decorates
the front of most of the churches here.   It is thus:
"Indulgences Plenary, daily and perpetual, for the
living and the dead, as often as *wanted*"; and this is
carved over the door as we write " Wigs to sell " over
a barber's.

These people are mad with religion.   When we
came from Barletta it happened to be Sunday; and

at one post-house we were catechised by everybody, from the master down to the ostler, whether we had been to Mass; not one word of reply but that could we get from them. "Pray make haste with the horses," said we. "Have you been to Mass?" was all we heard; and, take notice, notwithstanding this, that they were the most cheating scoundrels we had to do with on the whole road.

At last off we set, and in about three miles our straps broke, and lodged the crazy cabriolet we were in quietly in the dirt. I wish you had seen the crosses the post-boy made, and with what a rueful face he observed that if we had but gone to Mass the old straps would never have broken. The country for the last fifty miles is very cultivated, hilly, and beautiful. Indeed, the riches of it exceed all conception, and as they cultivate many vines, and in the most beautiful of all modes, by planting elms and training the vines by trellises from tree to tree, you may suppose what a charming effect these groves have, hung with the vines in such beautiful festoons, and the soil under them waving with corn or covered with every different produce so southern a climate produces. We are no longer in Greece and Turkey, with fine plains lying desert around us; and the fertility of this country makes us forget all the barrenness and wildness we are so used to.

Such is our history, and as it goes on I will from time to time send you *bulletins* of our proceedings. At present we are rather enjoying a rest and the comforts of good living than engaged in any undertaking of hobby-horse nature. Do tell Ann, however, that last night I was at the representation of our favourite opera, "La Zingara," in Fiéra, and liked it as well as ever, though I longed for Morellis and William Horton, without whom an opera loses more than half its charms. Next to the opera, the amusement here is a play, in which Punch performs a principal character. Not to confound matters, however, I must observe that there are very few traits of an English Punch in an Italian Polcinello, who really is a very witty and excellent buffoon, and certainly outshines plain Punch in every respect—no disparagement to him or his wife Joan, or to those excellent jokes about *hazy weather* and *going to be created*, which he has been in possession of time out of mind. He also figures in the streets here on the same footing as in England, and it is scarce an hour since we were called to our window by his soft and well-known voice, so that S. and I have been agreeing that he is the only one of our friends, perhaps, whose voice we should so soon have recognised. I do not know whether Punch, like the rest of his countrymen, has assumed this voice by way of being *à l'Anglais* or not, but I fancy in reality he is a native of Italy. Everybody else here might be English, and Naples has more the air of London than any place I have seen on the Continent. However, though most of them understand enough to look like Englishmen, there are a good many who are only *à l'Anglais*, a thing quite different, and their burlesque figures are delightful. If I had known what I now do, I should have saved myself the trouble of writing for a parcel of things my stupid servant told me I could not get here. Everything is to be got that can be got in London, and I was as stupid as him to believe a word of the story. My sheet grows near to an end, and I could prose on, but I will save something for my next. Adieu then, and pray write immediately in answer to your first part of this, and also to repeat what you wrote to Salonica.

Yours affectionately,
J. B. S. Morritt.

Naples,
December 1 *to* 6, 1795.

Dear Aunt,

In my letters to my mother, I told you all of our arrival here, and a little of what we saw. It is still, alas! the rainy season, and this *charming* climate, the theme of all Italian tourists, the wonder of all travelling Misses, who think it odd Italy should be hotter than England, has hitherto appeared to us, except for about two days, in the perfect character of a very bad English November. However, by all I hear, these rains are only to last a short time, and the rest of the year is fine weather, in hopes of seeing which I suspend my judgment, which at present would not be very like that of other people. About the situation and bay of Naples I join warmly in the general cry, for anything more lovely cannot exist, and the views in every part of the environs here are more enchanting than I ever had imagined. Our visits have hitherto been generally to paintings and statues in the town, but, favoured by the two fine days I have already mentioned, we got out twice to the coasts of the smaller gulf of Baiae, on the west of Naples, and visited Pozzuoli and the monuments that are left there.

The road there is curious, as from the end of the Quay of Naples it pierces by a long underground arched passage the promontory of Pausilipo, which separates the two bays, and through which an excellent broad road is made, arched above to the height of 24 feet in some parts and above 80 feet in others, and at least 770 yards in length.

Just above the entrance is the tomb of Virgil, which it is *proper*, you know, to see; but it is only a small brick ruin, with a few niches for urns, which may have been tomb to anybody, for I do not know why it is ascribed to Virgil alone, as it has evidently been that of a family, and he shares it with all the Masters and Misses Virgil, Mrs. Virgil, Mrs. W. Virgil, etc., etc., if there were such good people. Beyond the grotto, when we came again to the shore of the gulf of Baiae we were again delighted with the view. Cape Misenum runs out on the right, and made us think of the Aeneid—the islands Ischia, Procida, the castle of Baiae, Pozzuoli—all forms and situations whose happy

combination defies almost the imagination of a painter
to surpass this charming scenery.

At Pozzuoli, which is but three or four miles from
Naples, we climbed to the Solfatara. This, you know,
is the crater of an old volcano, and forms a small oval
valley, with a few shrubs and young trees on the
slope and foot of the low hills on one end, while the
rest is a sheet of white, crumbling earth and stone,
covered with flower of brimstone. The ground is
hollow, and a stamp echoes through the whole mountain. It is constantly on fire within, and we heard in
many places a bubbling of boiling water, the steam of
which flew out from two or three holes about with
astonishing violence and such heat that I could hardly
take up the earth round it, which is covered with
crystallised sulphurs. This steam shows a good deal
the principle of an eruption, I think; for suppose such
a current, by the falling in of any part, directed among
the red-hot entrails of the mountain, what calculation
could conjecture the explosion it must make, which
would continue as long as the stream of vapour was
driven that way ?

At the foot of the mountain in Pozzuoli we were
shown a temple of Serapis, buried in the side of the
hill. The front has been dug out, and three columns
are standing, but the interesting part to us was the
court before it, surrounded with cells for the priests
and small baths for the different lustrations. The
court is full of rain and other waters, and stepping-
stones are set all about it. In the centre is a raised
circular platform, which was adorned with statues now
at Portici, and in the middle has been the altar for
sacrifice, where we were shown the vases for the
blood and entrails of the victims, and bronze rings in
the floor to which they were tied. On going into a
part of the excavation which has been made by the
temple, I could feel the heat of the interior part of the
mountain very perceptibly, which shows how completely this whole country is on fire below. We were

shown an amphitheatre and some statues here, and a few columns of a very old temple in the wall of the cathedral.

Sacred and profane history is as delightfully jumbled, indeed, here as it is in other parts of Italy, and while the people of Pozzuoli pray above in a Roman temple, St. Januarius and a Roman Consul hold a *tête-à-tête* on opposite pedestals in the market-place.

As all carving and ornament is admitted into any church that finds it, and as the people are no connoisseurs, it may often happen that Jupiter and Apollo are still addressed for some saint or other, and the heathen goddesses and Roman empresses often come in for a pious Ave Mary by no means intended for them.

Naples at present is far from being the gay place it used to be, and the late plots, the war, and the continual arrests for treason, have made it quite dull. We do not see it to advantage, however, it must be confessed, as we have no letters of introduction but to our Ambassador, who, as well as the Court, is now out of town at Caserta. If you can get me any among your travelled acquaintance you will do us the greatest good you can imagine, as we are growing stupid, though there is so much to see here that we feel less the want of them, when we can get out, and we have not yet got to Caserta from the extreme bad weather. In the meantime I medallise, and look at statues and engraved stones all morning.

I have changed my duplicates and bought most of the coins of the Greek colonies in Calabria and Sicily, for I do not meddle with Roman ones, as they would lead me, like Johnny Gilpin, farther than I intend. I shall keep for you all of my own finding in the villages of Greece. I am also getting a charming set of sulphurs here, and have found a painter to finish our sketches, whose talent will, I know, surprise you, as I have seen scarce anything equal to his style of colouring from nature.

I told you that our draughtsman left us at Zante.

I sent him home on account of his health, which had suffered extremely in our tour, and he had been once so near dying we durst not risk him any longer. He would not, beside, have been capable of finishing his drawings well, though he did not want talent for sketching, but his coloured works were much inferior in every respect. I esteem myself, however, extremely fortunate now, and shall, I hope, bring home four or five of my principal views in a very masterly style, and the rest neatly finished in a suite of smaller drawings, much superior to most you may have seen, and exact, as I explain all the sketches leave doubtful.

To-morrow we mean to visit Vesuvius, whose ravages we have already seen in parts in the road to Pompeii. At Torre del Greco the lava last year entered the sea, and the whole town was buried under it to the depth of thirty feet. The steeple top, and a few buildings of the lower town which were rather guarded, peep up out of a large plain of scoriae and ashes. Not less than five or six streams of lava have passed over this situation at different times, and the town is once more rebuilding in exactly the same place.

This is more rational than it appears, for, the ground being so much raised, they presume the next streams will go either to the right or the left without hurting them. The place smokes still, and six months after the eruption the fire was seen running under it. In the lazaretto I amused myself with translating Greek (the only books I had worth it), and send you some of the shortest. I did into English a story of Leander and Hero, from Musaeus, but it is too long to send you. These others are only trifles, and like the others I gave you. They are from Theocritus and Bion. Tell me how you like them. Love to the Minster yard.

Adieu. Your most affectionate nephew,

J. B. S. Morritt.

NAPLES,
December 18, 1795.

DEAR ANNE,

I have just burnt a letter I had begun to you, and if I give you till I come to England to guess the reason I am sure you never will, so I will tell you. I had given you a long account of a lady you have heard described once by Mrs. Parsons, and had, as I thought, made it very exact. In the meantime we saw her again, and when I come to read it over it will not do at all, and I find it is not on a first visit one can do justice to so charming a subject. I shall now amend my style, no doubt, though seeing her only can give you an adequate idea of what she is, as you may suppose from the reason given by her husband for marrying her, namely, "that she only of the sex exhibited the beautiful lines he found on his Etruscan vases."

Every man has a reason for marrying, and this is certainly a new one, though perhaps as good a reason as most others. If one may judge from effects, the case is so indeed, for no creature can be more happy or satisfied than he is in showing her off, which he does exactly as I have seen a wax figure exhibited, placing you in the most favourable lights, and pointing out in detail before her all the boasted beauties of his *chère moitié*, and, luckily for him, without any more bad effects upon her than would happen if she were a wax figure ; which is wonderful considering the pains he takes and the country he takes them in.

We have met with the greatest civility from both, and if I were to say we did not admire her, the only excuse I could add must be that we were blind, for it can't happen to anybody that is not so. You may suppose her really an extraordinary woman, without education, without friends, without manners, when she came here ; she has added to all the outward accomplishments of a woman of education a knowledge of Italian, French, and music, which last, with a very fine voice, she executes divinely. Add to these the most difficult of all, the *ton* of society, which she has raised herself to, and though not the *most* elegant, she is certainly on a par with most women of the circles she is in. This would be alone a proof of very superior sense, but her conduct to her husband is a stronger one. As he does nothing but admire her, and make other people admire her, from morning till night, as he would a fine painting, it is a delicate point, and yet she manages it so well that without affectation and without prudery (which would only make people recollect how times are altered) she keeps him and everybody else in order and behaves in the most exceptional manner.

In her attitudes she exceeds herself, and joins every grace that ever was united to the greatest beauty of face and person, though I am told she was still more lovely two years ago. Such is Lady Hamilton, and as we knew her story you may conceive we did not expect so much. It is not that we have not heard *good stories* of her and him, but I can only tell you how she struck me, and I never was more surprised in my life. She was perhaps designed by Dame Nature for the stage, as, besides her wonderful talent for attitudes, she has that of countenance to a great degree. I have scarce known her look the same for three minutes together, and, with the study she has made of characters, she mimics in a moment everything that strikes her, with a versatility you have not a notion of. After this you may suppose her entertaining to a degree; I am told she is capricious, but we have not experienced it, " *et d'ailleurs tout est permis à une jolie femme.*" By their means we have been introduced to parties, of which I can scarce give you a more perfect description of than I can of her, and when I tell you I believe them the pleasantest in Naples it will never enter your head that I mean the Court. I do, notwithstanding, and will tell you how we have been presented.

We were invited some days ago to a boar-hunt of the King's by Sir William Hamilton, who asked permission, and presented us for the first time at the place of rendezvous in our frocks and boots, *sans cérémonie*. Here we met most of the gay world at a small palace of the King, breakfasted pell-mell, and therefore consorted with some very pleasant men and very pretty women. We were spectators only, and went to the field a party of six or eight in an open landau, of which party were Lady Hamilton and two of the prettiest women of this Court. This, you will allow, was as good fun as pig-hunting, or even as fox-hunting, and so will I, though once a Nimrod and a Yahoo. The hunt was very different from English notions, but really a pretty sight. About twenty gentlemen, divided in parties, stood round the cover, and dogs were stationed on all sides. At every moment roebucks and wild boars burst from it, as there were a large party of *chasseurs* beating it within. The dogs were slipped at them, and the gentlemen, armed with a spear, galloped and struck them when caught. We had at every moment pretty courses with the roebucks, and I was glad but few were killed.

The boars did not come off so well. We had horns, and, the day being beautifully fine, the scene was brilliant, and ended in our return to the palace and being invited to dinner. Before it was served the King came up to us, and, with an affability we little expected, took us all over the house and showed us the views himself, which are heavenly. You stare; so did I. But I was more astonished at him since, and will give you a curious history of our favour here before I have done. The table was King Arthur's round one, the dinner good, and the King forgot himself and remembered everybody else till I began really to make many moral reflections and comparisons between the first company here and the country parties in the *free* country of England. Oh that Sir Dilberry had learnt manners at the Court of Naples instead of the University of Padua! How many a formal dinner might have been made pleasant! In short, we enjoyed, as everybody must do, the company we were in, and before we left it the King himself asked us to another party two days after at another palace, where he has been doing more good than is often done by any King, in establishing a rising colony of manufacturers under his own eyes and introducing the machines of England, Genoa, and Lyons for working silk, which before was always imported from other countries.

If our first party made us admire his affability, our second made us love the heart it sprang from. He invited us to see his silk works, and we drove over in the morning with the Hamiltons. The rest of the party was only a young prince and his wife (one of the beauties of our first party). It was here we really saw the King of Naples. He showed us everything himself, and, for the good of his establishment, had made himself master of every part of the manufactory, which he explained from the first winding from the silkworms to the stuffs and velvets of Lyons, etc. The whole is very complete, and all his colony in a livery, which insures them so much a day according to their work, and as any of them are good manufacturers enough to get their livelihood by their work he marries them and gives them a house with weaving frames, etc., complete.

I wish you could have seen him here as we did, talking *patois* to all his people round him, playing with their children, commending some, encouraging all. You know I am not sentimental, but if you had seen him as I did, asking the children after their fathers or mothers who were ill, speaking of some others who were orphans of his old servants, and saying, with tears in his eyes, " *C'est moi qui suis leur père*," you would have felt, as I did, that he was there in a greater character than at the head of twenty armies. *Au reste*, we passed the morning with as much ease and happiness as at Rokeby almost, and drove about in his green landau, seated pell-mell with him upon it. His little colony is now near 700, and flourishes extremely, as the married couples manufacture children better, I think, than they do silk, which last, however, is very good.

The sights we saw lasted till near five in the evening, the King going with us all over, and no gentleman who thought himself our equal could be more amiable or more free. On our return he showed us the palace and a suite of his own private apartments, fitted up as a King's should be, entirely from his own manufactories of the country. As it grew dark, and we grew hungry, everybody was thinking of dinner when the dining-room next where we were opened, and we were shown into a charming room with an illumination of waxes bright as day. We dined with him and one or two of the Court, a party of ten, and he made us taste all the improvements he had made to bring to perfection the wine of the country. Whether it was the wine or the company I do not know, but he saw we were so satisfied and happy that after dinner he renewed our invitation to hunt in a small party on Sunday, and we are to have what he calls a *dîner de chasseurs* at another little palace. He has promised us horses and spears, and talked of asking us often, as he hunts the boar every week. Now are we not great people? and if we tell these stories do you not think Sir Dilberry and the travelled men about us will hide their diminished heads?

Be this as it will, I assure you we anticipate the invitation with more pleasure than you have a notion of, for we know now how pleasant the party is. Sir W. Hamilton says it is because we are not courtiers, and speak to the King as we do to other people, which he likes to meet with. Mark the advantage of not being too strange in a strange place, as very few English have been able to boast the same reception. And all this because we do not twirl our thumbs and look like fools when civilly spoken to. What a bless-

ing it is ; for it has made full dress and such like
caparisons almost useless, as we are always invited in
our morning dresses with or without boots, and I
should scarce have dined at Sedbury the figure I dined
at Caserta.   Could you believe that whilst the King is
universally beloved by the common people, yet a
considerable party of the principal nobles (who had
the greatest obligations to him besides), have had
impudence enough to raise the cry of democracy, and
intrigue for power under the pretence of freedom ?
Mind, the whole party was a vile, place-hunting set of
aristocrats, and the people that joined them a few
hireling foreigners, some of whom, to the shame of
humanity, had been brought from Lyons and Gascony
by the King himself when they were starving, and
provided for by him in the very manufactory where
his conduct would, one would think, have disarmed
his bitterest enemy.   One of these rascals belonged to
his hunt, and dined every hunting day at the King's
own table till he was taken up.   Now did you think
such ingratitude possible ?   These were the worthy
correspondents of the French Republic at Naples, and
I really think the story of the Lyonnese manufacturers
shows a Frenchman is capable of anything.   Besides
these parties, we have been introduced by degrees in
the town, and our time begins to be very gay again ;
we are, in short, once more embarked in the stream, and
have little more to do but to let it carry us, and I think
we shall not get away from hence till after the carnival.

Our first week or two was stupid, as we were not
immediately introduced to good company, and we
therefore preferred none, as I hope we always shall ;
but now we go on *à merveille*.   Among the sights to
be seen I have not yet been to the Royal Press, but if
you see Mr. Ingram, you may tell him that I believe
no more of the Herculanean manuscripts have yet
been published, though they are preparing some,
having made lately some progress in unrolling them.
You must tell him, too, that a particular friend of his

(Marchese Carletti), talked a great deal to me about him and made me promise to send his particular regards, on my saying he was so near a neighbour, by any conveyance I could, and I therefore choose this letter.

I would give the world to have you here, as I suppose you are up to the knees in snow, and we, after the rains, are enjoying a second summer, and sit all day with open windows, or ride lounging about in the finest country and climate nature ever formed. You have not a notion of the picturesque beauty of these environs—it beggars description, I assure you; and though I hate travelling Misses I long for you all day when I ride or walk. Apropos of travelled Misses, I hear a charming account of our Yorkshire belle, Miss Harrison, and am told she was extremely admired here; tell me how she is in England, as I shall speculate if she is so charming as they say. What restless animals your nephews and nieces would be! They would travel to the world's end.

Adieu, my dear Anne. Write me nonsense, and write often; nothing gives me half the pleasure. I hoped to hear to-day, but the English courier has missed twice, so your letters are on the road.

Your ever affectionate brother,
J. B. S. MORRITT.

I send you a French charade a lady gave me last night:

> Un enfant courant rencontra mon dernier,
> Fait mon tout, pleure, crie et montre mon premier.

NAPLES,
Tuesday, December 29, 1795.

DEAR MOTHER,
Long before this gets near England you will have heard over and over again from us, and you will I hope have entirely got over your fears, and the gloomy perspective you looked at us with when you

wrote to me last in November. When I wrote you word, my dear mother, that I *had been* ill, I certainly meant to say that I *was actually* very well, and not that I wished you to make yourself unhappy about me till you heard again; I do therefore enter a protest against all such readings in future, and desire my sentences may be understood in their plain and natural sense without the use of black spectacles or low spirits. When my letter was dated from a ship's cabin, and accompanied by contrary winds, you may suppose I did not write quite so happily as I am doing just now by a comfortable fireside after a good dinner, and I do not recollect any other cause that could make my letter low-spirited (as you supposed it at the time you received it). I have since that been much more ill, as I told you in my last letter to Anne, but the moment we brought ourselves to an anchor all was right again, and rest and good living have made us as lazy and as fat as pigs, therefore you need really be under no apprehension about us, for we find Naples agree with us extremely. As we go on here we find the place improves on us every day, and have found many acquaintances that promise to be very agreeable, and who make our stay more and more interesting.

I have told you, I think, most of the lions that we have at different times hunted in the environs, some of which have really afforded us great amusement. As we make some stay here beyond what is necessary for staring about us, we do not hunt lions every day now, and take them one by one, as parties offer to go and see them. You will be glad to know how we spend our time here so agreeably. At breakfast we are amused and cheated with medals, prints, marbles, etc., all which frequently attend our levee in form. We then call on the men we think it worth while to know best, if they do not call on us, and generally ride out till dinner in the environs. So many beautiful excursions you cannot imagine; the whole country is a Paradise, and as we strike out new roads every day, we are continually discovering new beauties. To-day we have been along the foot of Vesuvius, and coasted the bay of Naples. Yesterday we were in the spots so celebrated by Virgil, the Lucrine and Avernian lakes, Baiae, and Cape Misenum, of all which, if I could hope to give you the faintest idea as a picture, I would talk about them till to-morrow morning, but alas! it is as impossible as it is to give an Italian ideas of the comforts of a coal fire or the charms of a foxchase. It is in describing landscape, and not in forming it, that Dame Nature's uniformity is so striking, and here one may truly say, " Ring her changes round, her three flat notes are water, plants, and ground." The gulf of Baiae is nothing more upon paper, and therefore only equal to Mr. Cradock's fens at Smallways, which are also " ground, plants, and water."

We dine from three to four when we dine at home, and pass the evening generally either at a private assembly or at the theatres. These last are the places to visit the ladies of our acquaintance, and there we meet all the world in their different boxes, which serve only for this purpose, as it would be not only the most fruitless, but the most vulgar, thing in the world to attempt listening to the opera, which nobody does except to one or two favourite airs on the first or second representation. Besides this, there are now and then little episodes of balls, so that on the whole our time is spent as pleasantly as possible, and without any form or constraint, entirely after our own fancies. There are, this year, but few English at Naples, at least few have yet arrived here; as they come we all visit, and with some we are intimate, so that we easily make parties for our morning rides. The last person that has arrived, and whose card I have just received, is that renowned commander, Admiral Hotham. He is come here from Leghorn, where he left Signora Grassini to refit, and took Mrs. Newnham in tow for the continuance of his tour abroad. I do not know whether he thinks it

dangerous returning to England; but I should hope
by all accounts he will find it so, for the stories we
hear of his neglect of duty are scandalous, and I
believe the French are obliged to Signora Grassini
for keeping him windbound in port when they took
our Mediterranean convoy.   The ladies here are in
great uncertainty about their conduct to Mrs. Newnham, and he never stirs, I believe, without her.   As we
are not so shy of our characters, we shall visit the
Admiral, and perhaps shall improve our letters with
some entertaining particulars in consequence.   Besides
him we have made an acquaintance with a Suffolk
family who are here, Mr. and Mrs. Cullum, whom we
find a great acquisition to the place, as they are very
pleasant people, and, being thoroughly English, make
no disagreeable variety in the circle we visit.   The
other English are all single men, and we know less
of them excepting Rushout, a relation of the baronetcy.
His acquaintance we have formed some time, as we
were both medallising, but, however, in a very
different way, as his collection is upwards of twelve
thousand, and he gives up his whole time to it from
morning to night.   In short he is a most excellent
antiquarian, which I am not; has a smack of the
baronetcy, which I have not; and looks much oftener
at Julia Mammea and Faustina the younger than he
does at the pretty women about him—which I do not.

We have, however, received great civilities from
him, and an introduction to one of the pleasantest
houses in town, where we very often go in an evening.
This is the Russian Ambassador's, who has always
an assembly where at different times we meet all the
gay part of Naples.   From this mint was coined the
charade I sent Anne, which you may tell her was
Cul-bute, and I could send you a great deal of wit if
I thought it would bear transportation without growing flat.   As it is I shall keep it with me, and when
at Rokeby shine on a Sunday night with borrowed
plumage; but do not you tell people that it is not my

own. So much for our news, and if it is half as entertaining to you as yours is to us, I assure you it is not
written for nothing; for though an *Argus* or a *Morning
Post* is held so cheap by such saucy folk as Creswell
when within a day's journey, yet to us at the distance of
Italy they are very pretty reading, and the marriages
and broke-off matches of our friends in England are
almost as interesting as the welfare of Sling or Rover.
As for politics, we are now out of Turkey, and hear
enough of them—I had almost said too much; for by
all I read in the English papers parties run with you
higher than ever. Indeed, though no alarmist before,
I think you are right in your alarm now, and I will
tell you why I think so differently: from the charming
increase of popularity the abandoned part of the
democrats must acquire by the blundering expeditions
to Quiberon, and the choice commanders we make
use of, such as His Grace of York, Generalissimo by
land, and Mrs. Newnham in the Mediterranean. If
the war is to go on so, I do not wonder at anybody's
voting against its continuance, and, adding to this the
expenses on one hand, and the dearness of corn on
the other, I am much more nervous than I used to be
about the bonfires at Sheffield, and the rebellions at
Dundee.

The only good news of consequence since Lord
Howe's victory has been the taking of the Cape;
and, considering that we have bought it by taxes
without end, I own the war is no favourite of mine
now, and Mr. Pitt's promise of making peace as soon
as he well could was the best thing I thought he
offered. Your story of the insults offered to the
King on the day he opened the House was dreadful,
and his conduct was that of a hero, and well calculated
for the emergency; but I have again been staggered
in my faith by the bills to suppress public discussion
of political subjects, and was glad to read my uncle's
name in the minority, for I declare mine would have
been so too. I am afraid you are more loyal, at least

more afraid than I am; but notwithstanding consequences or party, I wonder at a majority ever being terrified into voting away a privilege of the people, which they did not give, and to which many of them owed their existence in that House. It is very true; and I believe all that was said about such meetings being at the bottom of the riot lately, and that many of them wrote and spoke treason; but that on that account the people at large should be silenced, and at a time when they are more than ever concerned, is a proposition which has more than ever disgusted me, with a Minister who, as Mr. Duncombe said in the House, owed his rise to the very influence he is destroying. The proposal was artfully timed when the people were shocked by the King's danger; but if I am to believe the lists of petitions against it, even many of the loyal part of the kingdom think as I do about the bills, that, under pretence of guarding the King, they are a prop to a Ministry growing weaker by the war. I think fully with you about most of the men that clamour in opposition, and the rascals who write and spread sedition, etc.; but really I cannot help thinking that the war as it has been carried on (and I only repeat the opinion of every impartial foreigner, when I say that has been not very brilliantly) will every day add weight to what once were idle clamours, in the minds of all the middle and lower ranks of people, and I think the alarm will originate not from the speeches of Messrs. Fox and Sheridan, but from every one's feeling the pressure of the war, and the scarcity, and from I hope an almost unanimous opposition out of the House to the Sedition Bills; for all which the Ministry may thank themselves, and the people will no doubt thank the Ministry. The war was undertaken to prevent French principles; and treason, etc., was prosecuted by Tory measures. Now, I only ask you if the alarm is not greater now from those measures than it then was from the clamour of a seditious party, while the great mass of the nation despised them, and then say that it is owing to *democratic* principles. To complete my long prose, which perhaps you all think treason, I own I believe the whole owing to the *Tory* principles, if not of Mr. Pitt, at least of the *ci-devant opposition* dukes and lords, and the blunders of the whole war, which out of England are *universally* laughed at.

That Mr. Fox means any good by the popular side he has taken I cannot easily believe, but, as a friend to measures and not to men, I do hope you are not grown so afraid as to like the Sedition Bills; but if you do, pray tell me something more of them (setting aside your fears), as I know that our creed and education used to be so much alike that I am curious to know how so good a Whig as you are can think so differently on the same things. My uncle's vote I was sure of before I read the list, and, whatever I thought before, I honoured him then, and think he would have been inconsistent if he had a moment hesitated; even had it been only till he wrote to Wyvill.[1] This long prose is a consequence of my just having read the newspapers, and, notwithstanding all I can do, the Sedition Bills will not square and settle with my principles, while the objections to them go down as smooth as possible, and Mr. Fox himself charmed me while I read those on the exclusion from petitioning they will give to copyholders and trades-men who at present have no other share in or mode of addressing the Legislature. Therefore reform will be more necessary; I wish I could say therefore more certain. As all this is treason, and therefore only meant for you, I beg you will not read any of it but to yourself, for I know Anne is so much an aristocrat she would flay me alive; but I talk to you, who ought to know better. So adieu, my dearest mother; believe me heartily and affectionately yours,

J. B. S. MORRITT.

[1] Chairman of the Yorkshire Association, formed to secure short Parliaments and equality of representation.

NAPLES,
February 14, 1796.

DEAR MOTHER,

From the charms of the situation we vegetate at Naples, though I must say the carnival has been as stupid as we had hoped to find it gay.   In a week or so we go to Rome, and so advance one step nearer Rokeby.   Since I wrote to you we have not seen many new sights, but one of those we have seen is fairly worth all Naples and Rome put together.   Not to puzzle you too much, I mean Lady Hamilton's attitudes ; and do not laugh or think me a fool, for I assure you it is beyond what you can have an idea of.   As I have heard them described and talked about fifty times, and had, after all, no idea of their excellence, I cannot hope for much better success ; however, I will tell you as well as I can what they were like. Her toilet is merely a white chemise gown, some shawls, and the finest hair in the world, flowing loose over her shoulders.   These set off a tall, beautiful figure, and a face that varies for ever, and is always lovely.   Thus accoutred, with the assistance of one or two Etruscan vases and an urn, she takes almost every attitude of the finest antique figures successively, and varying in a moment the folds of her shawls, the flow of her hair ; and her wonderful countenance is at one instant a Sibyl, then a Fury, a Niobe, a Sophonisba drinking poison, a Bacchante drinking wine, dancing, and playing the tambourine, an Agrippina at the tomb of Germanicus, and every different attitude of almost every different passion.   You will be more astonished when I tell you that the change of attitude and countenance, from one to another, sometimes totally opposite, is the work of a moment, and that this wonderful variety is always delicately elegant, and entirely studied from the antique designs of vases and the figures of Herculaneum, or the first pictures of Guido, etc., etc.

She sometimes does above two hundred, one after

the other, and, acting from the impulse of the moment, scarce ever does them twice the same. In short, suppose Raphael's figures, and the ancient statues, all flesh and blood, she would, if she pleased, rival them all. What is still better is that she acts with the greatest delicacy, and represents nothing but what the most modest woman may see with pleasure. It is extraordinary, too, that, when not acting, her manners and air are noble, and the moment she pleases her whole figure is elegance itself. We passed the day very happily, as we dined there afterwards, and in the evening had music and a new piece of acting in the character of Nina. With her hair about her *ears*, or rather her *ankles*, she sang a beautiful scene of Paenillo, where she is supposed mad for the absence of her lover, and acted till she made us shudder and cry. A quarter of an hour after, in the dress of a Neapolitan *paysanne*, she danced the tarantella with castagnets, and sung vaudevilles till she convinced us all that acting was a joke to her talents, and I assure you I never saw in my life *any* actress half her equal either in elegance or variety. A painter who was of the morning party when she performed her attitudes cried with pleasure the whole time. When one does a thing well, however, we sometimes misplace it ; and so she is rather apt to continue the acting in real life, where I think she approaches less to nature than when she acts professedly. Her conduct, *au reste*, is unexceptionable, and the *only* instance among the beau-monde at Naples (where morality is not at its greatest perfection, as you may have heard).

Most affectionately yours,

J. B. S. MORRITT.

NAPLES,
Begun Wednesday, February 23.
Sent March 8, 1796.

DEAR ANNETTE,

I have an idle hour or two, and must write to somebody, and I do not know how it happens, I can't begin anything like common sense, so now you know the reason why I write to you. I am so often in this sort of humour, that above half the letters I have begun lately have begun "dear Anne," but I was obliged in conscience to scratch it out and write to more *sensy* people, as Mr. Alderson calls them; but how can anybody write sober sadness when the history of their lives is eating, drinking, riding, and sleeping? For as to what we see, it has been celebrated, commented, critiqued, and lied upon till the subjects are threadbare; and as for the scandal of the town, it requires you to know the characters before you can derive entertainment from their description. I do not like much to introduce a Neapolitan party to your acquaintance, even by description, for really, to do them justice, it must be given in terms very apt to "give Virtue scandal, Innocence a fear," and they far overpass any sketch that falls short of this. In short, with nine out of ten I am now completely disgusted, and, from the situation of my Italian acquaintances, have seen so much and heard such stories, that I shall be not sorry to get to Rome, where we are going very soon; as, though not much afraid of our characters, we do not like a place where rogues and w——s compose the *whole* of society, and where, from the ignorance and generally confined education of both men and women, they have cultivated their heads as little as their hearts.

In short, one may fairly say here that, except with foreigners, "le libertinage général n'est pas racheté par aucun agrément," and in all our stay we have only known one or two good fellows among the men, and not one woman of character, or scarce common decency, among the ladies. Paris, Vienna, and most foreign towns were not famous for the constancy of their swains or the fidelity of the fair sex. Society, however, suffers little from it, and, from the general decency and elegance of manners, the most modest woman that is not outrageously good *might* live with them. At Naples, however, this is by no means the case, and I would just as soon send my wife (if I had one), or you, to improve your morals in the upper boxes of Drury Lane; for though as a young man I can bear a good deal, yet I do not like black-guardism on *any* subject. If ever I am asked whom I liked best among the men here, I shall always say the King, and make folks stare; he is the only jolly fellow amongst them, and never meets us without hollowing out a salutation, as I might to Abney or Duncombe, to the surprise and dismay of the English and others with whom we are in company. I believe they think us in high favour, and I wish we were, for I would rather have His Majesty for a neighbourly acquaintance than anybody here, as I almost adore his character, and wish he could change places with Sir Robert Hildyard, whom I do not adore at all.

Thursday.

Too much pleasure for one day. I, on my return home from a morning lounge, find a long letter from my mother and a card from whom do you think?—my *Lord Webb* himself, just arrived, loaded with all the wit of all the coffee-houses in London, and, I hope, with pardon and indulgences from Rome for the stolen puns and torrents of contraband *bons mots* that he will be sure to sport on his arrival when we see him. I never receive a letter but I immediately long to answer it; however, as it is not fair to cram your letter with messages to my mother, I shall perhaps add half a sheet enclosed to her, as I have a great deal to say to her about it. Think only, then, about our *rencontre* with Webb, and all the news he will have about the marriages of our Cantab friends ; for three days he will be as good as a feast.

You know he is always a favourite of the *old* women ; and so he continued, for before his arrival he was harbingered by a fine sitting figure lately arrived from Rome, who is about three yards circumference in the small of her back, and vows in broad Irish " he is a *swate* young fellow, my dear." It was good fun for us who know him to hear her vow that he was " so *swate*-tempered if you gave him a *stinking herring* to dinner he would not mind the difference."

Now when I recollected the dinners in London, where he always catered, and the generous indignation that fired his countenance when the cook had not done him justice, it gave me a great idea of his consummate civility, and I believe he is so bewitching a man that no old woman's heart in the world can withstand him.

An old, hypocritical varlet, to pretend to temperance, when if left to himself he never passes one day without a good dinner, and I should not wonder if his reason for travelling was the not liking brown bread in England.

My mother leaves all stories of fun, such as balls, plays, assemblies, and routs, to you. I expect, therefore, to hear everything of the sort, as the text is always amusing, and your comments upon them (like Coke upon Littleton) of equal authority.

Tell me if trousers are still the fashion in England, and if *you* ever wear them ; no use has yet accustomed my eye to them, and though very classical, and strictly *à la Grecque*, both ancient and modern, I still disapprove of ladies wearing the breeches. Pray tell me, too, in the dark, dreary, and ungenial months of December and January, what vertigo has seized at once all your acquaintance and mine, and set them all a-marrying, and *sattling*, as it is called in Yorkshire. Your late letters read like the end paragraphs of a newspaper, and record nothing but the fates of amiable gentlemen and ladies with genteel fortunes. How much more happy we men should think ourselves if we read "*genteel* young ladies with *amiable* fortunes"!

Adieu, dear Annette. Heaven keep you foolisher and foolisher.

I shall be more and more
Your affectionate brother,
J. B. S. MORRITT.

NAPLES,
Begun February 27,
Sent March 8, 1796.

MY DEAR MOTHER,

I have just received a long letter from you of January 24, which makes me want to prose to you, and so I begin, and if I do not fill my paper will perhaps enclose it in a scrawl I have just finished to Anne. Our letters of late have, it is true, turned upon gloomy subjects, and the bad news we have had to talk about has made them less entertaining to write than when we were sure of making each other happy by them. If you knew, however, the pleasure I have in receiving them from you I know you would not complain of having lost all the satisfaction you used to have in writing. To know it, however, you must travel in foreign parts as we do, and the full extent of it cannot be felt over a fireside in Yorkshire.

I forget, however, in all this that the subject of all others I want to talk to you about is poor little Robert. You will think me perhaps whimsical, and that I am choosing to have a way of my own in so often opposing my sentiments to what you resolve on from other intelligence; but let me beg and entreat you not to send him to Rugby. With respect to *it* I can speak with *certainty*, and Stockdale, who

is at my elbow, and as fidgety as I am about it, bids
me add his name, and say that he lives very near the
place, knows all about it, and has the *worst opinion*
of its morals, and no very good one of its teaching.
Rugby has already touched the meridian of its reputation, for which reason it is much cried up, but it
is not and will not again be so good as it was. I
only judge by effects, that is, the Rugby boys I knew
at Cambridge. Stockdale, who knows the place, says
the cause is this : James, who is headmaster, has been
a clever man, and brought the school to the reputation it had, but now, having made a fortune, and
grown old, neglects the office very much, and takes
no care of the discipline, which is riotous and
licentious, as any great school can be. All the men
I know speak of James as growing an old woman,
and as I have seen the decay of Manchester from the
same cause I know what a very bad school it became
latterly. In *learning* the Rugby men made no figure
at Cambridge. I knew several, some good fellows,
generally illiterate, and I think *always* idle ; and I had
in my own mind set Rugby down as nearly the worst
of all the large schools.[1] Judge, then, if I am not
heartily anxious to hinder Robert from going to such
a scene, and do not think me too capricious. I feel
how wavering and solicitous you naturally must be
on so important a subject, and beg you would make
inquiries, if you take no better determination, about
the school of Oakham, in the great county of Rutland.
Stockdale mentioned it to me, and recommends it
strongly. It is small in comparison of Rugby, but
has sent out some men who have made more figure
at Cambridge, and is an increasing and rising school,
especially since the decrease of Uppingham. This
was, he says, its character two years ago, and probably it continues so. He knows the undermaster,

[1] This opinion, right or wrong then, will surprise those who think of Rugby
in, and since, Arnold's time ; but Arnold was in his cradle when this letter
was written.

who was of Pembroke Hall, and he gives him a high character.

So much about my brothers. If they are not ungrateful they must own we talk about them, at least. To talk still about business, thank you for your conduct to my farmers. If you had not done it I would; for I hate great farms more than ever since they are become the nests of monopoly. When I am nearer you we will talk about what can be done both to relieve present misery, and prevent it in future as far as my power shall extend, and we will make little farms for little people, who, I hope, will not be such rascals as their greater predecessors. Our principles are so exactly alike on this point that I give you full commission to use the powers you have in my name, and turn off every man whose corn does not attend the markets. I will certainly not raise the farms, but I will not suffer fortunes to be made on the misery of the whole district, so I cannot but thank you with all my soul for what you have done, and beg you will proceed.

Your letters are full of marriages, and mostly of my friends, so things will have changed when I come back to England, and my London society will wear a different appearance—I hope at least not for the worse. Champneys in a black coat will be a melancholy object. My Lord Webb is here, more flimsy than ever, and talks more about Voltaire and the King of Prussia. Of the last he will probably hear at Naples many very interesting anecdotes, as one of the first luminaries of our society is Madame de Ritz, a left-handed wife, and long a favourite Sultana of his present majesty. This lady, you know, was said to have negotiated the Duke of Brunswick's famous retreat, being gained by the French; I do not know whether this was true, nor do I much believe it, for she is now quite anti-Gallican, and the English are honoured with every attention. We see her frequently, and dine there sometimes, as she gives very agreeable parties, and is, in fact, a very pleasant, lively woman. The *inamorato* people attribute to her is a curious one, viz. *Lord Bristol, the Bishop of Derry*, aged sixty-six, with whom she is very intimate, and travelled part of her tour. Now, as she is young, and also rich, I think the affair may admit of doubt, though as to my Lord, he is the strangest being ever made, and with all the vices and follies of youth, a drunkard and an atheist, though a *Bishop*, constantly talking blasphemy, or indecently at least, and at the same time very clever, and with infinite wit; in short, a true Hervey. As he courts every young and every old woman he knows, I suppose, like the Irishman who was *half*-married, that in the case of Madame de Ritz he has *his own consent*. He has been nearly dying, and I am sorry to say is better, and likely to recover.

We also are very intimate with Mrs. Newnham, the English lady who is "travelling" (for that is the phrase) with Admiral Hotham; and our party is enlarged for a few days by Lady Webster, who is also "travelling" with Lord Holland. So we are in good company, and shall make valuable acquaintances for future times, when our travelling, and theirs, ends in England. There are also four or five more of these "travelling" couples whom we shall see at Rome, Florence, etc., amongst whom I shall no doubt pick up stories that will set Frances's strange notions right about the advantages of travel for ladies. I fancy, before this, tidings of Wilbraham, whom his friends thought lost, are arrived in England.

A friend of mine, Mr. Toike, writes me word from Constantinople that he had forwarded letters from him to his friends, dated from Ispahan. What an interesting new tour he has made at last! I long to see him and compare notes. He is in company with a man I knew at Smyrna—a respectable, informed man—minister, I think, of the Swedish Lutheran Church, and speaking, with five or six other languages,

Arabian and Persian. This man had already travelled on foot through great part of the country, and was capable of making his way through any hardship; as I found Wilbraham was of the same *true stuff*, I hope they will see and do a great deal.

Have you seen his brother, Bootle? I am much mistaken if you will not love him, as I do, dearly. He is really a very fine young man; and I have made few friendships I wish and hope will last longer than with him and his brother. He is not, or at least he is more slily obstinate than Wilbraham; but has also a glorious firmness when he thinks he is right, which he also generally is. Now *that* I like.

I have been to Paestum; it is about fifty miles from Naples, not far from the shore in Calabria. We slept the first night at Salerno, after travelling along the bay of Naples and round the foot of Vesuvius—a succession of the finest scenery it is possible to behold. The temples are twenty-five miles farther, in a marshy plain. They are very perfect outwardly, though the cells and roofs are ruined; and we found them all three different, but all grand, plain specimens of early Doric architecture. One is particularly fine in its proportions, and has all the massy simplicity the order requires; they are all of stone, and are certainly of Grecian work. There are others in Sicily, and we had found similar ruins of marble in Greece; but these are the only specimens of the Grecian porticoed temple which are seen in Italy. It was this which at first made such *wonders* of them; they were none to us, though amply worth seeing from their very great beauty and majesty of architecture. They are, you know, without bases, as all old Doric is; and would have continued so, if modern architects had taste to feel the beauties which greater simplicity always gives this order, whose very essence is strength and solidity. I would as soon have dressed the Farnese Hercules in a turban cap and feather, like Miss D. Thank Miss Stanley for her care of us;

I know the regular English mode is always to have a cicerone to tell them this is a wall and that a pillar; but, having eyes, we spare, in these times of want, our *ounce* (half a guinea) a day, and imagine we see very well all that is to be seen at Naples without other assistance.   At Rome a cicerone may serve us.   Here nobody wants more than a *laquais de place*, and I myself am now more *au fait* than almost any of them. With *them* you always go one round.   With a horse apiece you see every corner of a country; and I have shown the country here to men, who thought they knew it all over, more than once.

Adieu.   Stockdale joins me in sincere good wishes, and believe me ever your affectionate son,

J. B. S. MORRITT.

CHAPTER XII

From Rome, through Trieste and Vienna, to Cuxhaven

MORRITT'S journey homewards from Rome was by no means easy or safe; and, as before, whether by luck or good management, he just got through in time. In 1796 Bonaparte began his victorious Italian campaign, arriving at Nice to take command of his army on March 27, a few days after Morritt reached Rome. By a series of successful actions, from Montenotte on April 10 to Mondevi on April 21, he had forced upon the King of Sardinia a treaty which gave the French a control of Piedmont, with free passage for their troops, and the possession of the fortified towns Cuneo, Ceva, and Alessandria. The victory at Lodi enabled him to occupy Milan on May 15. Brescia, then belonging to Venice, was occupied on the 28th; the passage of the Mincio forced and Verona occupied on June 3. Further south Bologna was entered on June 19. Meantime, in the north, the army of Sambre and Meuse had crossed the Rhine—Kleber's division on June 1 and Jourdan's main army by June 12— though they did not at that time maintain their hold on the right bank. Moreau, in command of the army of the Rhine and Moselle, crossed at Kehl, and established himself there on June 25.

The reasons therefore are clear which caused Morritt to give up his three or four weeks at Florence after he left Rome in April, to abandon his plan of going from Venice to the Tyrol at the end of May, and to travel instead by the Adriatic to Trieste; and why, when he reached Dresden from Vienna on June 23, he chose the passage to England from Cuxhaven instead of from a more westerly port.

Rome,
March 22, 1796.

Dear Aunt,

I write to you at last from Rome, and from the middle day of the Holy Week; therefore I hope my letter will carry with it all the salutary influence which so sacred an air can communicate. I wish I could think it would carry to England a little of the ancient fire that warmed their Fabricii and Scipios; it might be of some service against your beloved friends the sansculottes.

We arrived here on Saturday last, and opened the campaign at Rome, therefore, precisely at the right time, namely, with Holy Sunday. We took a last leave of Naples on Thursday last, after having spent the three or four last days of our stay in farewell visits to our favourite views, and in parties upon the water, which the weather is by this warm enough to make agreeable. You know how I admire this charming bay, and every object within fifty miles of Naples; the view of the town itself from the water, notwithstanding all that is said about it, is, however, certainly inferior to that of Constantinople and Pera, when not so near as to remark the badness of the buildings. The point of the Seraglio, and the numberless mosques and domes that rise above the town, are leading features which the other has not. Part of Naples, too, being flat, does not present itself as the other does, which is everywhere on declivities, and the town is at best scarce half so large. Your map will show you how much the beautiful canals of Pera and the Bosphorus must exceed a plain semi-circle in varying the scene as your boat moves to different points of view; but in every other beauty— of foliage, cultivation, outline, and prospect—the paradise round Naples exceeds not only it, but, I believe, every other country in the world—I mean when on shore. I assure you we left it with some regret, and a few of our friends with more, so that we hardly were consoled by the fine succession of beautiful scenery from hence to Terracina.

It is, I believe, our fate never more to travel like other people; for in a good chaise, with good roads and several good inns, we cannot get on without adventures. We slept at Mola di Gaeta, and left a good bed at half-past three in the morning, roused by the alarming news that a King's courier had hired, or rather ordered, all the post-horses in three hours from that time for Prince Xavier de Saxe, whom we had seen at Naples, and who told us he should not set off till the day after. We hurried off while it was time, and were very democratic in our remarks on people that had more horses than ourselves, till after breakfast, which rather softened us. At the last post, however, in the territory of Naples, where we arrived at seven, the postmaster, who kept also a miserable doghole of an alehouse, pretexted the king's order and stopped our course, as he chose to have our company. We did not like his, and his *room* still less, as one was dishonest, and the other full of fleas, lice, and bugs.

We therefore, after more growling at our superiors (which comes well out of a chaise-and-four, and sounds consistent), walked about to cool, and hoped for his arrival about midday; five hours being the variation between Court watches and common clocks ever since the time of King Stephen in England. In arbitrary government it is more, and Prince Xavier not coming, we undertook about one o'clock to walk to Terracina, where there is a good inn, and we had only one stretch of fourteen miles. To stay where we were was out of the question, so off we set, and left our carriage to follow. When we had advanced about two miles it began to rain, but, inspired by that quality men call perseverance in their own sex and obstinacy in yours, we continued our march. This, however, was stopped about two miles beyond, when we were almost wet through, as a guard-house is built on the frontiers of

St. Januarius's and St. Peter's dominions, where our passports were asked for. We had left them in the carriage, and were not sorry to be stopped and shown into a covered guard-room. This was better than the inn we had left, and we sat waiting patiently for events. At last the Prince passed, about six in the evening, and no horses were left for us. We had therefore to stay all or most of the night; so, making up our minds, we sent a note to my servants, and got some fish and salad which the soldiers had intended for themselves. They gave us a bed in the guard-house, and on the return of the Prince's horses, at last we got liberated at about two in the morning, and few people can say they have been so plagued and pestered between Rome and Naples. The next day we got here without more misfortunes.

March 29.

My letter has lain idle for some days: not so my legs and my eyes, which are here in continual exercise in this inexhaustible scene of curiosity and wonder: the functions of Holy Week are the general lounge for the English and foreigners who are here at the time; and Rome has lately been full of processions and Church ceremonies from morning till night. As more or less gold and silver lace makes all the difference of all the processions I ever saw, I own I was not infinitely struck with all this, neither did I even deign to be half squeezed to death to see the Pope wash the pilgrims' feet and serve them to dinner in the Vatican, which is reckoned a great sight. He washes feet like other people, and they eat much in the same way. I own, however, the grand Benediction from the front of St. Peter's has a fine effect, and that fine building is in its glory on these days when it is full of people, and the area before it covered with people and carriages. One can scarce help smiling in these days to hear the Bull of Excommunication against Heretics, which makes a part of the ceremony, and to see scraps of

paper thrown from St. Peter's, as if to carry the
anathema all over the world. I wish I could have
caught one for your entertainment. The music of the
Holy Week is more worth attention, and the *miserere*,
performed by voices alone without instruments, is one
of those fine effects of which hearing alone can convey
an idea.

When we had not any particular object of this sort,
we have been running from ruin to ruin and from
palace to palace. If I could tell you half what I have
seen I should be deservedly thought one of the best
describers in the world. I first saw St. Peter's. Of
its size and proportions I can say nothing new, but I
have looked at it a hundred times, and still can scarce
imagine it so large as St. Paul's or York Minster. The
first reason of this deception, which everybody feels, is
the symmetry and wonderful mutual dependence of its
immense parts, and the foreshortening of the beautiful
circular colonnade before it, which always makes you
appear nearer than you are. Within, the immense
dome, and the nave supported by only four immense
arches on each side, take off from its length, while the
long-drawn Gothic aisles of York Minster increase it
considerably. The thick, hazy smoke of London is
alone sufficient to make St. Paul's look higher, but in
ornaments and internal arrangement they fall every way
short of the Roman cathedral. In the front there are
great architectural blunders, and the miserable superstition of its forming a cross has fettered the noblest
plan ever conceived by man, and induced in many
instances a departure from the designs of Michael
Angelo, whose idea was to have shortened the middle
aisle and to have made it rather a grand portico, with
the dome rising over it. The circular colonnade before
it has the most chaste and noble effect, and no church
equals it in approach. I prefer, in point of architecture,
the principal façade of St. Paul's to that of St. Peter's,
exclusive of this, and I wonder such a front could be
built with the Pantheon before their eyes. The dome

is a glorious thing, and the building altogether is a study for a man's life. The optical deceptions are not to be enumerated, every object is colossal and seems diminutive, and the bronze pavilion under the dome is higher than any palace in Rome, and at the same time only strikes the eye at first as a common and proportionate ornament. This is the great beauty of the church: no glaring object catches the eye more than the rest, and no single dimension of any part seems the least out of proportion. I own, however, though I think it the most magnificent building in the world, St. Peter's fails in impressing the mind with the religious, gloomy awe one feels so naturally in the long isles of a Gothic building, for which there is no accounting; but it is impossible to walk in York Minster without a sensation which its namesake here does not produce, though more admirable in every way, perhaps.

A still more favourite sight of mine here has been the Coliseum by moonlight. You have seen descriptions over and over (again) of this enormous ruin of the Flavian Amphitheatre. Half of it is nearly entire, and the rest, broken into beauty by time, and overgrown with bushes, was lighted up or thrown into masses of deep shade by one of the finest moonlight nights ever beheld. How I longed for you to stare and admire it with me! It would not have been our first, or I hope our last, expedition at the same hour, and I have seen scarce any scene that ever struck me more. The shadows were so varied by the trembling light that shot through the arches, and the gradation so beautiful from the circular form of the building, that scarce any object was ever so calculated for an effect of this sort. I have seen nothing in Rome which has struck me so much, and I have seen most of the admired buildings in it. The Pantheon is the most entire and the most beautiful model of ancient architecture here. The portico is admirable, and the large, low dome is, I think, of a more pleasing shape than

the higher proportions of that at St. Peter's. I think
St. Paul's is nearly of the same shape with it; and
the Turkish domes, taken perhaps partly from Santa
Sophia, are all still flatter, and perhaps from that more
pleasing; at least I am not singular in thinking so.
The truth is, the Turks build in the simplest manner
with square tiles, and throw their dome without a
keystone, an art entirely unknown to Western architects, who were puzzled by the dimensions of Santa
Sophia, and could not build a dome of the sort. I do
not believe I told you—for I scarce believed it—the
square of the dome of Santa Sophia is considerably
larger than of St. Peter's, though the flattest of any;
this I have from certain authority.

> Believe me yours affectionately,
>   J. B. S. MORRITT.

ROME,
April 1 (no bad day for letter-writing).

MY DEAR ANNETTE,

I write to you from Rome—which, as my letter
to Frances last week would tell you, has now been our
residence some time, and answers our expectations in
every way; that is, both by the remains of ancient
magnificence and the dullness of modern society. We
have, for the last ten days, travelled post-haste over
almost everything worth seeing at Rome, and my head
is such a jumble of painting, sculpture, architecture
and antiquity that I do not know what my letters will
read like till the chaos comes to be a little *débrouillé*. I
have been driving this morning to at least ten different
bits of wall dignified with the names of tombs and
temples, and yesterday to as many modern houses full
of paintings and statues good, bad, and indifferent;
this will give you a notion of the exhaustless variety
of this wonderful place, where misery and depopulation exist in the midst of ecclesiastical palaces, and the
wonders of ancient and modern arts are united with
every sort of bad taste and ignorance. We drove this

morning to the ruins at the foot of the Aventine hill, and along the course of the Tiber; these are in great number, and I felt still more pleasure on this side of Rome, as the beauty and perfection of the arts are not the only considerations that give interest to these remains. I own, when I see a temple or an archway I admire, it takes a good deal off from the beauty of it when I am told it was built by Nero, or Heliogabalus; as, of all histories in the world, that of the Roman Empire is to me the most disgusting, and I cordially hate both the people and their rulers. On the other hand, an old wall-end grows into some estimation with me when some of the glorious names of the Republic are tacked to it, and I have some pleasure in seeing the works of a virtuous and free nation.

I saw, then, to-day the ruined ends of the Sublician Bridge, built in stone by Marcus Aurelius, but on the situation so gallantly defended by Cocles. Above it are the Palatine and Aventine hills, which were then almost the whole of the city; and the situation is at least guessed at where Romulus and Remus were found exposed, and where are still seen the remains of a temple dedicated to them. It was near the Tiber; and you know they were saved by being exposed in a flood, and left by it as the water subsided. One or two temples are shown of the times of the Republic, though I think most may be doubted. We peeped into the grotto, and drunk of the fountain of Egeria, which is still one of the finest springs I ever saw; and admired an old statue of the nymph, half broken to pieces, which is seen reclined over the stream. The grotto has been at different times repaired, but the vault seems to have continued since Numa's time. Another of our lions was the family tomb of the Scipios—a vaulted *souterrain*, with the remains of a small rotunda over it, still full of inscriptions, with the names of the different persons it contained. The sarcophagus, which is not elegant (as in the Imperial times), has been carried to the Vatican Museum; and it is singular that no inscription or urn was found with any allusion to the famous Scipio Africanus, and it is supposed he was buried on the shore at a place now called Patria, on the gulf of Naples, near Cumae, where he died in a sort of exile. The elegant tomb of Caecilia Metella, the wife of Crassus the younger, is very perfect, and is seen on the Appian road not far from hence. It is a rotunda on a square basement, with a frieze of bulls' skulls supporting festoons ; and this simple ornament has the most elegant effect.

Such has been our lounge to-day, without counting churches innumerable built with ancient columns or on ancient foundations. One, a little rotunda which was a temple of Vesta, charmed us. Round it was an open portico of twenty Corinthian columns, most elegantly worked of Parian marble. The walls are of the same materials. The friars to whom it now belongs have walled up the intercolumniations of the portico and whitewashed the marble, so it might as well be lime and hair. This side of Rome along the river, formerly the most populous part of the town, is now but thinly inhabited, and in summer is scarce habitable on account of the " bad air." This is ascribed to the exhalations of the wet ground about the Tiber, but I own I saw no marshes to which so violent an effect as this is said to be could be attributed. The truth is, that ground which seems good to us, and which would be perfectly wholesome in England, is, with an Italian sun, absolutely pestilential; and we have seen several places in our tour infected with this sort of *malaria*, as it is called, which would be fertile and wholesome with our climate. It is so with all the west coast of the Morea, and those of Epirus; and the heel of Italia, in l'Appulia. This is a good deal owing to the neglected state of culture these parts are now in ; and anciently there were no complaints of the bad air at Olympia and Elis, any more than Rome, which has now absolutely changed its seat and occupies most of the Campus Martius. If Italian suns were transferred to England, what a pretty desert there would be about the Lincolnshire and Cambridge fens; and how completely the population of the Isle of Ely, and the *hard ground* round Wilson's at Soham, would be reduced to its original inhabitants, the frogs!

I want to tell you more about what I see, but I shall bore you to death if I even attempt to describe the objects which strike us here. What possible language can convey an idea of Raphael's paintings, or do justice to the Apollo of Belvedere? We saw them and a thousand other beautiful things in the Vatican two days ago; of which the Laocoon is, I think, at the head. You will see this group and the Apollo in Spence's "Polymetis," and I wish you could for a moment see the originals. The Laocoon is the most difficult subject, and, being equally fine, has greater merit. It is really horribly natural. I saw, some day since, the fine charcoal drawing of Michael Angelo, about which Miss Bisset had a story. It is not in the Vatican, but in a casino belonging to the Farnese, and now to the King of Naples. Raphael was employed to paint this in arabesque, and Michael Angelo, who called on him when he was not at home, drew this head in one of the compartments as a critique on the smallness of his figures. His rival has worked a neat border round it, and would never suffer it to be touched; and indeed, this charcoal sketch is one of the finest drawings in Rome, and does Raphael's good character as much credit as it does his rival's genius.

I had not before an idea of the lions to be hunted down at Rome. There are at least eighteen or twenty houses, of which each has a rich picture gallery, and many fine collections of statues; add to these the antiquities, and the modern artists in all ways that deserve attention, and you will suppose how busy our mornings are. Our evenings are, on the contrary, idle. There are no public amusements, and few English in the place. A Roman conversazione, I am told, is stupidity itself—*il faut goûter de tout, pourtant*;

therefore to-night I shall make a sally and be presented to the Borghesi. When I have seen it, we shall know whether it is worth going again; though I have no great hopes, as the party meet in full dress, and I always find bags and swords are great dampers. One of the houses we have found most agreeable here is our own Prince Augustus's, who does the honours to Englishmen, *on ne peut pas mieux*, and has a general conversazione every Sunday. We dined there yesterday, and passed a very pleasant evening, as he is very civil and easy, without any humbug or nonsense in his manners. His wife is, you know, in England, and he is here *en garçon*, though I believe he wishes to have her over very much.

It is with no small pleasure that I reflect, my dear Anne, how fast our tour will now draw towards old England, and how much fun we shall have together and how much nonsense we shall talk in a very few months. I shall not stay at Rome one unnecessary moment after seeing all the objects most admired here, and shall then immediately go to the Ascension at Venice. We shall be detained three weeks or a month more at Florence, Bologna, and Milan, after which I follow my nose from Verona to Cuxhaven without turning to the right hand or to the left. We will be with you if possible in July, but you may set us fairly down for York races, all accidents included, I hope. Pray get the roans into good order, therefore, and I will drive you about in triumph on my return from foreign parts. You must for your own sake, however, make George break them till they are as quiet as old, for my driving talents have lately been much impaired for want of practice, and in driving a phaeton that was lent me at Naples I was frequently in scrapes, which, if I remember right, I used formerly to avoid pretty well. I hope to find Rover, King, the Greta Walk, and the Burgundy in equal good keeping, and then you know I shall be completely happy.

Adieu, dear Anne, till then. Stockdale desires to be

remembered to you and my mother ; give my best love to her, and believe me as much as ever, and I can't be more,

Your affectionate brother,
J. B. S. MORRITT.

VENICE,
May 8, 1796.

DEAR ANNE,

My change of date will show you the reason of my long silence, as we have either been extremely busy at Rome or in constant motion ever since I last wrote to you. *Eccoci quà in tanto, mia cara,* and the French seem to be taking good care that the little tour we meant to wind up with in the north of Italy should be as confined as possible, so that we shall certainly not make any very long stay there. You will have heard of their late successes, and here we talk of nothing else, but as English gazettes are seldom very alarming to your nerves, I will tell you what appears the plain truth.

The Austrians have lost in killed and prisoners about 18,000 men, and have evacuated all their posts as far as Mantua, where they, however, can assemble scarce the shadow of a defence. The Sardinians treat for peace with the enemy at the gates of Turin, and have *en attendant* surrendered Asti, Alexandria, Novi, Cuneo, Tortona, and all the posts which are almost impregnable if defended, and give them the keys of Italy. Milan is daily expected to be marched to, and, being defenceless, must fall ; the inhabitants also have long been Jacobins. The neutral states are laid under contribution ; the English are, we hear, to be sent from Leghorn, from which alone the fleet can be victualled, and Corsica preserved ; and it seems, in short, that Italy lies completely at their mercy, for they are in great force, and their enemies have now no army. All stories short of this are of Cabinet manufacture, and this is really, as far as I hear, not exaggerated.

At Venice we are quiet, but people are packing up their tatters in great haste from most of the other parts of Italy, as they fear, when the French have seized the mouth of the boot, that they may not be able to get out at the toes.   Besides the neutrality of Venice (which seems not to be treated with any great respect) we console ourselves that we have a nice back door to creep out at even though Verona is seized, for we can always get into a Trieste boat, and a very few hours sets the Adriatic between us. In the meantime we are going to-day to see the Doge marry that fair lady. The ceremony generally takes place at the Ascension, but his wife was not in the humour, and seemed to pout and fret so much that he dares not approach her. To-day she is in a more winning mood, though not very serene, and still what the Italians call *ritrosetta*. To say the truth, I was acquainted with Mrs. Adriatic so much last year, that I am not at all sure of the Doge's opinion as to choosing his wife, for we found her a sad, cross-grained, capricious, *cantankerous* female, besides the infidelities she commits with Turkish and Barbaresque pirates.

I left off my nonsense here to go to the wedding, and embarked in our gondola for St. Mark's Place. We here found the Doge and Senators filing two by two on board the *Bucentaur*, the large state galley used for this purpose. This galley is covered with a red velvet canopy, and every part of it very fine, with a prodigious quantity of carving and gilding. When they were all on board it was rowed and towed slowly out to the Lido, after having run foul of some ropes and anchors of other vessels, to the dismay of many, though, we hope, without anything ominous. It was attended by thousands of gondolas and other barges, which made the scene very gay and pretty, especially as several of the Venetian ladies were in them, and were no bad change after the ugly faces we have been used to at Naples and Rome.

At a church, which is on one of the islands about

two miles off, the Doge and his train descended after
the ceremony of dropping a ring into the Adriatic, and
heard High Mass, during which we amused ourselves
with walking about and looking at people's pretty
faces on the island.

> We then sailed back amid the cannon's roar,
> As safe and sage as when we left the shore.

The fair in St. Mark's Place is a pretty and gay scene
at this time, and the temporary wood buildings in the
middle, with shops and coffee-houses of all sorts, recall
to our recollection the Palais Royal in the days of its
splendour. To enjoy Venice, however, a man must
be a little amphibious and partake a good deal of the
otter, for the water comes up to every door, and,
except a walk through narrow alleys to St. Mark's
Place and along the shore beyond, we never stir but
in our gondola. It is possible, I am told, to walk by
land to every part of the town by knowing the bridges
and back lanes of the place, but all the direct communications are by water, and you have no idea of
how very singular an air this gives the place. The
gondolas are the nicest lounging carriages possible,
though, from their all being black, they look a good
deal like hearses laid on a long canoe. The boatmen
are excellent, and you pass each other and turn corners
really much more adroitly than with any carriages.
The hours of their amusements are insufferable, and
we find it a great bore to go to the opera, which does
not begin till eleven and lasts till three or four ; and
what do you think must be the spirit of the public
balls which are given after the opera sometimes ?
Now I could forgive people's turning water into
land, but when they come so completely to turn night
into day they make too great a change in the old
system. We dined yesterday at Sir Richard Worsley's,
who is Ambassador to the *Serenissima* Rep, and he
showed us some very fine things in the way of sculpture and painting, and gave us a gallop on our own

hobby-horse through the plains of Greece and Asia, of most of which he has good drawings. I own I could not help now and then thinking of the *peeping* scene and I was rather surprised at him, as, from his conversation and ideas, he by no means seems as if he had been such an ass. Being Grecian travellers, he has shown us great attention, and has given us free ingress and regress to his cabinet, which is very well worth seeing, and particularly rich in cameos and antique stones.

I have dabbled at Rome in this way, and have at last wound up by buying two most beautiful cameos this morning, which were part of a Roman collection, now selling off. The one is a very well cut head of Brutus with the dagger, and the other a most superb gem of a Medusa, in full face and very high *rilievo*, upon which I mean to establish my fame. These I shall sport as rings when I dine at Sedbury or in places of the sort, and expect to show them off with no small *éclat*. I have bought a picture or two likewise in Rome, so that if I get clear away before I ruin myself, you may think me well off; for, to say the truth, I cannot resist temptation. I shall have something good at least to show for my money, I hope, and so shall content myself, as a good many people spend theirs without.

I read over my letter and find it all full of Venice, without telling you how we got there. We crossed the finest country almost in the world from Rome to Loretto, always in rain and mist, so that we saw about as much of it as you have. We did, however, visit the cascades at Terni, and saw a very charming and picturesque fall of water. Before we left Rome, however, we made an excursion to Tivoli, where the different falls, the round temple, the woods and plain form a combination of more picturesque scenery than was ever put together anywhere else. At Loretto we saw the black Lady and her wardrobe, for form's sake, as, to say the truth, the sight is easily managed, and the riches in the

church, with the poverty out of it, are a melancholy
proof of what fools men may be made into. The
country from it to Bologna is beautiful, and the trees
and cultivation on the water edge are not to be seen
in many countries. From Bologna is a dead flat, and
the whole country a most striking resemblance of
Holland. We did not stop, as we wanted to arrive for
the Ascension, and shall make a trip on this road after
leaving Venice, then through the Tyrol home, for
which reason I can give you no directions to write, as
we shall move very quickly, and seeing you once more
will be a better thing. Adieu. Loves, etc., to everybody.

Your affectionate brother,

J. B. S. MORRITT.

VIENNA,
June 15, 1796.

DEAR MOTHER,
   I am afraid you have been some time without
hearing from us, but when you read my date you will
see we have been doing something more to the
purpose than writing, and that is making a long stride
on our road towards England. We stayed at Venice
waiting for something decisive between the Austrian
and French armies, to determine whether we should
risk a trip to Florence to visit the Venus de Medicis,
considering, like prudent generals, that if we undertook it rashly, General Buonaparte would probably
cut off our last retreat by Venice and Trieste, as he
had already cut off our communication with the Tyrol.
At last he decided us completely, for on the first or
second of this month he gave General Beaulieu a
second drubbing, and, after dispersing the whole
army, marched on the Venetian territory to Padua,
from which, of course, all obnoxious persons moved
off to Venice, and, in order not to be stopped by a
general scramble for post-horses, we directly took ship
to Trieste, and made the best of our way hither, all

touring in the north of Italy being out of the question. We had a very quick and fortunate passage to Trieste, which gave us the start in the bustle, and so we came on very smoothly to Vienna.

The country between Trieste and this place, which is not often taken into the tour of Germany, is, however, one of the most pleasing in Europe. It crosses the lower chains of the Carniolian and Styrian Alps, which are covered with wood and a verdure our eyes had been quite unaccustomed to in warmer climates. The water is beautiful, and the country abounds in trout streams, which are useful as well as ornamental. We have, therefore, not so much to regret in losing the Tyrol, which, however, I hear is still finer. With us the account is balanced by having again an excuse in seeing Vienna; you know how we liked it last time, and it has lost none of its charms. We shall not stay above ten days, and certainly when we leave it nothing will stop us till we see you in England. We have found most of our acquaintance, and all our favourites, in high preservation, and having seen Italian towns which are talked so much about, we know how to do justice to Vienna, which is the only capital fit for a gentleman to live at. In summer here one really lives in the country, for there are six or eight public and private gardens, to which everybody makes parties to dine, and there are balls two or three times a week always at casinos four or five miles out of town. By this means we never think of passing an evening in town, but meet all our friends riding and driving on the promenades in the *faubourgs*.

You may, after all this, think it lucky if we get away before Christmas. However, we are good boys, and will certainly set off on Tuesday or Wednesday next. We shall certainly, therefore, see you before York races, and possibly, I think, in about six weeks, as there is nothing from hence to Hamburg which can possibly detain us. Of the northern Courts we had a sufficient sample at Dresden, and though they may be very good practice for a courtier or an Ambassador who is not quite broken in to his bag and sword, yet they are not so agreeable to us, who probably never shall be broken in to either, and, I hope, never shall need it. I am going to take a lesson, however, to-day, for we dine with Sir Morton Eden, who is, I hear, a perfect master of diplomatic *Hummery*; it is the only dinner of the sort we mean to have before our return, so pray wish us well over it.

By all accounts it will be much the same sort of party as a dinner at Sedbury, and I wonder Sir Dilberry, after his studies at Padua and his tour of Europe, did not enter into the Corps Diplomatique, or never occurred to the Minister as a proper person for the employment. As a man of virtu I shall now stand very high in the neighbourhood, as within a few days of my leaving Vienna I bought an antique cameo in a ring that is so large and showy it must attract all eyes and give great weight to my observations every time I lay my hand on the table. It is really an extremely fine head of a Medusa, on an Oriental stone, and though I dare not tell you how much I gave for it, yet I am told by connoisseurs that I got it much below its value. It was part of a very fine collection at Rome which was selling off, and had first been offered me at Rome for just five times the sum I paid for it. I bought a picture or two besides at Rome, and with my drawings and sulphurs have really a very pretty little collection to show after my tour, which I think you will be glad to rummage over.

Before I left Italy I began to be a good deal like my Lord Webb, who asked me one day at Rome, " Morritt, are there any fine pictures in this house ? " " No." " God be thanked, nobody will plague me to look about me." Vienna is a charming relaxation after seeing a great deal; for here is nothing to *see*, and a great deal of amusement, exactly the contrast of Rome, where your eyes are the only sense you ought to employ. I saw here a day or two ago a cousin of the

man who married Anne Cradock, who had met you
at Hartforth, I believe, so we had the pleasure of
talking about you and Yorkshire; he is a little bit
of a literary coxcomb, and came to talk about Greece,
where he says he means to go. The best part of the
story of his tour is that he set off with Webb to make
the whole tour together, and after a passage of a week
they got sick of each other's company, and parted at
Hamburg by mutual consent.

I did not tell you that we were intimate at Venice
with two men who were just setting off for Constantinople—the one of them an oldish Mr. Meynell of
Yarm, who had seen you, I think, at Sir John Lawson's.
He is travelling with a son of Lord Stourton's, whom
we liked extremely, and lived a great deal with during
our stay there. We talked so much about Yorkshire
it has given us the *mal du pays*, which you will not be
sorry for, as it makes us now think every moment
longer and longer till we see you. You will not be
able to write to us again easily; you may, however,
direct to us poste restante Hamburg, and tell us how
you do; we shall probably get the letter in time, but
everywhere else we shall move too rapidly to hear of
you, I hope. So expect us to escort you at York and
Richmond races, and tell Anne I expect she has the
roans in complete order, if she values my neck and
her own. I shall bring her over all sorts of pretty
knick-knacks if she is good and pretty-behaved.

If you see Mr. Ingram soon after receiving this, pray
give my best compliments to him, and tell him that
there are no additional volumes printed of the books
he desired me to inquire after at Naples. I am
extremely obliged to him for his attentions, as he
mentioned us to his friend Parr at Venice, from whom
you may tell him we received every kindness, and
were extremely glad of the introduction. We shall
now be a match for W. Horton after visiting the
schools of Italy, and shall be as great connoisseurs as
he is when Mara sings out of tune. It is rather

curious, however, that, while we are fools enough to
send for the Bunti, Morichelli, etc., etc., Mrs. Billington
is singing at Venice, and is allowed there on all hands
to be the best singer of the present day.   Nobody is
either a singer or a prophet in their own country, but
I think we must pay some deference to Italian tastes,
which certainly ought to know best when their own
music is well executed.   I think she is improved with
being there, for I really never heard anything like
her in the opera she played in at Venice.   Marchesi
acted at the other theatre, and was deserted.   Adieu
now, for I have come to the end of my paper; I hope
you will soon hear from my own mouth, which is
always better than writing how much
            I am your affectionate son,
                    J. B. S. MORRITT.

                                    YARMOUTH,
                                    [*July*] 1796.
DEAR ANNETTE,
        This is to inform you we are safely arrived
at Yarmouth, and that it may be quite ready for the
post office I write it before we set off from Cuxhaven,
like a true Paddy; for at present the wind is so contrary to our passage that when we shall touch English
ground I have not an idea.   If it lasts we must amuse
ourselves here some time.   We have now been on the
water's edge these six days, and have during that time
eyed old ocean very often, and with many a longing
look towards England; that crusty old gentleman,
however, regardless of our ogling, has not once been
favourable to our wishes, so if we have made you wait
longer than you expected, you must ascribe it to his
doing, and not to ours, for the charms of Cuxhaven
are not what detain us on the Continent.
After getting our chaise into repair at Dresden, we
set off again the day after I wrote you my short letter.
We had been detained in port to refit, for the roads
between Prague and Dresden are indescribable, and,

besides breaking our pole and wheels, we ourselves were almost bruised to a jelly by gentle taps against the four sides of the carriage. We then went to Berlin. By way of variety, the road was a heavy sand up to our axle, and we proceeded at the rate of about two miles and a half in the hour for three long days, in the middle of these barren sands, where the only varieties are forests of scrubby fir and sand oaks. We found Berlin one of the prettiest towns in Europe. The late King filled it with public buildings, and the streets, by his order, were built regular and open. The houses are low, and their fronts stuccoed, which has a much better effect than the high houses of six stories in Italy and France, casting a gloom over the narrow streets they shut out the sun from. Architecture is in a pretty taste there, and some buildings on chaste antique plans; and it was with some pleasure we saw revived in the new gate towards Potsdam the plan of the ancient propylaea of the Athenian citadel. This is at the end of a long mall, the middle of which is a public walk, divided by double rows of trees from the carriage road on each side of it, and, as the houses on either hand are regular, this approach and entrance is one of the prettiest I know.

We stayed at Berlin four days, and made an excursion to Potsdam. This is a town in the same taste, and we were shown the famous château de Sans Souci and some other palaces, where Frederic has shown that he understood comfort very well. There are some good pictures *par ci par là*, which repaid us for our trouble. Except the exterior, Berlin is melancholy, dull, poor, and ill-peopled, and Potsdam a mere garrison, at least in summer; but four days are not enough to talk of society and manners. We were five more coming to Hamburg through the same agreeable sands.[1]

[1] The last letter, posted, no doubt, on arrival at Yarmouth, ends here without signature.

INDEX